PRAISE FOR THE BOOKS OF COLIN EVANS

THE CASEBOOK OF FORENSIC DETECTION

"[A] well-organized compendium . . . Even the most dedicated devotee of the genre will find much that is new in these brief but exciting accounts of the brilliant and persistent scientific work that brought murderers . . . to justice."
—*Publishers Weekly*

"Pithy, concise, and remarkably accurate."
—*Science Books & Films*

"Written in a popular style as clear as it is brief."
—*Library Journal*

"An interesting read."
—*NewScientist*

THE FATHER OF FORENSICS

"True-crime readers, historical division, are served a full plate of murder with this biography of a forensic pathologist who was once one of the most famous people in Britain. . . . Evans proves to be a verbally agile narrator of the macabre, figuratively shaking his head about toxic love triangles and murder-for-insurance schemes that produced dismembered bodies and charred corpses. Crediting Spilsbury for making medical evidence acceptable to British courts, Evans delivers a page-turner for fans of the hot genre of criminal forensics."
—*Booklist*

BLOOD ON THE TABLE

The Greatest Cases of New York City's Office of the Chief Medical Examiner

Colin Evans

BERKLEY BOOKS, NEW YORK

THE BERKLEY PUBLISHING GROUP
Published by the Penguin Group
Penguin Group (USA) Inc.
375 Hudson Street, New York, New York 10014, USA
Penguin Group (Canada), 90 Eglinton Avenue East, Suite 700, Toronto, Ontario M4P 2Y3, Canada
(a division of Pearson Penguin Canada Inc.)
Penguin Books Ltd., 80 Strand, London WC2R 0RL, England
Penguin Group Ireland, 25 St. Stephen's Green, Dublin 2, Ireland (a division of Penguin Books Ltd.)
Penguin Group (Australia), 250 Camberwell Road, Camberwell, Victoria 3124, Australia
(a division of Pearson Australia Group Pty. Ltd.)
Penguin Books India Pvt. Ltd., 11 Community Centre, Panchsheel Park, New Delhi—110 017, India
Penguin Group (NZ), 67 Apollo Drive, Rosedale, North Shore 0632, New Zealand
(a division of Pearson New Zealand Ltd.)
Penguin Books (South Africa) (Pty.) Ltd., 24 Sturdee Avenue, Rosebank, Johannesburg 2196, South Africa

Penguin Books Ltd., Registered Offices: 80 Strand, London WC2R 0RL, England

BLOOD ON THE TABLE

This book is an original publication of The Berkley Publishing Group.

Copyright © 2008 by Colin Evans.
Interior text design by Kristin del Rosario.

PRINTING HISTORY
Berkley trade paperback edition / March 2008

Library of Congress Cataloging-in-Publication Data

Evans, Colin, 1948–
   Blood on the table : the greatest cases of New York City's Office of the Chief Medical Examiner / Colin Evans.
      p. cm.
   Includes bibliographical references and index.
   ISBN 978-0-425-21937-9
   1. New York (N.Y.). Office of Chief Medical Examiner.   2. Homicide investigation—New York (State)—New York—Case studies.   3. Criminal investigation—Case studies.   4. Forensic pathology—Case studies.   I. Title.

HV8079.H6E927 2008
614'.1097471—dc22

2007042358

PRINTED IN THE UNITED STATES OF AMERICA

10   9   8   7   6   5   4   3   2   1

ACKNOWLEDGMENTS

I am greatly indebted to several people and the numerous organizations that have assisted me in the preparation of this book. These are Dr. Vincent DiMaio, Ellen Borakove at the New York City Office of the Chief Medical Examiner, the New York Police Department, Hugh M. Cook at the University of Illinois Alumni Association, the Occupational Safety and Health Administration, the marvelously helpful staff at the British Library, and their colleagues just a few miles up the road at the British Newspaper Library in Colindale. Samantha Mandor and Shannon Jamieson Vazquez, at Berkley Books, have been unfailingly supportive; while a vote of special thanks goes to my agent, Ed Knappman, and all at New England Publishing Associates. David Andersen once again put his exhaustive private library at my disposal, and Greg Manning helped in more ways than he knows. As always, the final thank-you is dedicated to Norma. Needless to say, while all the above contributed enormously to this book, any errors are the responsibility of the writer alone.

INTRODUCTION

Each year approximately sixty thousand people die in New York City.* Most do so quietly and unnoticed, except by grieving families and friends, carried off either by old age or diagnosed illness. These are what we might term "normal" deaths. But New York is no ordinary city. And each year around fifteen thousand of its citizens die in extraordinary circumstances. In broad terms these deaths fall into one of three categories: sudden, unexplained, or violent. The only unifying thread is that all these bodies will ultimately find their way to the New York City Office of the Chief Medical Examiner (OCME).

Since its inception at the end of the First World War, the OCME has investigated well in excess of one million deaths. Most are found to be not at all suspicious and can be cleared up with an experienced eye, an external examination, or else a helpful telephone

---

* The number used to be far higher, but improved health care has slashed the mortality rate in recent decades.

call to the most recent attending physician. But around half—approximately seven thousand per annum—only give up their secrets on the mortuary slab. Of these, the overwhelming majority never make the headlines. Those that do—murders, mostly—have a knack of grabbing national attention. The roll call of killers reads like a *Who's Who* of American homicide: Francis "Two Gun" Crowley, Ruth Snyder and Judd Gray, Robert Irwin, Raymond Fernandez and Martha Beck, Alice Crimmins, David Berkowitz ("Son of Sam"), Joel Rifkin, Vincent Johnson ("the Brooklyn Strangler") . . . The list goes on and on and on. Even nowadays, at a time when its per capita homicide rate has plummeted to levels not seen since the early 1930s, New York still manages to murder more of its residents than any other major city in America. Little wonder, then, that its medical examiners are so highly regarded: they get to see more homicides in one year than most forensic pathologists experience in a decade.

Overseeing what has become a well-oiled operation is New York City's chief medical examiner (CME), arguably the most influential position in American medical jurisprudence. It is a post that combines prestige and pressure in equal amounts. You'd better have a lot of talent and the hide of a rhino if you want this job. Get ten thousand cases right and the media will just yawn; botch a single investigation and they will be at your throat like jackals. In the ninety years or so of the OCME's existence, the rank of chief medical examiner has been held by just seven men (women have yet to crack this particular glass ceiling on a permanent basis). In background and education, five CMEs enjoyed a commonality, being New York born and educated, while the remaining duo had very close ties to the region. But that is where the similarities end. Their personalities were carved from all kinds of different rock. Some were close drinking buddies; some couldn't stand the sight of each other. Some were magnetically attracted to the reporter's notebook or TV camera; others made Calvin Coolidge look positively chatty. At times, their feuds and battles for succession wouldn't have looked out of place in a medieval European royal court. But one thing's for sure: the OCME has never been dull, and many of the homicide cases it has investigated have become medico-legal classics.

As it developed new methods of tracking down killers, the OCME helped change the face of forensic science across America. This came about through a combination of technological innovation, top-quality personnel, superb science, and painstaking diligence. Oh yes, and the odd inspired hunch. (Dr. Milton Helpern, in particular, was always very big on "hunches.") The biggest beneficiaries of this forensic bonanza were the residents of New York City itself. And none too soon. To put it charitably, New York's earliest settlers had a fairly relaxed attitude when it came to the willful removal of human life. Especially if the killer was white. The state's first recorded execution took place on June 25, 1646, when a black slave named Jan Creoli was first choked to death and then "burned to ashes" for the crime of sodomy, and yet we have to wait until 1673 before we find anyone paying the ultimate price for murder. On this occasion the culprits were two Native Americans. Astonishingly, another hundred years would pass before we have the first verified case of a white person being hanged for murder. (Treason, buggery, counterfeiting, and horse stealing were a different story. Several white people were hanged for these offenses.) Given the freewheeling nature of colonial life—and the fact that a century-long moratorium on homicide flies in the face of human nature—all we can assume is that New Yorkers had one standard for Caucasian killers and another for the rest. Unlike their cousins to the north. Inhabitants of Massachusetts, for instance, had been hanging homicidal descendants of the Pilgrims since as early as 1630.

But all that changed in the nineteenth century. The tidal wave of immigration that hit New York brought about a quantum shift in public sentiment. As the population rate soared, so did the crime figures and, with it, demands that the authorities crack down hard. Punishment, where it was exacted, was harsh and retributive. When it came to meting out capital punishment most, though not all, of the racial inequities were ironed out, but one serious problem remained: how to catch the bad guy? Across the Atlantic, western Europe's law enforcement agencies had pinned their crime fighting future on scientific analysis. It was a stratagem that had brought spectacular success. Killers and other criminals who left their fingerprints at crime scenes were paying a high price for this sloppiness, as the magnifying glass came into its own, and the fingerprint expert did the rest. Blood grouping and sophisticated ballistics analysis had also been added to the forensic arsenal. But it wasn't that way in the New World. When it came to catching criminals they were decidedly old time. For two decades at the start of the twentieth century, frustrated American scientists, medical men, and criminologists banged the drum to play catch up. Eventually in New York State they created enough clamor to force Albany's hand and in 1918 the Office of the Chief Medical Examiner was created in Manhattan. The OCME might not have been the first dedicated medico-legal facility in America—that distinction belongs to Boston—but it soon became the most powerful and the most emulated, as it uncovered ways of closing off many of the loopholes through which killers had been wriggling free.

As we noted earlier, the OCME has never been concerned solely with murder. Besides homicide, there are countless ways of prematurely abandoning the mortal coil—train wrecks, illness, airplane crashes, bombings, suicide, auto wrecks, domestic accidents, and falls, to name just a few—and the OCME has seen them all. Some of the more esoteric often occur during so-called sex games. Autoeroticism, with its nooses and lethal lack of muscle tone, is always a chancy business, as hundreds have discovered just a second or so too late. So, too, is "playful strangulation" between partners, where many a dominant partner had stared down disbelievingly at the lifeless flesh beneath his or her fingers. In both of the foregoing examples, the participant is driven by the belief that cutting off oxygen to the brain will trigger the ultimate orgasm. What many fail to appreciate is that while interfering with the flow of oxygen to the brain may or may not elevate sexual pleasure to Olympian levels of ecstasy, it does tend to play havoc with various other minor bodily functions—such as the ability to breathe. Incidentally, while we're on the subject of dangerous liaisons, how about a special mention for the housewares enthusiast who became amorously attached to his vacuum cleaner. You've guessed it. One consummation too many and his heart called it quits. The OCME has dealt with all these deaths and more, but overwhelmingly, when people think of the OCME they think of murder, and that is where the core of this book lies.

It is worth remembering that at the start of the twentieth century, New York City had approximately three hundred murders each year, an incredibly low total by modern standards. By 1990 this had soared to 2,245 per annum. Fast-forward to a ghastly September morning in 2001, when 2,749 people were murdered in a matter of minutes. When the first World Trade Center tower collapsed and the rubble began to fly, an advance guard from the OCME found itself caught in the killing zone. The blast literally took them off their feet. Almost miraculously all survived with nothing worse than broken bones and cuts. Patching up their injuries was the easy part. What lay in front of them, buried beneath the smoldering ruins of the Twin Towers, was the most daunting forensic puzzle that any medico-legal team has ever faced. It would be their job—the pathologists, the forensic biologists, the

THE EARLY YEARS

A "Coroner's Quest" is a queer sort of thing!
—R. H. Barham (nom de plume: Thomas Ingoldsby), 1788–1845

On January 1, 1898, something quite remarkable happened. The biggest city in the United States suddenly became very much bigger. Overnight, New York City quadrupled in area to three hundred square miles and boosted its population by approximately 65 percent to almost 3.4 million. This meticulously planned demographic explosion was detonated when Manhattan and the Bronx, hitherto known collectively as New York, merged with urban Brooklyn and the largely rural areas of Queens and Staten Island to form the modern-day conurbation we call New York City. It was a bold, brash move in readiness for the new century, one that instantly catapulted this sprawling archipelago of more than five hundred islands and a snatch of mainland—the Bronx—into the front rank of world cities.

And, like most metropolises, New York City had more than its share of dead bodies. They turned up everywhere. Leaving aside the natural wastage generated by old age, death was depressingly commonplace. Construction sites, road accidents, disease in all its forms, indifferent medical care, premature births, and food poisoning—restaurateurs appear to have been alarmingly lavish with the toxins they served up on their menus—all combined to send the mortality rate skyrocketing. And this was without factoring in homicide.

By law, every death from anything other than natural causes was supposed to be investigated fully, and for that New Yorkers turned to the coroner, a post that could trace its lineage to medieval England. Although the job description dates back to pre-Norman times, it was King Richard I who gave the office statutory authority. This came about in September 1194, when a group of traveling judges who dispensed justice in the absent king's name—he was château-hopping somewhere in his beloved France—fetched up in the county of Kent, and there issued the Articles of Eyre, number twenty of which stated, "In every county of the king's realm shall be elected three knights and one clerk, to keep the pleas of the Crown." In the original Latin this office was called *custos placitorum coronas*, and from this the title coronator or crowner evolved, from which we get the word *coroner*.

At the outset the coroner's primary function was to protect the king's financial interests, something very close to Richard's heart. For despite what popular legend would have us believe, there was nothing especially endearing or honorable about "Good King Richard." In reality, he was a grasping opportunist with an appetite for expensive and ruinous wars. Moreover, he utterly loathed England. In a reign that lasted ten years, fewer than six months were actually spent in the "sceptred isle," which probably explains why he never even bothered to learn the language. Richard used his kingdom like an ATM, plundering its citizens' pockets to finance weaponry and pay soldiers, then disappearing on the latest crusade. In his absence these fund-raising activities were delegated to the coroner.

From being little more than a revenue gatherer, the coroner

gradually extended his authority into other areas. An early addition to his duties involved making sure that the property of executed felons—which meant pretty much everyone convicted of a serious crime at this time—was confiscated for the Crown. But gradually, as Parliament became stronger and more influential, especially in matters of tax collection, the powers of the coroner waned, until they became almost solely confined to the investigation of suspicious death. In this capacity, over the next several hundred years, the office of coroner became thoroughly entrenched in English law, so it was only natural that when the early immigrants arrived in America, they brought the coroner system with them.

New York State, like the rest of the thirteen colonies, embraced wholeheartedly what became known as "crowner's quest law." Unlike its English forebear, the New York coroner was an elective office, rather than appointed, although by the end of the nineteenth century the benefits of this egalitarianism were somewhat muted. As the Democratic Tammany machine tightened its grip on the political landscape, graft and corruption ran riot, and the coroner's office was no exception. Overwhelmingly it degenerated into a sinecure for party hacks brought in to balance a political ticket. Few had any legal training, and fewer still knew anything about medicine, but to a man they knew how to turn a blind eye and a quick buck. Even if dear old Uncle Silas had been found sucking coal gas through a rubber tube, it was a rare coroner indeed who wasn't prepared to ease the bereaved family's grief and shame by ruling that death to be natural—provided, of course, that a few bucks changed hands. Ten dollars was reckoned to be the going rate. Rumors abounded that for fifty dollars even an inconvenient homicide could be overlooked.

Such wholesale corruption wasn't to everyone's taste. As early as 1852, the *New York Times* was praying for "some ingenious gentleman [to] inform us of what possible use are coroner's inquests as they are habitually conducted." The press had a point. Some of the abuses were eye-catching. Although coroners were notorious for impaneling juries unnecessarily—at five dollars a sitting—this enthusiasm didn't always extend to letting jurors actually view the body. Not that this omission troubled most panelists, especially those who gained access to the exclusive Jurymen's Ring, as it came to be known. Every coroner had his favorite jurors. One gentleman, an Albert B. White, served on no fewer than 208 panels. As he had a sideline of supplying dead bodies or "material" to medical colleges, his ubiquity cannot be considered coincidental. Nor did the coroners delve too deeply into their jurors' antecedents. Yet another gentleman, J. J. McDonald, a veteran of 118 juries, was revealed to be a vagrant who, during one morgue visit, had been caught taking rather too intimate an interest in a recent female admission. Despite this lapse, he continued to serve and receive his juror's fees.

Records show that in 1868 when a skilled laborer counted himself lucky if he made $2.00 a day, a New York coroner pocketed from all sources, on average, $27.75 per body. It was the kind of return that made dead bodies valuable items indeed. So valuable, in fact, that some coroners would go to almost any lengths to gain possession of a cadaver. On one infamous occasion, when a body was spotted lying in the Hackensack Meadows, it sparked off what amounted to a human gold rush, with three coroners converging from various cardinal points, all desperate to lay claim to the corpse. Only some smart work by the coroner in whose jurisdiction the body actually lay—he had wisely sent some retainers on ahead and they encircled the trophy, holding off the interlopers at gun and knifepoint—prevented him from losing what would have been a good pay day. Occasionally tempers could really fray. In another incident, on an otherwise quiet Sunday afternoon in lower Jersey City, the local coroner was backing up his wagon to the front of his establishment to unload a boxed corpse when his attention was distracted by the crunch of metal-rimmed wheels on cobblestones. Glancing up, he spotted a hated rival coroner reining his own horse-drawn carriage to a halt just yards away. An edgy standoff ensued. The newcomer waited until the box was lifted out, then sprang down from his seat, bellowing that the body had been found in his district and that he was staking his claim. Within seconds the two coroners were tugging at the box in a furious fight for its possession. Such was the vigor of their dispute that the box fell to the sidewalk, pitching its contents out face first onto the pavement. Each of the warring officials made a grab for the corpse. Strong hands grasped hold of the coat so firmly that the body was raised to its feet. When tugging failed to decide the issue, punches were aimed over the dead man's shoulders. This way and that his frame twisted and whirled. Mortified churchgoers, watching from a distance, cringed in ashen-faced horror as the dead man seemed to take as lively a hand in the affray as the rival claimants. Cries of "Shame!" and loud hissing fell on deaf ears as the two protagonists continued trading roundhouse rights until a detachment of police arrived and put an end to the unseemly brawl. History doesn't record who won.

Across the Hudson, New York audiences were more hardnosed. When a similar dispute broke out on the East River—this time a drowning victim, or "floater," was the prize—chortling spectators thronged the shoreline as coroners from Brooklyn and Manhattan launched dinghies and then waged a pitched battle in midstream, each clubbing the other with oars. Finally, exhaustion set in. One of the combatants lost his balance and tumbled headlong into the river, allowing the victor to haul in the dead body and row back to shore, a chorus of raucous and appreciative cheers accompanying his every stroke.

Being paid by the body led to some creative corpse management. For instance, it was not unknown for a coroner to yank a body from the river, issue a John Doe certificate, and then heave the body back again. A few minutes later, it would be retrieved a second time, a second certificate issued, and a second $11.50 of taxpayers' money would promptly vanish into the coroner's back pocket. Sometimes the tactics bordered on the psychopathic. Certain coroners were known to personally bar a funeral's progress, muttering threats of impromptu and wholly unwarranted inquests, and refusing to permit the weeping cortege to proceed until an appropriate emolument had been handed over. Such extortion was as profitable as it was unethical. A coroner would count it a bad year if he made less than $11,000; most pocketed much more.

For cold-blooded larceny, though, the coroners of Staten Island were unbeatable. In October 1893, when the Warsak family of Elm Park called Dr. F. E. Barber to tend their six-week-old child, he diagnosed the illness as brain fever, declared that death was imminent, and said that he would write up the necessary certificate. As Barber was leaving the house he was confronted by the coroner's physician, Dr. J. Walter Wood, who had just caught wind of the infant's potentially fatal illness. Wood barged past him into the house. He cornered the parents, demanding to know what arrangements they had made for their impending bereavement. They told him and then he left. That night the child died. Shortly after dawn the next day, Wood returned with a seven-man jury. He swore them in, they viewed the body, and then they promptly disappeared. Wood was now authorized to do his worst. And he didn't disappoint. In a loud, portentous voice he announced his intention of performing an autopsy. Mrs. Warsak, uncertain whether to scream or faint, eventually did both, dual displays of emotion that clearly unsettled Wood, who threatened to call the police. Over her hysterical complaints, he conducted the autopsy with utter disregard for the family's feeling. After the most perfunctory examination—he singularly neglected any investigation of the cerebral region—Wood billed the county for twenty-five dollars, with another twenty-five dollars for his boss, coroner Stephen E. Whitman. This was no isolated incident. Whitman and Wood were notorious body snatchers, hated for a clutch of unnecessary and profitable autopsies.

The consolidation of New York's five boroughs in 1898 did nothing to arrest these abuses. Coroners' juries were packed with cronies, favored undertakers continued to snaffle most of the business, and even insurance companies got sucked into the vortex. (Because life policies rarely paid out in the event of a suicide, coroners kept a mental list of those underwriters prepared to pay handsomely for a favorable death certificate.)

But it was the area of crime investigation that really exposed the coroner's shortcomings. Although exact figures are difficult to come by, in the early twentieth century New Yorkers were slaying around three hundred of their fellow citizens annually. In terms of murder per capita, it worked out at around six per hundred thousand. (Compared with some southern cities, this was positively pedestrian: Memphis, at this time the most dangerous city in America, had a murder rate of sixty-four per hundred thousand per annum!) But murder was clearly a problem in New York, and its newfound status as a global city demanded that something be done.

Envious eyes were cast across the Atlantic, where Europe was in the midst of a forensic science revolution. Slowly at first, and then with greater rapidity, Old World law enforcement agencies had warmed to the notion of laboratory-led crime detection. In 1901 the Austrian scientist Karl Landsteiner developed the ABO blood grouping that later won him the Nobel Prize. One year earlier in Germany, Paul Uhlenhuth had devised his precipitin test for distinguishing human blood from that of other animals. These two advances added further muscle to what had unquestionably been *the* great identification breakthrough of the nineteenth century: the discovery that no two humans have the same fingerprint. Blood grouping, fingerprint analysis, and blood typing united in a tripronged attack that utterly transformed crime fighting. Killers in Europe were now going to the gallows or guillotine, convicted on the evidence of their fingertips or bodily fluids, while detectives processing crime scenes suddenly found themselves down on their hands and knees alongside scientists with magnifying lenses and trained forensic pathologists.

It was all so very different in the United States. Crime solving here, for the most part, was still rooted in the old traditions of eyewitnesses, informants, posses, and confessions. Science played virtually no part in the law enforcement process. The field of forensic pathology was no better. Any frustrated student who yearned for the latest advances in legal medicine needed some seriously deep pockets in order to travel to the great universities of Berlin, Paris, and Vienna, where the study and teaching of forensic science could be traced back to the eighteenth century.

With a murder rate ten times higher than that of its great rival, London, New York City clearly needed all the help it could get. Here, as in the majority of America, responsibility for the early stages of any homicide investigation still resided with the coroner. Only one state bucked the trend. As early as 1877, Massachusetts, fed up with the corruption and graft that went hand in hand with the old system, had voted to replace the position of coroner with a properly trained medical examiner, appointed by the governor for a seven-year term. The intention was that being nonelective, the post would be impartial and objective.

New York City could only dream of such independence. As the twentieth century entered its second decade, Gotham's coroners were as inefficient, corrupt, and autonomous as ever, with no sign of a shift in this balance of power. One particularly egregious example of their misconduct occurred on March 9, 1914, when a character named Eugene Rochette, holed up in a cheap hotel that had been under police surveillance, somehow managed to sustain a bullet wound to the head. A coroner's physician summoned to the scene had no hesitation in declaring it to be a case of suicide. But two doctors at Bellevue Hospital, who'd taken a much closer look at the body, disputed this finding. They were baffled by the absence of powder burns or scorching on the skin around the entrance wound. Most suicides who shoot themselves in the head hold the gun either against or very close to the skull. As the bullet is fired, explosive gases also belch from the barrel, often traveling many inches. These blacken and scorch an area around the entrance wound. The further away the muzzle is from the skin, the less noticeable are the powder burns. Although ballistics analysis was still in its infancy at this stage, the two Bellevue pathologists—and it should be remembered that Bellevue in the early 1900s saw more cases of shooting than any other U.S. hospital—already understood this correlation, and what they saw convinced them that the fatal shot had been fired from some distance, certainly not by Rochette himself. On their recommendation, the matter was referred to the district attorney. He agreed that it sounded fishy and ordered an immediate inquiry. However, the investigation never even got off the ground. Unbeknownst to everyone except the coroner's office, Rochette's body had been cremated forthwith. And there the matter was closed. Little wonder that Dr. James

Ewing, the eminent professor of pathology at Cornell Medical School, shook his head and sighed, "New York gets along with practically no aid from the science of legal medicine."

But all that was about to change.

On January 1, 1914, John Purroy Mitchel was sworn in as mayor of New York City. The election of a candidate who had run on a Fusion (Liberal and Republican) reform ticket sent shivers through a Tammany political machine that had run the city as its personal fiefdom for over a century. Just thirty-four years old and bursting with vigor, Mitchel was brilliant, abrasive, and *honest*! And he wasted no time in getting out the broom.

He ordered his Commissioner of Accounts, Leonard M. Wallstein, to conduct a root-and-branch investigation of New York's coroner system, to see if all the rumored corruption and excesses were merely the product of partisan political pamphleteering or if they were grounded in the truth. Wallstein opened his inquiry on June 13, 1914, little realizing the difficulties involved. After seven months spent weathering and not always overcoming just about every form of prevarication and obfuscation known to man, he finally submitted his report in January 1915.

It made for mighty uncomfortable reading. Wallstein cataloged a string of ineptitude and blatant dishonesty that shocked even hardened New Yorkers. Describing the current coroner system as a "public scandal and disgrace," he showed how of the sixty-five men who had held the office of coroner since consolidation, not one was thoroughly qualified, by training or experience, for the adequate performance of his duties. By occupation, nineteen were general physicians without any formal training in legal medicine, eight were undertakers, seven were politicians, six were real estate dealers, two were saloonkeepers, and two were plumbers; the rest were, respectively, a lawyer, a printer, an auctioneer, a contractor, a carpenter, a painter, an expressman, a dentist, a butcher, a wood-carver, a marble cutter, a labor leader, an insurance agent, a musician, and a milkman. The remainder had occupations that were unknown.

With so much medical ignorance on display, coroners generally relied on hired physicians to establish the cause of death and took their verdicts without quibble. This created its own set of problems. For instance, Wallstein discovered that in 1913 the Manhattan coroners recorded only one case of infanticide but found an abnormal number of alleged stillborn and premature births. Such a discrepancy made it hard to escape the notion that baby killers were operating with impunity in New York City. Another feature that disturbed Wallstein was a curious uniformity in causes of death; each coroner tended to have his own favorite. In Brooklyn, over a three-day period, he found that one acting coroner's physician reported four deaths owing to valvular heart disease and four owing to acute cardiac dilation. In each case only the most superficial of examinations was performed. Elsewhere, another death certificate recorded an impressive list of ailments that included chronic nephritis, myocarditis, and pulmonary edema, though nowhere did it confirm police and hospital reports that showed the poor fellow had committed suicide by gassing himself.

Further frustration attended the discovery of a man found dead in a lodging house, with a clearly visible bullet wound in his mouth and a .38-caliber revolver clutched in his right hand. The gun contained three loaded cartridges and one expended shell. An ambulance surgeon pronounced the man dead at the scene and the body was removed, on the orders of the coroner, to the morgue. By the time the coroner had tidied up his papers, the cause of death had mysteriously transmuted to a "rupture of thoracic aneurysm," and all reference to a bullet wound had been excised. In this manner, yet another suicide was swept conveniently under the carpet. Nor were these anomalies uncommon. Of the 320 cases that Wallstein reviewed, approximately 40 percent displayed a complete lack of evidence in the official papers to justify the cause of death.

One of the Manhattan coroners singled out for particularly "scandalous" conduct was Herman Hellenstein, and he was dragged kicking and screaming before the commission. It soon became evident that not only was he on the payroll of several insurance and railroad companies, but that his predilection for corporate arm-twisting had secured lucrative jobs for several of his friends. After a miserable grilling, Hellenstein, white and visibly shaken, conceded that the office of coroner should be abolished. Another coroner called to testify added little to his already murky reputation by declaring that he always declined to refer to legal books for fear that they might "confuse him."

At the time of Wallstein's review, Manhattan had four coroners; there were two in Brooklyn, two in Queens, two in the Bronx, and one in Staten Island. Those based in Manhattan, Brooklyn, and the Bronx each received $6,000 per annum, while coroners in Queens and Staten Island had to make do with $4,000. In addition, each office employed a coroner's physician who was paid $3,000 a year, and a clerk who received another $2,000. Wallstein estimated that the coroner system was costing New York's taxpayers approximately $172,000 a year. By contrast, the Suffolk County medical examiner's office based in Boston, Massachusetts, operated efficiently on just $32,500 per annum. Wallstein recommended that the old elective coroner system, with its graft and political quid pro quos, be replaced by a system based on the Suffolk County template, whereby a medical examiner was appointed—in New York's case, by the mayor—for seven years.

Mitchel took Wallstein's recommendations on board (although the seven-year term was not adopted; the New York position would last until retirement), and on April 7, 1915, a bill passed the New York legislature abolishing the coroner system. The small print stated that current holders of the post would be replaced when their engagement ended on January 1, 1918. After that, the city of New York would have its first chief medical examiner. Qualification criteria for the new post were rigid and trifold. Each candidate needed to be a physician, a trained pathologist, and an expert microscopist. Applications would be vetted and then the final candidates would sit a competitive exam. The successful applicant would be based in Manhattan and receive an annual salary of seventy-five hundred dollars and the power to appoint deputy medical examiners in each of the other four boroughs, all of whom would be under his authority.

It was clearly a step in the right direction and that same month offered further proof that New York was finally taking its murder problem seriously with the formation on April 19, 1915, of the Homicide Squad. This meant that jurisdiction over a dead victim of crime would now reside with the police rather than boneheaded coroners.

Not everyone was thrilled by this upheaval. One of the fiercest critics was ex-coroner Dr. Patrick Riordan, a well-connected Irishman whose whisky-laced appearances at countless crime scenes were the object of considerable humor and no little awe. Although Riordan was exactly the type of shady operator that the new system was designed to eradicate, that didn't prevent him from applying for the new job. Initial chuckles of disbelief soon gave way to a storm of criticism, all of which washed off Riordan's back like rain off a roof. When the list of candidates was whittled down to a final three, Riordan's name was still in the mix. Up against him, coincidentally, were the two physicians from Bellevue Hospital whose intervention in the Eugene Rochette case had created such a furor. Not that Riordan was worried. He had bluffed his way through the examination, worked the smoke-filled rooms like the old pro that he was, and was noisily confident of landing the new post. Even the electorate seemed to be on his side, for when it came time for the position of chief medical examiner to be filled, New York had itself a new mayor.

Despite having been a first-rate chief executive, Mitchel had paid the price for his infamous lack of tact. In the 1917 primaries he failed to win Republican support and ran for reelection on the Fusion ticket alone.* His Tammany opponent, John F. Rylan, a lawyer who mixed mediocrity and malleability in equal measure, buried him. Bumbling and ponderous, without wit, warmth, or wisdom, Rylan took office on the very day that the post of coroner was abolished, January 1, 1918. One of his first acts was to appoint Riordan temporarily to the position of CME, on the tacit understanding that confirmation would be forthcoming at the end of that month.

Riordan wasted no time in making his presence felt. He ordered that his name be placed on the door of every office occupied by the old Board of Coroners in all five boroughs. In the Bronx office alone, there were nineteen doors and embossed on every one, in fancy gold letters, was the legend DR. PATRICK J. RIORDAN, CHIEF MEDICAL EXAMINER.

Just one month later, the sign writers were inscribing a new name. For reasons that remain shrouded in mystery, Riordan suddenly found himself in very bad odor at City Hall and out of a job. (He didn't even get paid for his month in office). Instead, Rylan offered the post of chief medical examiner to one of the most extraordinary characters in the history of American forensic sci-

---

* After his defeat in 1917, Mitchel enlisted in the U.S. Army and received a commission in the air service. On July 6, 1918, at Camp Gerstner, Lake Charles, Louisiana, while training before being sent to fight in World War I, Mitchel fell five hundred feet from his single-seated scout plane and was killed. An investigation blamed his death on an unfastened safety belt.

ence, an East Coast blueblood who combined an impeccable social pedigree with outstanding credentials in the field of legal medicine. His name was Dr. Charles Norris.

At the time of his appointment, Norris was director of laboratories at Bellevue Hospital. That vacancy was now filled by his deputy, Dr. Douglas Symmers, who had placed third behind Norris on the civil service list for the post of chief medical officer, and was the other physician who had stood shoulder to shoulder with Norris in controversially asserting that Eugene Rochette had not died from a self-inflicted gunshot wound but had instead been murdered by an unknown assailant (for that, read "the police").

With his deep-set eyes, commanding bulk of more than two hundred pounds, and a glossy Vandyke beard that looked as if it had been polished and then sanded into shape, Norris looked more like a Shakespearean stage actor than America's premier forensic pathologist of the early twentieth century. But there was real substance behind the showy appearance. He was born into a wealthy Hoboken family on December 4, 1867, and attended Yale before going on to study medicine at the Columbia School of Physicians and Surgeons. He received his medical degree in 1892. Most unusually for medical graduates at that time he was drawn irresistibly to pathology—the "beastly science," as many derided it—only to suffer the same frustration as that endured by fellow students on his side of the Atlantic: all the best teachers were in Europe. For most this was an insurmountable hurdle; for Norris, with his ever-open checkbook, it provided the chance to soak up the sights and splendor of Europe's greatest cities while receiving top-flight instruction. In 1894 he pitched up in Germany. There he enrolled for two semesters in Kiel and one in Göttingen, before traveling to Berlin, where he fell under the influence of the legendary pathologist, Rudolf Virchow. From 1895 to 1896 he collaborated with two outstanding Viennese teachers, Eduard von Hofmann and Alexander Kolisko. The final leg of Norris's forensic jaunt across Europe took him to Scotland, and the hothouse university faculties of Glasgow and Edinburgh, where he studied under the Glaisters and the Littlejohns, two academic dynasties that had revolutionized British forensic science. By the time he returned to his homeland, Norris knew more about legal medicine than anyone in America, and he was eager for a chance to demonstrate his new-found skills.

In 1904 he was offered the post of professor of pathology at Bellevue Hospital and soon began conducting autopsies in criminal cases. The police trusted Norris. They liked his calm, deliberate manner of speech, and the way he delivered testimony, clearly and succinctly with none of the windbag pompousness that afflicted so many so-called expert witnesses. But like everyone else in the medico-legal system, Norris was hamstrung by the coroners' hegemony. Their fondness for "in-house" autopsies kept him on the sidelines in many big cases, but when incompetence, arrogance, and a general sense that something needed to be done eventually combined to bring about the coroners' downfall, the professor from Hoboken was waiting, scalpel poised.

When Norris officially took over his new role on February 1, 1918, the job parameters were sharply delineated: the CME was an appointed post that lasted until the incumbent's retirement, and only one person could remove him from office—the mayor. Over the years more than one resident of Gracie Mansion would seek to avail himself of this privilege. But for now, thoughts of failure didn't even enter Norris's mind as he set about organizing his department. He housed his headquarters in the pathology building of Bellevue Hospital at 400 East Twenty-ninth Street, thus beginning that establishment's long association with the Office of the

Chief Medical Examiner, a relationship that endures to the present day. Bellevue, besides being home to the New York University School of Medicine, is the oldest public hospital in the United States, able to trace its roots back to 1735. Because of the bountiful supply of violent and unexpected death in New York, it had always been in the vanguard of American pathology, both general and forensic. It welcomed Norris, but no special provisions were laid on. He and his assistants shared the large, skylit autopsy room on the second floor with the hospital pathologists. Some found the close proximity of the four marble tables claustrophobic; others preferred it, taking the view that so many colleagues so close at hand amounted to having access to a human reference library should an especially tricky situation arise. On a more pragmatic level, if the elevator that transported bodies to the second floor happened to break down, then a room in the basement could be pressed into service as a makeshift mortuary. Although bodies were stored in a room lined with centrally refrigerated storage compartments, a lack of air-conditioning elsewhere in the department meant that sometimes, especially at the height of summer, the OCME could be a sensory nightmare, particularly for distressed relatives who had come in to identify a deceased family member.

One of Norris's most important innovations was the introduction of a telephone switchboard, manned twenty-four hours a day. Whereas in the past, coroners had sauntered up to a crime scene, either at their leisure or after they had sobered up, Norris expected a professional response at any hour of the day or night.

The establishment of the OCME coincided with a period of enormous social upheaval, both on the home front and abroad. Just nine months earlier, the United States had entered World War I against Germany, and the number of doctors volunteering for active service overseas left many sectors of the medical profession dangerously understaffed. But Norris was fortunate in having good people around him. While he oversaw the Manhattan department, the post of deputy medical examiner for Queens went to Dr. Howard Neil, the Bronx to Dr. Karl S. Kennard. After a fitful start Dr. Carl Boettinger assumed responsibility for Brooklyn, leaving Dr. George Mord free to oversee Staten Island. The pay was nothing to write home about. Each deputy received an annual salary of $3,000, except Mord, who, for some reason, had to scrape by on just $1,950 a year. The total package turned out to be one of the best bargains New Yorkers ever got. For $50,000 a year less than the rickety old coroner system had cost them, they had, at long last, a modern cohesive investigative unit, purpose-built to fight crime.

They also had one the most remarkable medico-legal experts in history as their CME. Norris had brio to burn. His Runyonesque flamboyance came quite naturally to him, as did the patrician air of elegance that infused his every action. Where other pathologists had to make do with cabs or else hitch a ride to the latest crime scene, Norris would invariably sweep up in a lustrous, chauffeur-driven limousine. Alighting in his beautifully tailored frock coat, wing-collar and the trademark bow tie, looking for all the world as if he'd just stopped off en route to a cocktail party, he would then go about his work. Blessed with a razor-sharp intellect, Norris was a stickler for accuracy and demanded nothing less of those around him. Sloppiness was not tolerated. It was surprising how often back-alley crime scenes transmogrified into ad hoc classrooms as the CME instructed ham-fisted police officers in the correct methods of evidence processing.

He also possessed enviable reserves of compartmentalization. Most mornings found him in the morgue, dealing with the overnight admissions, but come midday—barring any emergencies—he would down tools, peel off his rubber gloves, and head for a long and often very liquid lunch at one of the glitzy hotels on Park Avenue.

These were the early days of the newspaper "gossip wars," a time when columnists such as Walter Winchell and Ed Sullivan were slugging it out for the best copy. For those who covered the Broadway beat, larger-than-life characters like Charles Norris were money in the bank. The press loved him and he loved them. But it wasn't all about ego feeding. Norris, pragmatic down to the soles of his gleaming wingtips, knew the value of "good press," and in the years to come, as his relations with City Hall soured to the point of disintegration, he went out of his way to cultivate the fourth estate. As a result, reporters were better informed than ever before, the OCME got some great coverage, and Norris gained some powerful allies.

Not everyone approved. Norris's elegance or arrogance—it all depended on the point of view—raised plenty of hackles. As early as 1921, a well-organized lobbying campaign designed to strip him of his powers and transfer them to the New York County district attorney's physician, Dr. Otto H. Schultze, came within a hair-breadth of success. Schultze, a fussy, self-important man with a knack for insinuating himself into high-profile cases—he would later gain prominence in the unsolved Hall–Mills murders of 1922 and the baffling death of Starr Faithfull in 1929—despised Norris. The antipathy dated back to Schultze's days as a coroner's physician when, like scores of others, he had been roughly handled by the Wallstein report. Dark hints about his probity, or lack thereof, meant that when the mayor was casting around for candidates to fill the post of CME, Schultze's name got spiked almost immediately. It was a stinging rejection, one that Schultze never forgot nor forgave. And he was a world-class grudge bearer. For the rest of his increasingly erratic career, he sniped and fumed incessantly at the man whom he believed had robbed him of his medical birthright.

If Norris was able to shrug off Schultze's maledictions like so many unwanted flies, then he was allowed no similar luxury when he found himself almost overrun by the consequences and the victims of Prohibition. Passage of what became popularly known as the Volstead Act (after its promoter, Congressman Andrew J. Volstead), might have been implemented with the best intentions, but it played havoc with the nation's health and gave the OCME a decade-long hangover. Thirsty Americans had no intention of modifying their behavior just because of some government diktat. They crowded into chic speakeasies if they were rich, and sleazy backrooms if they were not, and guzzled whatever was shoved in front of them. For many it was the last drink they ever swallowed. Some of the fluids that masqueraded as whisky or gin would have powered a Model T Ford. In 1920 an estimated 1,064 persons died from poisoned liquor in the United States. By 1925 that figure had soared by more than 400 percent, although the true figure will never be known, owing to the fact that many sympathetic doctors—unwilling to compound a bereaved family's grief with the possibility of legal action—excised all mention of alcohol from death certificates.

Norris autopsied hundreds of these hooch victims. An unashamed bon vivant himself, he found the human toll depressing and avoidable. To his way of thinking, just about the only beneficiary of Prohibition was organized crime. Certainly the OCME's workload came under increasing strain, as trigger-happy mobsters battling for control of the bootleg market pumped bullets into each other with lavish disdain.

This surge in gun crime forced a radical rethink in the way that gunshot wounds were investigated. Norris and his assistants fired all kinds of guns into different materials from various ranges and angles, studied the gunpowder marks and shot patterns, and then applied this knowledge to cases. The recent invention of the comparison microscope, which allowed two bullets to be viewed side by side, had transformed ballistics analysis, and Norris was one of the first to grasp its potential. Drawing on the power of the comparison microscope, and combining it with his own experiments, he was able, on one occasion, to disagree with a former coroner's physician (who was now working in law enforcement) and successfully establish that a death previously considered a suicide was actually a homicide. It also worked the other way. In another case, Norris was successful in changing an apparent homicide to a suicide.

With departmental problems multiplying exponentially, Norris refused to lose sight of his strategy. "My only object is to run the office efficiently and to obtain results along medical lines," he declared. "I mean by this the establishment of a medico-legal institute which would do research work along the lines being done in the larger central European cities. There is no reason why a city of the size and magnificence of New York should not do this work." And in 1922, the OCME got the chance to demonstrate just how much leeway it had made up on its European counterparts.

CASE FILE:
Becker and Norkin (1922)

Harry Becker was only eight years old but he sensed—no, make that *knew*—something was seriously wrong. For the past several months, ever since Pop had deposited him and his brother, Alexander, age nine, at the Hebrew Orphans' Asylum in Manhattan, Harry had been begging the welfare workers to find their mom. The hard-pressed staff told Harry what Abraham Becker had told them: their no-account mother had hightailed it with another man, and he just couldn't cope with four kids on his own. Harry didn't believe that. Mom had loved her children too much to just abandon them. In between pestering the nurses and wardens, Harry fretted over his twin sisters, Celia and Sarah, just three years old, anxious for news of their whereabouts. Last he'd heard they were at the Home for Hebrew Infants up in the Bronx, but that was months ago; they could be anywhere by now. At the back of his mind lurked an icy dread—he'd heard the other kids' taunts—that they'd probably been adopted. When prospective parents came to the orphanage to view the children, eight- or nine-year-olds like him and Alex rarely got a look-in; cute little twins, barely age three, now that was a different story. Harry, old beyond his years, shuddered at the prospect. More than anything else, he wanted the family back together. Which is why he kept bugging the staff. In the end, his nonstop badgering paid off. Someone from the Asylum contacted the police.

It turned out that Harry Becker wasn't the only person concerned about the disappearance of his mother. Just a few days earlier, two women from the Bronx—longtime friends of Jennie Becker—had also taken their concerns to the police. An investigation was promised. Without any great conviction or indeed desire, a couple of detectives began going door to door in Home Street where the Beckers had lived. It was routine stuff at first, but by nightfall their investigative antennae were twitching. Just about everyone they talked to—or so it seemed—told the same story: Abraham Becker had gotten fed up with his wife, murdered her, and buried the body close by. The detectives were staggered. For months this close-knit community had managed to bottle up these rumors and keep them from official ears, but gradually, as suspicions waned and tongues loosened, the officers were able to piece together the whole, incredible story . . .

Abraham Becker's antecedents had a familiar ring. He'd been born in Russia in 1888, at the height of the vicious pogroms. As a youngster he saw mobs attack Jewish homes, loot businesses, burn synagogues, all without hindrance from police or soldiers. Murders, too, went uninvestigated. Those able to flee this tyranny did so, and these included Becker's family. While still an infant, he joined millions of others on the long trek westward. His journey to the United States had been haphazard. He'd traveled first to Johannesburg, South Africa, and then on to London, which is where he met and married Jennie Karbritz, who was some nine years his junior. A short time later the couple booked passage for America. After clearing immigration at Ellis Island, the family settled in the Bronx where Becker found work as a chauffeur/truck driver. Each month was a struggle to support his rapidly expanding family. Not that Becker was overly concerned. Although functionally illiterate, he was blessed with a quicksilver tongue and a brash, cocky attitude, useful traits for a serial lecher wholly disinterested in monogamy. He also had a mean streak. Judging from the tearful letters that Jennie wrote her mother in London, she suffered regular beatings from her violent, philandering husband, although, according to some friends, at five foot three and almost two hundred pounds, Jennie was more than capable of landing a few solid blows of her own when the occasion demanded.

By 1919 what had always been a shaky marriage was teetering on the abyss. In August of that year Becker was hired to drive a party of day-trippers out to Coney Island. Among the passengers was a twenty-year-old woman, with blond, fashionably bobbed hair and gullible eyes that blinked fast behind thick, tortoise-shell-rimmed spectacles. Her name was Anna Elias, and while her co-passengers squealed with delight on the various rides and amusements, the curvaceous Anna sat spellbound beside the driver. Becker, amusing and handsome in a coarse sort of way, tossed compliments around like confetti, and was, by his own admission, single and unattached. When he asked to see her again, she jumped at the chance. Pretty soon Anna realized she was hopelessly in love. As summer mellowed into fall and their relationship ripened into promises of a January wedding, Becker even applied for a marriage license in the names of A. Beck and Anna Elias. What should have been the happiest day of Anna's life came to an abrupt conclusion when her sister, Carrie Rosenweig—who hated and distrusted Becker—burst into the ceremony, grabbed hold of the startled bride-to-be, hauled her outside, and dragged her away. Anna was nothing if not resilient. Laying this disaster to one side, she sneaked meetings with Becker throughout 1920 and that same year took the life-changing step of running off with him to Cleveland, where they set up home as man and wife. With this course of action, Anna knew she had crossed the moral Rubicon, at least so far as her family was concerned. Henceforth, she was a pariah to them, hated and reviled for the "shame" she had brought on their name.

So Cleveland it was. And this was where Anna's world crashed in flames. Somehow—it was never made clear how—she got wind that Becker had a wife and four children back in New York. Heart-broken, she listened as the man she loved finally admitted his deception. Not that she got the full story—far from it. Even now, Becker ducked and dived, insisting that he and Jennie had never legally married. Maybe this is why, when Anna and Becker returned to New York after just three months, she continued to sleep with him. But more trouble was brewing. Jennie had found out where Anna lived and one day turned up unannounced, catching her husband in *flagrante delicto* with his young mistress. Once again the punches started to fly.

Anna had reached the end of her tether. Brutalized and humili-ated, she would have severed all contact with Becker at this stage, except for one thing; she was now pregnant. In early 1921 she gave birth to a little girl. Each week the occasional father stopped by to pay Anna five dollars toward the upkeep of their daughter, Marie, and to beg her to continue the relationship. As Anna's will wavered, her parents stepped up their campaign against the two-timing Becker, insisting that she dump this jerk who had ruined her life. The soul-searching was long and deep, but in the end Anna yielded to their advice, upping sticks and moving to Staten Island.

Becker was furious. Like most egocentrics he was unable to stomach any hint of rejection. New York might have been bulging with seven million citizens, but it didn't take Becker long to track down his missing lover. Once the initial anger wore off, he showered her with protestations of undying love. But Anna would have nothing to do with him, not even when he asserted that he would "get rid of" his wife and marry her. The emptiness of this promise was soon apparent, for it was about now that Jennie finally made good on her oft-repeated threat to leave him. Given the opportunity at last to square what had become a hellish love triangle, Becker flinched. He wasn't about to swallow another dose of rejection, unpalatable and bitter. No surprises, then, that it wasn't Anna, but Jennie, whom he ran after, begging his long-suffering wife to return.

As reunions go it was limp and lackluster, certainly not happy. All through 1921 the tension festered; Becker was stealing assignations with Anna whenever he could, still fighting nonstop whenever he was in Jennie's company. His notoriously short temper was shrinking by the day. And then, in the spring of 1922, a sudden and wholly unexpected thaw warmed Becker's glacial home life. Friends were astonished to see that instead of hitting each other, the couple were now hitting it off. There was a newfound gaiety in the Becker household, so much so that when they attended a friend's party on the night of Friday, April 6, 1922, the hostess was delighted to see the Beckers acting more like love-struck teenagers than grizzled veterans of the matrimonial wars. Jennie Linder clucked around the Beckers all night long like a mother hen, ensuring that their plates were never empty for long. The conveyor belt of food—fruit and canapés—continued unabated until Jennie Becker was forced to laughingly hold up her hand and cry,

"Enough." Abe, too, seemed to be enjoying himself. As midnight neared and the party drew to a close, Mrs. Linder waved good-bye to the Beckers and watched as their Dodge sedan disappeared into the chilly spring night, heading north toward the Willis Avenue Bridge.

She never saw Jennie Becker alive again.

The next day Abe went to the police with a curious tale. He'd gone off to work that morning, he said, and left Jennie at their apartment; when he'd returned at noon his wife had vanished. He could offer no explanation for the mysterious disappearance. The description he provided ran as follows: "Mrs. Becker was born in England twenty-five years ago and lived up until the time of her disappearance at 819 East 150th Street . . . She had blue eyes, blonde hair and good teeth." He went on to describe the outfit she had worn to the party. "A dark gray overcoat, a white waist [blouse], brown skirt, black lace shoes and black silk stockings and . . . a dark brown cloth hat. She wore a wedding ring, but no other jewelry, and carried twelve dollars in her purse." The desk sergeant wearily noted the details, before mentally filing them in the "Forget It" file. Spouses went missing all the time. No big deal. Mostly they came home, and if they didn't, well, good luck to them. Experience told him that ninety-nine times out of a hundred, the disappearance would be of no interest to the authorities.

For someone who'd just been elbowed unceremoniously into the single-parent column with four youngsters to care for, Becker took the dislocation with enviable equanimity. Indeed, those who knew him well couldn't recall him looking so upbeat. On April 10, he called on Mrs. Linder and let her in on a secret—Jennie had actually run off with a lover. "He said he didn't care, that his wife was no good anyhow," was how she recalled it later. At a subsequent meeting he did affect more concern, telling Mrs. Linder that he was still searching for his wife, this time "in the cabarets," a clear implication that she was hitting the nightspots and living the high life. Mrs. Linder frowned: that didn't sound like Jennie at all.

With Jennie apparently out of his hair, Becker set out to reclaim Anna. But when he showed up at her house in Staten Island, he received a body blow—she'd started walking out with a new man. Barely able to contain his fury, Becker produced what he said was a telegram from Jennie in England, stating that she'd left America for good. He thrust the telegram into Anna's face and delivered an ultimatum: him or the other guy. She chose Becker.

So notorious was Becker's reputation as a womanizer, that few in the neighborhood expressed any open surprise when he moved Anna into the apartment on 150th Street. But behind his back the whispers had begun. Word got around that Becker knew a whole lot more about Jennie's disappearance than he was letting on. Significantly, most of this gossip was sparked off by Becker's reckless boasting when drunk. His vanity was boundless and so was his tongue. Insulated from all this gossip—most neighbors shunned her—Anna just got on with her life, thankful that her fortune had turned at last. Once his divorce came through, Becker promised, they would get married. First, though, he needed to straighten out a few details.

One week after Jennie's disappearance, out of the blue, he sold the Dodge for three hundred dollars and bought a cheaper Studebaker. The hundred-dollar balance, so he would later claim, was earmarked for something else. As the days passed and Becker went about reconstructing his life, the clamor about Jennie's disappearance kept mounting. The story just wouldn't die down. Desperate to sweep the gossip under the carpet, he told Anna's sister, Carrie Rosenweig, who lived just a few blocks away, that Jennie had returned to England and that he intended to get a divorce. She called him a liar, told him to get the hell out of it, and slammed the door in his face.

Others were equally skeptical. Leading the charge was Mrs. Linder. Toward the end of April she confronted Becker with the rumors. He countered by producing a letter, ostensibly written by Jennie and mailed in Philadelphia. It read: "Dear Husband Abe— A few lines to inform you am leaving with another man to whom I was married before I married. [sic] He threatened that unless I do this he will have me arrested. I hope you will be a better father to the children than I have been mother. Your ungrateful wife, Jennie."

Mrs. Linder, who had known the missing woman for a good many years, studied the letter closely. To her untrained and admittedly jaundiced eye, the handwriting bore no resemblance to that of her friend's. Nor could she reconcile the sentiments expressed in the letter with the loving mother she had known. Becker? Now he was a different kettle of fish altogether; she could believe anything of that putz—hence her lack of surprise when the amorous truck driver first farmed out his four kids onto some friends, then shooed them into various orphanages.

With his children out of sight, Becker really let down his guard. A few drinks was all it took to loosen his tongue to suicidal levels. Not that he'd ever been circumspect; it wasn't in his nature. As early as April 7, the day of Jennie's disappearance, he'd lurched drunkenly up to a friend, Harry Simonwitz, proffered his hand, and smirked, "Congratulate me. I have got rid of my wife." Simonwitz, nonplussed, had scurried away. On another occasion, when Becker was touting around for someone to adopt his children and a friend, Yetta Weinberg, mentioned knowing a woman who was prepared to adopt one, but was put off by fear of the birth mother's coming back and claiming them, Becker had leered triumphantly. "Tell the lady to take the child," he gloated. "I'll guarantee that the mother will never come back."

Such intemperance did little to staunch the flow of gossip—which by now had reached flood level—linking Becker to the disappearance of his wife. The stories varied, but some were remarkably detailed, with one version claiming that Jennie had been murdered in a taxicab crossing the Willis Avenue Bridge and then buried somewhere in the Bronx. Viewed from a distance of time, it beggars belief that such rampant gossip did not somehow filter through to the authorities but early immigrant neighborhoods were homogeneous, close communities, deeply distrustful of any outside interference. Many of Becker's neighbors had grown up in the shadow of the tsar's terrifying secret police, the Ochrana, and for such people the thought of taking any problem, no matter how grave, to the authorities was unthinkable. This was the dilemma that confronted Mrs. Linder. All summer she twisted and turned, but by mid-November she could bottle up her suspicions no longer. Accompanied by a friend, she went to the police and unburdened herself. Coincidentally, just days later, staff at the Hebrew Orphans' Asylum decided that little Harry Becker's persistence deserved at least a token airing, and they too called at the nearest precinct station . . .

When detectives had completed their initial inquiries into the disappearance of Jennie Becker, they submitted a report to the district attorney's office. On November 24, 1922, the assistant DA, Albert Cohn, decided that enough evidence existed to question Becker and he was taken into custody. Once behind bars, and denied the damaging impact of liquor on his tongue, Becker clammed up tight. His reticence forced investigators to widen their search. As they delved deeper into Becker's background, one anomaly leaped out at them almost immediately. According to the employment records of the Empire Fireproof Door Company, where Becker worked, on

April 7—the day of Jennie's disappearance—Becker had not showed up at work, contrary to what he'd told the police at the time of filing his missing persons report. Clearly, he was a liar; but did this make him a killer?

Desperate to answer this question, detectives now switched tactics. In the course of their inquiries, one name had cropped up repeatedly, that of Harry Monstein, a close friend of Becker. Monstein was pulled in for questioning and given one of those old-fashioned "interviews," the kind that last well into the night, unencumbered by the stultifying presence of any defense lawyer. It worked. By morning Monstein was spilling his guts. He revealed that on April 22—two weeks after Jennie's disappearance—Becker had begged him to write a letter, making it appear to be from his missing wife, on the pretext that he needed such a document to speed up the institutionalization process for his children. Monstein agreed. To add a flourish of verisimilitude, Monstein acceded to Becker's suggestion that he travel to Philadelphia, where he duly mailed the letter and topped it off with a telegram, also designed to convey the impression that Jennie had decamped to the City of Brotherly Love. For this little bit of evidence tampering, Becker paid Monstein just ten dollars.

By June, Becker's confidence had swollen to bursting point. That month, over a shared bottle of booze, he decided to confide in Monstein. Jennie hadn't run off at all, he slurred. Two men had killed her and buried her body "in the woods." Monstein's befuddled brain registered this admission with neither shock nor abhorrence; he, too, had heard the neighborhood scuttlebutt and part of him wondered if this wasn't another helping of Becker's braggadocio. Even so, he wasn't prepared to take any chances: priority number one was self-preservation, and that meant keeping his mouth shut. Until now.

Officers leaned in close over the perspiring Monstein. Long

experience told them that the critical psychological moment had been reached. The threats were stark: cooperate or else face a charge of accessory to murder—maybe worse. Monstein, greasy with sweat and scared witless by the thought of a possible appointment with "Old Sparky," jumped at their offer of immunity if he would turn stool pigeon. On November 27 he was thrown into the Bronx County Jail, and locked in a cell opposite Becker. Monstein's was the first familiar face Becker had seen in three days. His relief was palpable, and, being Becker, he began blabbing. Although the two men talked in hushed whispers, decibel levels were still high enough for them to be overheard by a detective and a police stenographer who had been stationed in adjacent cells. Monstein stuck to the prepared script, telling Becker that he'd been arrested on suspicion of complicity in Jennie's disappearance, and that searchers were looking in the dumps all over the city for her body. "They'll never find it," scoffed Becker. "It's not in the dumps."

Monstein didn't press. Instead, he mentioned that the police had dug up a woman's body in the North Bronx. Becker seemed to find this amusing, in light of the fact, he chuckled, that Jennie was buried in the *South Bronx*. Furthermore, her body was covered with lime and therefore unrecognizable.

Every word entered the stenographer's notebook, and listening ears really perked up when Becker's tongue finally severed all contact with his brain and he bragged that someone named Norkin had killed Jennie and buried her "so deep they couldn't find the body in 100 years." Just a hundred bucks it had cost him, Becker crowed, best deal he'd ever made.

He'd barely finished talking before he was hauled back into the interview room. For the next twenty-four hours, he was "questioned vigorously," according to the DA; Becker saw it rather differently, later claiming that he'd been beaten like a rug for hours on end. Whatever the means employed, the information obtained proved decisive.

That same day, Reuben Norkin, aged thirty-one, who owned an auto repair shop at 140th Street and Southern Boulevard, close to where Becker worked, was arrested on suspicion of murder. When told of Becker's accusation, Norkin erupted like a volcano, swearing it was all a crock and he'd done nothing wrong. But a night in the police cells in 1920s New York could have a wondrously liberating effect on the memory, and by morning, looking considerably the worse for wear, Norkin was a changed man. Determined—or so he said—to set the record straight, he led officers to his shop and began pointing out various spots in the ground. Detectives grabbed shovels and started digging. But each spot came up blank.

Eventually, Norkin tired of the parrying and directed officers to an adjacent two-acre vacant lot, once a junkyard and now surrounded by billboards and hedges. Neatly sidestepping the scraps of iron, twisted axles, and broken wheels, he led detectives to a slightly raised area of earth. A tentative prod with a stick released a distinctive odor. At 5 P.M. on November 29, the search for Jennie Becker came to an end.

Exhumation of the remains was overseen by the assistant medical examiner for the Bronx, Dr. Karl Kennard. Since gaining his medical degree in 1899 at the University of Kentucky, Kennard had worked mainly in the New York area and had taught pathology at the Fordham Medical College until financial difficulties had forced that institution's closure on June 16, 1921. He watched keenly as diggers uncovered a disused pit that had three walls made of brick and the fourth of soil. Judging from the amount of ash, it had once been a boiler vault. At a depth of four feet, shovels struck into some mattress ticking, beneath which lay a sack. Inside this sack were human remains. Lime had been liberally scattered on the corpse, though not enough to complete decomposition or mask the foul smell. The body was dressed in a coat, sweater, and dress, all falling to pieces. Once Kennard had completed his preliminary examination, the body was removed and taken to the Fordham Hospital morgue, where the OCME maintained its Bronx headquarters. There, Kennard conducted an autopsy.

He began by stripping away the rotted fabric of the garments. As he did so a clay-encrusted object fell to the floor. He bent to pick up what looked like a wedding ring. Careful washing revealed an inscription on the inside of the ring, but even under a magnifying glass the lettering was too worn to be deciphered. There was little to be gleaned from the clothing: a brown knee-length overcoat, a light dress of blue and white check, and a sweater worn over the dress. The only other items were a pocketbook that contained $1.18 and some keys.

Now it was a question of establishing the cause of death. It seemed clear enough, the skull had been fractured by a single blow behind the left ear made by some blunt object; a hammer or iron bar was Kennard's best guess. However, despite being fractured, the skull was still intact, which led Kennard to think that the blow might not have killed immediately but rather that the victim lived for several hours after the attack. When he cut into the bronchial tubes, he found what looked like traces of ash and earth. This added an entirely different, more horrific dimension to the murder equation: that the victim might have been alive when buried. Decomposition made it impossible to tell if any other external injuries had been inflicted.

When Kennard opened the stomach he found a small quantity of undigested food. While this could tell him nothing about how long the body had been in the ground, it did provide a clue as to how long after her final meal Jennie Becker had died. By and large, digestion is a fairly predictable process. As one later New York City medical examiner puts it, "Very little interferes with the law of the digestive process. It is not precise to the minute (no biological process is), but within a narrow range of time it is very reliable. Within two hours of eating, ninety-five percent of food has moved out of the stomach and into the small intestine. It is as elemental as rigor mortis. The process stops at death." This is fine so far as it goes, but like rigor mortis, any number of variables can affect the digestive process. Fatty food takes longer to digest, as does a large meal. Mood, health and emotional state can also play their part. But nothing is more likely to disrupt the digestive process than sudden trauma, either physical or psychological. Extreme terror can play havoc with the body's metabolism. Fear, fright, injury, pain— all of these can hamper digestion. For example, after severe head trauma sustained in a road accident, food may stay in the stomach for several days, looking as fresh as when it was swallowed. These, however, are exceptions. As a rough rule of thumb, the average meal evacuates the stomach after a couple of hours or so.

What Kennard saw here convinced him that the victim had met her death shortly after eating food of some description. According to the case notes, on the night of her disappearance Jennie had been seen at the party, gorging herself on snacks. Mindful of the possibility that the soupy stomach contents he had extracted might well be the residue of those snacks, Kennard sent them, along with numerous other bodily samples, to Alexander O. Gettler, New York City's chief toxicologist since 1918, for chemical analysis.

Once Kennard had completed his autopsy, Becker was brought to the mortuary and asked if he could identify the body. Under Kennard's watchful gaze, Becker viewed the rotting remains with no more emotion than if he had been checking out a used car, then shook his head. Too small, he said, and his wife had much better teeth. Also, Jennie never wore a sweater, and the shoes were all wrong. At this point, Becker's original missing person's report was produced, included in which was a comprehensive description of these very shoes. He shrugged his indifference. And it was the same with the pocketbook: never seen it before.

None of Becker's denials cut any ice with the DA's office, and, on November 29, he was charged with murder. The following day, Norkin also found himself facing the capital charge. He was furious. Sure, he might have furnished the shovel used to bury the dead woman, but that was the extent of his involvement. Any suggestion Becker made to the contrary was a flat-out lie! While Norkin fulminated and Becker schemed, Detective James I. McCarton took the keys found on the dead woman to the Beckers' apartment. To no one's surprise, they fitted various locks, including the front door, a dresser, and the mailbox. Any iota of doubt that the body was that of Jennie Becker had evaporated, certainly as far as the police were concerned.

With his already perilous situation darkening by the hour, Becker now buckled and admitted what everyone knew—that his long-lost wife had been found. But still he wriggled like an eel, piecing together a story that flirted first with the surreal, then lurched into the downright fantastic. Norkin, he insisted, had been the lone killer, a vicious psychopath motivated solely by revenge. "He killed her to get even with me because we had a row over an automobile," Becker told detectives. The two men had argued over payment after Norkin repaired Becker's truck. Norkin had then killed Becker's wife and declared the debt wiped out. After this, said Becker, the two men shook hands and resumed their friendship!

The district attorney, Edward J. Glennon, was incredulous. "Why didn't you report the crime?"

"Because he had killed a lot of other people and would kill me, too," was Becker's lame and unsubstantiated response.

Elsewhere in the county jail, Norkin was dishing up his own version of events, and—surprise, surprise—this painted the teller in an infinitely more favorable light. He said that Becker had first broached the subject of murder around Christmastime 1921, but he'd thought it was just Becker running his mouth as usual, so he'd paid him no mind. Over that winter and into spring Becker piled on the pressure, nagging Norkin at every turn to help him and always receiving a negative response. Finally, in early April, Becker had asked to borrow a shovel. He didn't say why he needed the shovel, but Norkin had lent him one anyway. Only later did Becker reveal the truth: that he'd killed Jennie and buried her next to Norkin's repair shop.

Investigators didn't buy Norkin's story at all and cranked up the level of questioning. Hour after hour of relentless grilling finally produced the desired effect. Norkin broke under the pressure and changed his tale. This version contained an admission that he *had* helped Becker to conceal the body, though he still refused to budge from his adamant denial of any involvement in Jennie's actual death.

As the two former confederates did their damndest to strap each other into the electric chair, it was all too easy to forget the other victim in this tragedy. For Anna Elias the past week had been a living nightmare. Just hours after Becker was charged with murder, she was found wandering the streets at midnight, half out of her mind, babe in arms. Tearfully, she told the sympathetic officer that she had been thrown out by her landlady. Her own family, too, had turned their back on her. With nowhere to go, she spent that night at Tremont Police Station.

Anna's plight was brought into sharp relief two days later, on December 1, when she was called before a grand jury investigating the death of Jennie Becker. Misty-eyed jury members choked back their emotion as she detailed her appalling predicament. In a spontaneous gesture of charity, they struck up a collection to help the poor woman, with one talesman throwing in a hundred dollars. (This was later refunded when it became apparent that Anna's circumstances, through the kindness of friends, had improved.)

Once this poignant interlude was concluded, the grand jury got to hear some startling testimony. Much of this came via a signed confession by Reuben Norkin, in which he claimed that Jennie Becker's death had been no sudden domestic flare-up that spiraled into tragedy but rather a deliberate murder, planned down to the very last detail. According to Norkin, Becker had first suggested poisoning his hated wife, then drowning her, only for the hesitant and fearful Norkin to each time dissuade him from such drastic action. But persistence won out. Subjected to weeks of incessant pressure and motivated by a sense of loyalty that he now bitterly regretted, Norkin folded and reluctantly agreed to help. The conspirators next scrutinized the neighborhood for a suitable murder venue. After much scouring they finally decided that Norkin's repair shop, a small building with no dwelling within two hundred feet, was the ideal spot. The icing on the murderous cake was provided by the abandoned junkyard next door: perfect for burying a body. With the details finalized, on April 5 Becker told the unwitting Jennie that he was taking his car for Norkin to fix, because the engine had been misfiring. Instead, the two men used this time to dig the pit, piling up the ash and clay close by, ready to shovel in once the deed was done. The next afternoon—the day of the party—they carried out a full-scale rehearsal of the crime; then Norkin went home to await his assignation with Becker.

That night Becker drove Jennie home after the party, along a prearranged route that wended northward on Southern Boulevard. As they neared Norkin's shop, Becker put his driving skills to devious use. By crafty use of the gas pedal and the brake, he managed to contrive the impression that the car's engine trouble had returned. Pounding the steering wheel in frustration—dammit, he'd paid Norkin good money to fix this car just a couple of days earlier!—Becker thundered that he was driving to Norkin's to get this sorted out right there and then, even though it was 1:30 in the morning. Whether Jennie expressed skepticism over the likelihood of Norkin's being at work at this unpromising hour we don't know, but we do know that when Becker reached Norkin's place, he found the big front gate locked. Leaving Jennie in the car, he strode angrily to a nearby lunch wagon, one of Norkin's favorite hangouts. As arranged, Norkin was waiting. Quite by chance, two men witnessed this meeting. After exchanging a few words, Norkin accompanied Becker to the car, where their victim was waiting, then drove it into Norkin's yard. According to Norkin, the yard's bleak desolation really got to Jennie. "Oh, my, I don't like this place," he heard her say to Becker. "Let's get away from here."

Becker pooh-poohed her concerns, insisting that it wouldn't take long, and for a few minutes Jennie shivered inside the car while the two men tinkered with the engine. When Norkin announced that he needed to fetch some extra tools and wandered off, Becker summoned Jennie from the car and asked her to listen for "knocking" sounds from the engine, while he adjusted the carburetor's fuel mixture. As requested, Jennie bent low over the engine and put one ear to the block.

A thunderous blow knocked her senseless.

Becker threw his club to one side and stood, panting, over his stricken wife. Norkin, who had watched this scene unfold from by the gate, where he was standing guard, glanced anxiously in both directions along the deserted street. Even if any passerby had chanced along at this late hour, he or she wouldn't have seen a thing as the murder scene, on the south side of the premises, was completely hidden from the street by billboards. Then, Norkin alleged, Becker grabbed his wife by the coat and dragged her like a sack of potatoes around to the north side of the building, into the adjacent vacant lot where the yawning pit lay in wait. With Norkin still acting as lookout, Becker heaved his wife's body into the makeshift grave, doused it with lime, then filled the hole with the accumulated ash and clay.

Only now did Norkin become actively involved, or so he claimed. For the next few minutes he helped Becker throw dirt over the blood on the ground where the blow had been struck, then he washed the auto thoroughly, before joining Becker in the car and driving back to the lunch wagon. Harry Series, who worked the night shift at the wagon, and Nicholas Carbo, a customer, were still swapping stories when the two men returned sometime between 2:00 and 3:00 A.M. Becker, obviously pleased with his night's work, ordered cigars.

According to Norkin, Becker later gave him one hundred dollars for his part in the crime. Asked why someone who owned a thriving business, that employed five mechanics, would carry out such a deed for so paltry a sum, Norkin shrugged and said the money had played no part in his decision. "I did it out of friendship for Becker."

Investigators didn't buy Norkin's story at all. Gut instinct—the kind gleaned from a thousand interviews—convinced them that Norkin controlled the partnership. His was the brain that had fashioned the cunning scheme, and if the boastful Becker had been able to keep his lip zipped, then, most likely, both men would have gotten clean away with murder.

There was also a sense that Norkin was telling prosecutors what they wanted to hear. For instance, when told that Kennard thought Jennie Becker might have died from suffocation rather than the blow to the head, Norkin suddenly and miraculously recalled that, yeah, the victim was still groaning as Becker shoved ash and clay on top of her body in the pit. Unfortunately for Norkin, as the grand jury now heard, Kennard was no longer prepared to defend that opinion. He didn't really have much choice: his boss had decided to intervene.

As the chief medical examiner, Charles Norris had the authority to investigate any case of unnatural death in the five boroughs, and something about this case just didn't smell right to him. The fact that the body had lain, unpreserved, in the ground for eight months was crucial. Decomposition and postmortem staining made any observations tricky. His own examination of the body left him convinced that Kennard had overstepped the mark. And he decided to say so before the grand jury. "I don't see any *medical evidence* that suffocation was the cause of death," [italics added] Norris told the packed courtroom. "It may or may not have been." Poor Kennard could only squirm in impotent silence as he listened to this. As public humiliations go, it was right out of the top drawer. Under the old system, coroners' physicians were used to having their opinions rubber-stamped, not countermanded, by superiors. For Norris it was a brave step; any blunder and the mayor would have his head. The DA's office wasn't too impressed either. Not that Norris gave a damn. He knew how the legal game was played, how much an election-conscious prosecutor—always with one eye fixed firmly on his conviction rate—would try to wring every inch of emotional mileage out of a killer *burying his wife alive, for God's sake!* Such game playing irked Norris. So far as he was concerned, forensic science counted for nothing if its objectivity was undermined by political expedience. Norris saw what Kennard saw, the same contamination of the bronchial tubes, and he would have defied anyone to say that this provided categorical *proof* of suffocation. He was equally scathing when it came to vague rumors that Jennie might have been drugged or poisoned, prompted mainly by Norkin's claim that she seemed drowsy, making him wonder if Becker had doped her, saying, "There has been no evidence of poisoning . . . No evidence has been found of any wound except the wound on the head."

In the five years since Norris had taken office, this marked the first occasion on which he had really exerted his authority. In the past, district attorneys had bullied coroners and physicians alike into giving them the evidence that best suited their ends. Norris was having none of it. While his intervention probably made little impact on the grand jury, which indicted both Becker and Norkin on charges of first-degree murder, it did have a sobering effect on the investigative team. Chastened detectives returned to the junkyard, and this time recovered an eighteen-inch length of gas pipe that clearly could have been the murder weapon.

By the laggardly standards of modern day, 1920s justice moved along at breakneck pace. Consider this: within fourteen days of Jennie Becker's body being unearthed from its temporary grave, a grand jury had been convened, indictments had been returned against two men, and one of those defendants—Abraham Becker— was standing trial for his life (it was decided to try Norkin separately). Little wonder that Assistant DA Cohn was able to boast to reporters, "We are going to make a record in this case."

Even during this hiatus there was scarcely time to catch a breath as, on December 10, New York City witnessed one of the most astonishing private funerals in its long and colorful history. Upward of fifty thousand people, many wailing and sobbing, jammed the streets as Jennie Becker's funeral cortege treacled its way through the Bronx. Every yard of the journey was fraught with grief. Some mourners, more frenzied than the rest, had to be physically restrained from wrenching off the coffin lid so that they might have a sight of the victim. Police managed to restore order by the time the cortege reached the orphanage where the twins Celia and Sarah Becker still lived. After a brief service on the orphanage steps, Jennie Becker's coffin moved on to its final resting place, the Riverside Cemetery in Hackensack. Such a remarkable outpouring of public grief for someone, who just two weeks beforehand had been virtually anonymous, gives some idea of the extraordinary level of publicity that this case generated. So heavily charged was the overwrought atmosphere that jury selection for Becker's trial, which had been scheduled for the following day, was delayed until December 13.

When the trial did open, the state's case was crystallized in one simple sentence: Becker had enlisted the assistance of Norkin to murder his wife in order that he might live with Anna Elias. For the defense, attorney Alexander Mayper decided that his only hope, however faint, lay in resurrecting Becker's initial argument that no incontrovertible evidence existed to prove that the body found at the vacant lot was that of Jennie Becker.

Kennard testified first. He gave his evidence clearly and well, describing the blow to the head, but was expressly forbidden by the judge from offering an opinion as to whether the woman had been buried alive. Then came Anna Elias. Looking stiffly ahead—not once did she glance at the defendant—she outlined her personal tragedy in terms so graphic and personal that at one stage she dissolved into hysterical screams and the court had to be recessed. Other witnesses followed. Monstein told his story, then came a chain of bit players, all of whom claimed that Becker had bragged repeatedly of having got rid of his troublesome wife.

When the state rested its case, the defense moved for a dismissal on grounds that the prosecution had failed to prove that the victim was Mrs. Becker, a motion that was unsurprisingly denied by county judge Louis D. Gibbs.

Then Becker took the stand. Looking haggard and drawn, he gave a confused performance, one minute resolutely denying that his wife's body had been found and then in the next breath leveling venomous accusations against the absent Norkin. He claimed that five or six days before his wife's disappearance Norkin had burst into the Becker home, threatening to "fix" Jennie because she had blabbed to Norkin's wife of his adultery with his sister-in-law and with other women. All Becker could think was that Norkin had kept his malevolent word. As for himself, he reiterated his claim to have brought his wife home safely from the party on the night of April 6, that she was there when he arose next morning, and that she had vanished when he returned at noon. As for Monstein's testimony, Becker dismissed it all as "a tissue of lies."

Exhausted though he may have been, Becker refused to buckle under cross-examination. Even the sight of the clothing and other articles found on the dead woman failed to shake his nerve. First, he denied that the coat was his wife's, declared that the lock of hair was too dark for Jennie's. And then, having originally stated that Jennie hadn't worn a sweater, he now had the barefaced temerity to claim that she had actually been wearing a *brown* sweater, rather than the gray one found in the pit! What proof was there, he ranted, to show that this was his wife?

Plenty, was the prosecution's response. And it all came down to those stomach contents. The samples that Alexander O. Gettler had been asked to analyze showed clear traces of grapes, figs, almonds, and meat paste—the very items Becker had so lovingly fed his unsuspecting wife at the party.

Becker, obviously shaken by these discoveries, blustered that any woman could have eaten such food, until Gettler administered the coup de grâce: examination of the meat spread found it to be identical to the canapés served by Mrs. Linder—prepared, said the party hostess, according to an old family recipe. Gettler's testimony ripped the admittedly feeble heart out of Becker's defense. Surely now there could be no gainsaying the fact that the human remains found buried in the vacant lot were those of Jennie Becker?

In his closing, attorney Mayper struggled manfully, turning both barrels onto the investigative team for using a stool pigeon, ending with, "It is a well-known fact that this is not the first time a policeman has said more than his prayers. It isn't the first time a policeman has gone out of his way to fasten the guilt upon an innocent person." But when Mayper took his seat, few felt that Becker's chances had been advanced one jot.

Courtrooms were more rugged venues in those days, used to long sittings, and it was well after midnight on December 23 when the jury retired to consider the verdict. After an hour's deliberation jurors returned at 1:47 A.M. with a guilty verdict. Becker listened stony faced to his fate. He retained his Keatonesque impassivity three days later when Judge Gibbs sentenced him to the electric chair, and he was led away to become the twenty-seventh resident on Sing Sing's death row.

The New Year was just five days old when his erstwhile partner stood trial. While Norkin readily admitted helping to conceal Jennie's body, his defense pivoted on the argument that he was an innocent dupe, deceived by Becker's Machiavellian scheming. Norkin claimed to have had no foreknowledge of the murder, telling the court he was "petrified" and "dazed" when Becker suddenly clubbed his wife senseless. Quaking from panic, Norkin waited until Becker began dragging the body round the back, then ran, only for the enraged attacker to chase him down. The two men grappled for a moment. As Becker got the upper hand, he drew a flask from his pocket and forced it to Norkin's lips, snarling, "Here, take a drink. Don't be yellow." When Norkin refused, he said, Becker grabbed his right hand, yanked it upward and swore him to silence. So terrified was Norkin by this experience that for weeks afterward, so he said, his trembling nerves wouldn't allow him near the shop after dark. Not so, said Harry Gerner, a mechanic who worked at Norkin's shop. He testified that just two nights after the crime he saw his boss working on an auto, unconcerned and cheerful as always.

Unlike Becker, Norkin was rock solid on the stand; he told his story and stuck to it, unwilling to give an inch in cross-examination, but it was useless. Another late-night court sitting—this one dragging on until 1:50 A.M. on January 19, 1923—came back with an identical verdict. Ten days later, Norkin's previously icy resolution melted in a convulsive spasm as he was sentenced to death, then hauled away, trembling violently, to join his confederate at Sing Sing.

From all accounts the two men mended their differences during their spell in the "Dancehall," as inmates quaintly termed the cluster of cells that comprised Sing Sing's death row. Becker passed the time playing checkers, shouting out the moves to a fellow condemned prisoner, who would then reciprocate, while Norkin followed the match with keen interest from an adjacent cell. But all the while the judicial process was ticking, and for Becker it ended on December 13, 1923, when, with all his appeals exhausted, he died in the electric chair. His last reported words were: "If there is another world and I have any influence there, I'm going to do something to District Attorney Cohn!" His ire might have been better directed at Gettler, but this was not a time to appreciate the subtleties of science. The following April it was Norkin's turn to shuffle those last few terrible yards. As he was being strapped in, he told the witnesses, "I am innocent of any part in that crime . . . I am guilty of no crime except keeping a secret." Then the switch was thrown.

*   *   *

With this case, Norris's dream of an integrated European-style approach to medical jurisprudence in New York City had come one step closer to reality. He had staked everything on a sincerely held belief that the future of crime detection lay in the laboratory, and Gettler hadn't let him down. Although there is little doubt that Becker and Norkin would have been convicted anyway, given the totality of the evidence against them, Gettler's painstaking analysis of the stomach contents removed any lingering doubts about identification, and it was his role in their downfall that generated the biggest and boldest headlines. Not that it made a penny's worth of difference to this modest, unassuming Austrian-born chemist. Unlike so many in the medico-legal field, Gettler deliberately shunned the media spotlight, preferring the reflective anonymity of his lab in the grounds of Bellevue Hospital. (Oddly enough, despite holding the rank of chief toxicologist for New York City, he was actually paid by Bellevue.) Given the frequency of his courtroom appearances, however, where his tersely delivered testimony sent dozens of killers to the electric chair, it was no surprise that the press dubbed him "one of the world's greatest test-tube detectives," a verdict that Norris would not have disputed. In temperament and attitude the two men might have been polar opposites, but they enjoyed a warm kinship and a shared intellectual vigor that served the city well.

Which was just as well, considering New York's soaring body count. As the numbers swelled, the exploits of Norris and his team, fanning out across the city to investigate suspicious death of every color and stripe, became regular newspaper fare. The sensational murder cases still took center stage, of course—particularly Gettler's devastating intervention in the Snyder–Gray case of 1927, and the mysterious shooting death of gambler Arnold Rothstein the following year*—but it was still the running sore of Prohibition that exercised Norris like nothing else. In one four-day spell in 1927, Norris himself autopsied no fewer than twenty-four victims of alcohol. By 1930 the carnage was mind-boggling. Norris's annual report for that year listed 1,295 liquor-related deaths in New York City, with the author adding sourly, "And there are probably hundreds of alcoholic deaths we never know of." Road accidents, too, were going through the roof. In 1920 Norris recorded 692 deaths in traffic accidents. Seven years later, that number had soared to 1,138. Norris attributed much of this rise to rotgut booze. And not all the drunks were behind the wheel. Scores of jaywalkers, reeling half blind from the latest skinful, were staggering out in front of cars, giving themselves and the unsuspecting drivers virtually no chance of survival.

With such a caseload, it is hardly surprising that by the end of the 1920s, the OCME was close to a meltdown. Each year it was investigating more than thirteen thousand suspicious deaths on a wafer-thin budget that worked out to around eleven dollars per body. Facilities, too, were stretched to breaking point with just three municipal morgues—one in Manhattan at Bellevue, one in Brooklyn at Kings County Hospital, and one in the Bronx at Fordham Hospital. After ten years Norris's dream of building a world-class operation was still being thwarted at every turn by City Hall. They resented his self-serving manipulation of a compliant media; he despised their venal self-interest. A remorseless battle of wills ensued as both sides dug in their heels.

And then Wall Street crashed.

The Depression that gripped America tore the financial heart

---

* Because Rothstein, who survived the gangland shooting for several hours, never identified his assailant, it was popularly reckoned that he was adhering to the traditional underworld code of silence. Norris took the view that Rothstein never even saw the person who shot him. Whatever the truth, Rothstein's killer was never apprehended.

out of the Office of the Chief Medical Examiner. Salaries were slashed to the bone, so deeply that Norris frequently dipped into his own pocket to supplement staff members' wages. And it was the same whenever new equipment was needed—microscopes, cameras, and the like—invariably it was Norris who cut the check. Such generosity did wonders for inspiring staff loyalty, but it also presented City Hall with a gilded opportunity to tighten the financial screws to choking point. Even so, Norris's munificence did little to stem the tidal wave of criticism. He was still catching it in the neck from all quarters.

In 1931 one particularly hostile source of censure did run dry, for it was in September of that year that Norris's old nemesis, Dr. Otto Schultze, took it upon himself to deliver one of the most entertaining and suicidal courtroom performances that anyone could recall. He'd been in bad health for some time, and when asked to testify before a Long Island inquest that was investigating a recent murder, he threw a tantrum and refused to appear. Even though a threatened subpoena for contempt did provoke a change of heart, it did nothing to improve his demeanor. Obviously grumpy, Schultze took the stand and raised his spirits by first favoring the jury with a rousing hymnal chorus. Next, as open-jawed court officials looked on powerlessly, or seemingly unwilling to stop him, he delivered a homily on the relative merits of salt and sugar in the American kitchen, denounced the English system of numerals as vastly inferior to that of the Romans, dismissed with a contemptuous wave suspicious marks found on the victim's body—"Oh yes, those little things"—before suddenly standing up, bidding the jury good-bye, and disappearing from public view for good.*

---

* A hastily convened commission in lunacy decided that Schultze was sane, but he never fully recovered his faculties and died on July 4, 1934.

Schultze's spectacular self-immolation marked a severing of all ties with the old coroner system. Not that Norris felt much like celebrating. The wearisome and ongoing quarrel with City Hall was rubbing his nerves raw. With frustration on all sides building to volcanic levels, something had to give, and the eruption came in 1932.

It began with a regular enough occurrence: Norris tackling the then acting mayor Joseph V. McKee about a further 20 percent cut in OCME funding. McKee had only been in office a matter of days, taking over from the disgraced Jimmy Walker, after that mayor's fondness for willowy showgirls and unexplained additions to his bank account exhausted the patience of even hardened Tammany block captains. McKee might have been a makeshift mayor, but he was obviously feeling his oats and he showed Norris the door. Norris's patrician nature rebelled. No damned carpetbagger was going to push him around—or make him grovel for funds!

On September 20, after fourteen years in the job without a pay raise, Dr. Charles Norris quit. Being Norris, he made sure that the press got his side of the story first, and the media went to bat for him big time. Sympathetic editors reminded their readers of the OCME's many successes, contrasting them vividly with the shady old coroner system that it had replaced. As the groundswell of protest began to surge, calls for Norris's reinstatement from the Medical Alliance, an organization of physicians, were echoed by the many doctors and scientists who worked under him.

In the end, the pressure overwhelmed McKee. Backed into a corner, his nerve gave way and through gritted teeth he was obliged to ask Norris to reconsider. Never one to gloat—at least not in public—Norris accepted the capitulation with his customary good grace and returned to work on September 27. McKee put his own spin on it for the reporters, saying, "We felt the doctor was too valuable a public servant to lose." One very public humiliation for McKee was followed shortly by another. Barely a month later his brief tenure as New York mayor was brought to an abrupt conclusion when a specially convened poll saw Tammany candidate John P. O'Brien elected to power.

So far as Norris was concerned, it was the hollowest of victories. He returned to an OCME in which virtually nothing had changed; the budget was still risible and the end of each month still found him plundering his own bank account in order to keep the ship afloat.

But one shaft of sunlight did illuminate the gloomy horizon. For years Norris had been on the stump, noisily urging the abolition of Prohibition to anyone who would listen—"There would be less crime and less need for inquests, if the bootleggers and the speakeasies were destroyed"—and on December 5, 1933, his prayers were answered. That was the date when Utah became the thirty-sixth state to ratify the Twenty-first Amendment to the Constitution, thus ending state-sponsored teetotalism in America for good. (Within nine months, the rate of alcohol-related deaths in New York State had plunged to a twelve-year low. Suicide, too, fell to levels not seen since 1928.)

Any exultation that Norris felt over this reduced caseload was tarnished, however, by the bizarre happenings at an autopsy that took place on May 1, 1934. The circumstances were mundane in the extreme, an unidentified man struck down and killed by an automobile. Only when Norris entered the morgue did he realize that the man on the slab was thirty-six-year-old Dr. Ladislaus Schwarz, who just one day earlier had been appointed as Norris's assistant at the newly created Department of Forensic Medicine of the New York University–Bellevue Hospital Medical School, the first establishment wholly dedicated to medical jurisprudence in

America. The incident jolted Norris to his core. "One of the greatest shocks of my life," was how he described it. What should have been the crowning achievement of his career felt oddly marred. Ever since taking office he had campaigned for a teaching facility to rival those in Europe. The path to that goal had been rocky and strewn with setbacks. But Norris had stuck to his guns. Now, with his dream a reality at last, came the painful reminder that forensic science does not exist in a vacuum. No matter how revolutionary the technology, how smart the physician, forensic pathology is all about hurt. That body on the slab has died in unnatural circumstances and the grief tends to radiate concentrically, affecting all it touches. This time it reached Norris.

His health, never the best, now began a rapid decline. As early as 1925, Norris had been forced to take four months off work and travel to Europe for treatment. Thereafter the job interruptions were frequent and lengthy. His lifestyle, uncompromisingly hedonistic, did little for a flagging heart or a wheezy respiratory system, and on September 11, 1935, it was the former that finally gave up the ghost. He was age sixty-seven.

At Norris's funeral, thirty patrolmen from the NYPD formed a guard of honor, and it was their boss, Commissioner Lewis J. Valentine, who best captured the mood of general loss: "Probably no one in our generation has contributed more from the standpoint of science to police work and its correlated activities." The *New York Times*, one of the most enduring and vociferous critics of the old coroner system, lauded Norris as "incorruptible and free from political influence of every kind. When he said a man had committed suicide, that was the truth of the matter. When he said that a man had been murdered, even the doubting police usually came to his way of thinking."

Norris was a fine pathologist, a great administrator, and an even more remarkable person. His was the era of noblesse oblige, a time when many in the privileged classes felt the weight of social responsibility on their shoulders. Certainly it bore heavily on Norris. With his background it would have been all too easy to slide seamlessly into the Social Register circuit—Broadway first nights, sailing off Rhode Island, sipping cocktails at Saratoga in August, that kind of thing. Instead, he dedicated his life to finding out why others had died. Immaculately tailored physicians bent low in some alleyway over a corpse writhing with maggots are not common sights. But Norris was a most uncommon man. He was also blessed with an unquenchable humanity. Nothing better demonstrates this quality than an incident from May 1920, when Ernest Goetz, a seventy-year-old German immigrant, crippled and half blind, was found dead by his own hand at Bellevue Hospital. Just two years before, Goetz had retired from that selfsame hospital where he had worked as a morgue assistant. Norris knew him well and had paid for an operation to relieve Goetz's glaucoma. Now, in a letter to the *New York Times*, Norris expressed his outrage that after thirty-seven years of devoted service to Bellevue Goetz—this "personification of honesty"—was pensioned off at just $362 per annum, not even a dollar a day. When found dead, he had just forty-five cents in his pockets. "Is it to be wondered or is it strange that he committed suicide?" Norris mused sadly. "The city should indeed deplore the loss of such a servant."

Much the same could be said about Norris. There would never be another CME like him. The advantages of his birth—his estate was valued at almost a half-million dollars at the time of his death, not including several properties squirreled away in Pennsylvania— meant that he enjoyed a uniquely enviable immunity when it came to dealing with meddling mayors and the other inconveniences of public life. Norris didn't need the job and everyone knew it. This gave him unusual bargaining strength. As we have seen, he didn't win all the battles with City Hall—in fact, he probably came out on the short side more often than not—but he was able to fight every crusade without regard to career advancement or financial reward. By doing so he acquired for the OCME an invaluable degree of autonomy when it was needed most. New Yorkers were lucky to have him.

The only problem now lay in finding a replacement for Charles Norris. Transitions in power are often tricky, and this one was no exception. McKee might have been history, but politics goes on forever, and by 1935 New York City had a new mayor. Fiorello La Guardia was now the man in charge, and, as events would show, "The Little Flower" was no shrinking violet when it came to sowing seeds of discontent at the OCME.

TWO

A QUIET HAND ON THE TILLER

Even before the dust had settled on Norris's grave, La Guardia was trumpeting his vision of a radically enhanced OCME, much broader in scope than before, with a far stronger emphasis on teaching. In a speech delivered on September 18, the mayor said, "This office provides more material and opportunities for pathological research than can be found anywhere else in the country. It would be of great value to science and to medicine if a model, fully equipped laboratory could be provided for autopsies. Such a laboratory should be constructed like an operating theater, so that scientists could gather and watch the work being done." On one point, La Guardia was emphatic. Finance. While fulsome in his praise for Norris's generosity in repeatedly digging into his own pockets to bail out the ailing department, La Guardia decided to set the record straight: the expenses of a city agency were proper charges upon the city and should therefore be paid from taxes. He promised that whoever took over as CME would be in charge of a fully funded, fully functional investigative unit that would be the envy of the world.

So far so good. It was toward the end of La Guardia's speech that things turned decidedly murky. Although the mayor paid lip service to the notion of a competitive exam for the vacant post—as stipulated in the 1915 bill—he also made absolutely no attempt to disguise the fact that he had already singled out a favored candidate. If the intent of the legislators had been to banish the bad old days of cronyism, then someone obviously forgot to tell La Guardia. Here he was, touting the office like it was his own personal gift.

No one doubted that Dr. Harrison S. Martland was superbly qualified for the job. Since being appointed the first full-time pathologist for Newark City Hospital in 1909, and later the ME for Essex County, New Jersey, he had distinguished himself in dozens of notorious criminal cases, where his expertise in the effects of bullets on the human body was unparalleled. Outside the courtroom, he was equally formidable. When the police were baffled by the mysterious deaths of several women who worked at a New Jersey watch factory, it was Martland who tracked down the cause. All the victims, he discovered, used a brush to apply luminous paint to the watch dials, bringing the brush to a fine point by applying it to the lips, ignorant of the fact that luminous paint contained radium. With every touch of the brush they poisoned themselves just a little more. Martland's groundbreaking clinical research into radium's lethal qualities found its way into the *Journal of the American Medical Association*. And it was also Martland who, in 1928, coined the term punch drunk to describe those prize fighters who were suffering from a brain injury caused by the rupture of blood vessels. In 1933 he was made professor of forensic medicine at New York University. On every level, Martland was the obvious candidate to fill Norris's shoes, an ideal mix of the solidly practical and the academic. There was just one problem: he didn't want the job. Not only would assuming the role of CME put a serious dent in his teaching schedule, but it also thrust him headlong into the cauldron of big city politics, with its clamoring headlines and relentless scrutiny. The cut and thrust of Essex County he could handle; he had little appetite for those heartaches across the Hudson.

Martland's "thanks, but no thanks" knocked La Guardia sideways. Suddenly he was scratching around to fill the vacancy. To buy himself some much needed breathing space, he opted for a temporary replacement. He settled on a long-standing servant of the OCME, someone who'd joined at its formation in 1918 and who would remain there until the day he retired.

Dr. Thomas Gonzales was low key, tall, and spare, with a rather forbidding scholarly appearance in marked contrast to the flamboyant Norris. In background and upbringing, he could not have been more different from his predecessor. His father was a Cuban leaf-tobacco merchant, who had immigrated to the United States in the nineteenth century and settled in New York. The family prospered in their new home country and, by the time of Thomas's birth in 1878, were well on their way to achieving their small slice of the American dream. There was enough money for Thomas to attend Bellevue Medical School, and after graduation the young man took a position as assistant pathologist at Harlem Hospital; two years later, in 1906, he was named chief pathologist there. Over the next decade he honed his skills in a variety of fields, and in 1918 he was appointed to the position of assistant at the Office of the Chief Medical Examiner.

Like all his colleagues, he toiled in the considerable shadow of Charles Norris, but Gonzales had too much talent to stay hidden for long, and from the 1920s onward we find his name featuring ever more prominently in some of that decade's most sensational cases. There was the curious death in 1923 of wealthy socialite Gertie Webb, where Gonzales went toe-to-toe with the infamous Dr. Otto Schultze (according to Schultze, Mrs. Webb had been poisoned with mercury; Gonzales found nothing except natural circumstances; the grand jury believed Gonzales); Paul Hilton, the "radio burglar" who shot a police officer in 1926 en route to the electric chair; and the blood-drenched 1932 gang murder of hoodlum Vincent "Mad Dog" Coll.

As an assistant medical examiner, Gonzales echoed Norris's loathing of the old coroner system. New York City might have banished this medieval relic to the scrap heap, but other regions of the United States were not so enlightened. In a 1934 address to the Science Forum of the New York Electrical Society, Gonzales snorted his contempt: "The appalling ignorance of most of our coroners is responsible for sending many innocent men to jail, while keeping many criminals out of prison . . . Accurate medical knowledge in the determination of the exact cause of death is one of our greatest needs toward curbing crime."

In almost every respect, Gonzales was Norris's true disciple. His outstanding ability, allied to a tenacious work ethic, saw him steadily work his way up through the system, until, at the time of his mentor's death, he was deputy CME in charge of Manhattan and the Bronx. For many—certainly those who worked alongside him—Gonzales was the natural successor to Norris. But La Guardia could be an awkward cuss at times. When he'd appointed Gonzales acting CME on September 18, 1935, he had done so in the expectation that it would be a purely holding position, a stopgap until Martland's coronation. Now that he'd been thwarted in that ambition, La Guardia was in no rush to make the position permanent. For more than a year he kept Gonzales dangling in limbo. All the acting CME could do was knuckle down, grit his teeth, and do the job. Which was just as well, really, because during this inter-regnum one of the most sensational murders to hit New York City in decades took place, one destined to become a forensic classic. If Gonzales could get this one right, then his chances of nailing down the permanent job would be almost guaranteed. Get it wrong, and the scrap heap beckoned.

CASE FILE:
John Fiorenza (1936)

When the report came through, Assistant Chief Inspector John A. Lyons must have shuddered. Jeez, not again! After all, murders in swanky Midtown apartment buildings were scarcer than January heat waves. But on Friday, April 10, 1936, for the second time in a matter of months, New York's premier detective found himself having to quarterback yet another high-profile Manhattan homicide. Just one week earlier Lyons had looked on in utter disbelief as Vera Stretz, twenty-three years old by her own reckoning—you can add at least a decade on to that, sneered most who knew her—ash blond and gorgeous, had walked free from General Sessions Court after having been acquitted of murdering her wealthy German lover, Dr. Fritz Gebhardt.

Lyons had been crestfallen. Like just about everyone connected with the case, he had assumed that Vera's conviction was a slam dunk. The spectacularly sordid details of the case had kept New Yorkers salivating for months on end. Although Gebhardt had a wife and two daughters back home in Karlsruhe, these domestic encumbrances had not prevented him from installing Vera, his part-time bookkeeper and full-time mistress, in luxury rooms at Beekman Towers, a ritzy hotel that stood on Mitchell Place, near Forty-ninth Street. Gebhardt also stayed at the Beekman, but mindful of the need to maintain at least a thin veneer of respectability his own quarters were two floors up. For the times, their relationship was steamy in the extreme. But it was also twelve months old. And in those twelve months, according to rumor, Gebhardt had begun to tire of the persistent Vera. She would later deny any such thing. Hence her concern when, on the night of November 11, 1935, Gebhardt had summoned her to his room, complaining of feeling unwell. Throwing a coat over her dressing gown, Vera hastened upstairs. Her arrival seemingly triggered a miraculous recovery. According to Vera, far from feeling ill, Gebhardt was like a rutting stag. When she refused his advances, he had gone berserk, throwing her down on the bed, tearing at her clothes, and forcing himself on her. As a final indignity, he then yanked up his nightshirt and demanded that she fellate him. So appalled was she by this suggestion that she shot him.

Or so she said.

Those hard-bitten detectives who were first on the scene took the view that the coolly possessed—and still fully dressed—Vera was no demure daffodil who'd gallantly defended her honor but rather a jealous killer who'd burst into her lover's room and shot him because he was about to dump her. Considering that, when arrested, she was carrying a handbag that contained a .32-caliber pistol and a box with forty-six cartridges, this was a not unreasonable assumption. When the autopsy showed that Gebhardt had been shot four times—twice in the back—things looked black indeed for Miss Stretz. Faced by the prospect of an appointment with Sing Sing's least inviting item of furniture, Vera did the smartest thing possible: she hired a lawyer. Not just any old lawyer, mind you, but arguably America's greatest defense attorney of the midwar period.

Samuel L. Leibowitz might have lacked Clarence Darrow's campaigning zeal against the wrongs of society, and some picky souls might have grumbled that his client list was a tad top heavy with gangland luminaries, but when it came to getting people acquitted against the odds, the feisty New Yorker was unbeatable. He knew better than anyone that most trial verdicts were won in the heart, not the head. Pity the poor prosecutor who came armed with mere facts when Leibowitz was on the brief. For years he had buried his opponents under an avalanche of emotion and obfuscation. His strong suit was nailing that "unique selling point," something to feed the jury's prejudices, and it didn't take him long to work out where Vera's best chances of survival lay. Just recently, dark reports of Hitler's anti-Semitic ravings had begun to figure prominently in the American press. These gave Leibowitz his opening. In court, by the time the little Jewish lawyer had finished his closing address, Gebhardt had been transformed from wealthy German financier into Aryan monster, a closet Nazi, someone so perverted by sexual excess that shooting was too good for him. The jury swallowed every overwrought word, and Vera walked free. Outside the court, mobbed by reporters, a triumphant Leibowitz tallied up the score: by his reckoning, Vera Stretz was the 116th defendant he had saved from the electric chair.

Now, one week later, as Inspector Lyons leafed through the details of this most recent murder, he was haunted by the Stretz fiasco. The call had come through at 4:30 P.M. A body had been found at 22 Beekman Place, just one block north of the Gebhardt shooting. And this time the victim was not some shadowy financier from a deeply unpopular foreign country but rather a demure young woman with strong connections to Manhattan's exclusive inner circle.

The last day of Nancy Titterton's life had begun just like most of the others. After breakfast, her husband, Lewis, had kissed her good-bye and taken off for his job at NBC, where he headed the literary rights department. (In his spare time, he doubled up as a noted book critic, whose reviews featured in several newspapers, most notably The *New York Times*.) Shortly after arriving at work, at 9:00 A.M., he had phoned Nancy at home. She had seemed happy enough, with no hint of distress in her voice. At age thirty-four, life had assumed a comfortable course for the quietly spoken woman from Dayton, Ohio. She had met Lewis while working in the book department of Lord & Taylor and after a whirlwind courtship the couple had married on October 5, 1929, just three weeks before Wall Street went south. They had survived the crash better than most. Lewis's job as a radio executive meant there was plenty of money to ride out the slump, with enough left over to fund an opulent lifestyle in one of Midtown's most desirable addresses. Their candlelit dinners frequently hosted Lewis's friends from the media glitterati, who dished up the kind of sparkling conversation that Nancy was able to work into her own fiction. Like her husband, she also wrote literary reviews, but her dream was to pen her own novel, and most days were spent striving to turn that dream into reality. A great lifestyle, a great husband, and a promising future, yes, everything on life's horizon glowed beacon bright for Nancy Titterton.

Until the morning of April 10, 1936.

From what the police were able to piece together, the last person to speak to Nancy that morning was a close friend named Georgia Mansbridge, who had phoned sometime between 10:30 and 11:00 to set a dinner date for the following evening. She confirmed that Nancy had seemed perfectly normal, not at all agitated, quite cheerful, in fact.

At 11:30 A.M., Wiley Staughn, a seventeen-year-old courier for the London Valet Company, arrived to deliver a dress for Nancy. From down on the sidewalk he rang the bell to the Tittertons' fourth-floor apartment. Then again. And again. One final ring was no more successful than the previous three. Only then did he notice that the vestibule door was slightly ajar. Rather than traipse up the four floors on foot—the building had no elevator—he took refuge in the fact that, on a previous visit, Mrs. Titterton had instructed that if there was no answer on the bell, then he should not leave anything outside her apartment door. Making a mental note to return later, Staughn left to continue his deliveries.

The next noteworthy incident at Beekman Place came around midday. A maid, working in an apartment one floor below the Tittertons', heard a woman's voice shout, "Dudley! Dudley! Dudley!" Since calls for Dudley Mings, the building janitor, were an everyday occurrence, she had thought no more of it. Besides, instinct told her that the cry had come not from upstairs but rather the garden.

For the next few hours Beekman Place remained quiet, with no apparent visitors. When a local tradesman named Theodore Kruger arrived in the late afternoon, he found the vestibule door still ajar. Kruger ran a furniture upholsterer's store, and the previous day had collected a sofa that required repadding from the Tittertons. It had been a daylong job. Finally, at four o'clock, he and his assistant had loaded the couch into a truck at Kruger's place of business at 386 Third Avenue, for the short drive to the Tittertons' residence. They reached the five-story brownstone at 4:15 P.M. Like Staughn before him, Kruger received no answer when he rang the bell. Rather than make a return journey the following day, he told his assistant that they were going to heft the couch up the carpeted stairs to the fourth-floor apartment anyhow.

Perspiring and out of breath, they finally reached the Tittertons' flat. Kruger frowned. This door was also ajar. He knocked and got no answer. Hesitantly, calling out Mrs. Titterton's name, he edged into the apartment. This was the third time that Kruger had called on Mrs. Titterton and he was familiar with the apartment's traditional shotgun-style layout. There was a small kitchen abutting the living room, next came a library, then the only bedroom. The last door along the corridor led into the bathroom. Kruger, calling out all the while, worked his way along the corridor until he reached the bedroom. This was the only room that showed some untidiness in the otherwise immaculate flat. Both beds were made, but the one nearest the bathroom was rumpled and strewn with clothing. By now convinced the place was empty, Kruger decided to leave the couch in the living room.

After positioning the sofa, Kruger suddenly had an idea: if he took a note of Mrs. Titterton's telephone number, he could call and let her know that the bill had come to $7.50. Maybe she could mail him a check? The phone was along the hallway. To reach it, Kruger had to pass the bathroom. The door was open, the light was on, and he glanced inside. What he saw next jolted him to a standstill.

Sticking out of the bathtub was a human leg.

Senses reeling, Kruger swayed in the doorway, struggling to absorb the horrific scene. Nancy Titterton lay facedown in the tub. Her slightly built body—she weighed only one hundred pounds—was nude apart from a torn white silk slip and rolled-down stockings. Some kind of material had been knotted tightly around her neck.

Protectively, Kruger shepherded his young assistant away from the hideous view, and gasped, "Something has happened to the missus." Without another word the two men ran downstairs where they breathlessly enlisted the help of Dudley Mings. He in turn contacted the janitor of a nearby building, Swan Fredericksen, and all four men returned to the apartment, from where they phoned the emergency service.

Within minutes the building was swarming with police. The officer in charge, Inspector Francis J. Kear, was a veteran cop with almost thirty years of service. While technicians and other detectives bustled about him, Kear stood back and coolly surveyed the scene, trying to gain some sense of how this crime had unfolded. The bed nearest to the bathroom was covered with torn and disheveled clothing, a torn gray skirt, a garter belt, and, incongruously, a fountain pen. Hooks and eyes from the underwear were scattered across the bed and the floor, presumably the result of the attacker tearing the clothes off his victim. Because there was no sign of disorder anywhere else in the apartment, Kear reasoned that the attack had been confined to the bedroom. Probably the unsuspecting Nancy had been jumped in this room, thrown down on the bed, and strangled. That attacker had then dragged her— alive or dead, Kear didn't know—the four feet or so to the bathroom and dumped her body in the bathtub, presumably in an attempt to drown her. Although the bathroom window was open, the shade had been pulled down, and while this would have prevented any inquisitive eyes, it meant that had Nancy screamed in the bathroom, she would probably have been overheard. A check of other residents had already confirmed that apart from the probably unconnected cry of "Dudley! Dudley! Dudley!" mentioned earlier, no one had heard anything out of the ordinary.

This didn't surprise Kear. His experienced eye could detect no signs of a break-in, no jimmied locks, no shattered windows; nor had the place been ransacked. And there was another inconsistency: if the killer had been a burglar, surprised by the hapless Nancy, then surely after silencing the only witness, he would have stolen something to make his visit worthwhile? All the signs indicated that whoever killed Nancy Titterton had gained access to the apartment by the front door, carried out the murder with willful deliberation, then left by the front door.

While Kear was piecing together this scenario, Dr. Thomas Gonzales arrived. After studying the bathtub from every angle, he began his examination of Nancy Titterton's rapidly cooling body. First, he carefully cut the ligature from her neck. It was three feet in length and had been fashioned from the victim's own pink pajama top and a flimsy red dressing jacket, twisted together. Above and below the left eye were ugly weals that might have come from a beating. With the body lying on its left side, Gonzales leaned in more closely. He could make out contusions on both wrists. Either the killer had grabbed Nancy's arms with particularly vicious strength or—and Gonzales thought this much more likely—he had bound her wrists with some kind of rope or twine at some time during the attack. Once she was dead, he had then removed the bindings. Gonzales glanced about him. There was no sign of the restraints in the bathroom. He asked Kear to check the rest of the apartment. When that came up blank, Gonzales concluded that the killer must have taken the bindings away with him.

Like Kear, Gonzales also believed that the attack had originated in the bedroom and had terminated in the bathroom. But he noticed something else: although the body was moist, the soles of the feet were still dry. Whether the killer had intended to drown Nancy, only to change his mind for some reason—perhaps he'd been disturbed?—or whether the moisture was due to the dripping shower, Gonzales couldn't tell.

Kear pressed Gonzales for an approximate time of death. Even nowadays, this is an area fraught with difficulties, and probably nothing in the annals of medical jurisprudence has provoked more controversy and more heated debate, but within certain broad limits it is possible to hazard a guess. Here, measurement of the rectal temperature, allied to the level of rigor mortis present in the body, steered Gonzales to the conclusion that Nancy had been murdered that morning, at around 11:30, give or take one hour. Without the benefit of an autopsy it was impossible to say whether Nancy had been raped, but Gonzales had little doubt that Nancy Titterton had been subjected to the full rigor of the killer's lust. Death, he said, was caused by strangulation. A new test devised by Gettler would be able to let him know whether Nancy had been alive or dead when placed in the bathtub.

Preliminary examination over, Gonzales gave orders for the body to be removed to the Bellevue mortuary. Only then, as the slight frame of Nancy Titterton was being raised from the bathtub, did the most significant clue in the apartment come to light. Scrunched up beneath the body lay a single length of cord, about thirteen inches long and a quarter inch thick. It had been cleanly cut at both ends. Gonzales examined the rope closely, then compared it with the marks on Nancy's wrists. He had no doubt that at least part of the bindings had been found. Most likely, the killer in his haste had slashed through the restraints, intending to take the rope away with him, only to overlook this single strand. The rope was similar to that used on venetian blinds, but a quick check around the apartment showed all these cords to be intact. Since some indentations had been found on the wooden frame of the disheveled bed, Kear asked if the killer could have used the cord to tie Nancy's wrists to the bed. Gonzales replied affirmatively.

The two men were still deep in discussion when Lewis Titterton reached the apartment. The scholarly British-born executive could barely countenance what had happened. His face was chalky white and he looked broken by the dreadful news. When shown the length of cord, he shook his head; it meant nothing to him. He was asked if he kept large amounts of money in the apartment. Again, Lewis shook his head dumbly. Gathering his fuzzy thoughts, he recalled that just the day previously he had given Nancy ten dollars, out of which she had paid a maid three dollars, and another couple of dollars had gone to a local cleaners. Since Kear had already found Nancy's purse and found it empty, Lewis could only assume that the killer had stolen the remaining five dollars. After looking round the apartment, Lewis confirmed what Kear already suspected: nothing else had been taken. The bureau drawers were as tidy as they always had been.

Most of all, Lewis was baffled as to how anyone could have gained access to the apartment. Nancy, he said, was almost pathologically shy, timid and soft spoken; the notion that she would admit a stranger was unthinkable. The killer must have been someone known to her.

Kear was thinking along the same lines. This bore none of the hallmarks of a random or opportunistic break-in that had escalated into homicide. Whoever killed Nancy not only managed to inveigle their way into the apartment without attracting the suspicion of anyone else in the building but had also come prepared with the means to tie her up. That smacked either of premeditation or . . . ?

Kear let his imagination wander. By his own admission, Lewis worked long hours at the office, rarely home until early evening. All those hours alone might have left Nancy feeling neglected and lonely—perhaps lonely enough to seek solace in the arms of another man? It was an angle worth considering.

Gonzales, meanwhile, was expanding on reasons why the killer had dumped the body in the bathtub. If the intent was to create the impression that Nancy had drowned, then why wasn't the tub full of water? All Gonzales could imagine was that the killer had been disturbed and fled before he completed the task.

Kear already knew about Staughn's abortive visit at 11:30 A.M., slap bang in the middle of the time frame that Gonzales had estimated for the time of death. Had his ringing of the doorbell interrupted the killer?

While Gonzales and Kear hypothesized, other detectives continued scouring the apartment for clues. They found no useable fingerprints but the counterpane on the bed did provide a lead; a smear of what looked to be either paint or mud. This counterpane, together with a blue smock, a lavender bathrobe, a bedspread, a pillowcase, a pair of pajamas, and a bra apparently wrenched off during the attack, were sent for analysis to the Police Research Laboratory in the shadow of the Brooklyn Bridge, together with clothing from the body.

The possible paint smear in the bedroom was viewed as extremely significant, given the fact that four painters had recently been employed in the building, and one, a Daniel Kaplan, had actually worked in the vestibule that very day. But when officers rounded up the men quickly, it soon became apparent all four could be eliminated as suspects.

At the end of day one, Kear had no clear leads, no clear suspects, and a whole bunch of headaches. He knew that like most things in life, homicide has its pecking order. Nancy Titterton wasn't some anonymous wino beaten to death in a back-alley brawl, barely mentioned in the metro pages, with no relative or friend to care whether the crime was solved or not. No, this was entirely different. Nancy Titterton might not have been a household name before her death, but the cocktail-chinking circles in which she—and more especially her husband—moved carried a lot of clout and they would expect a quick resolution to this case. The press, too, would run and run with this story until her killer was found.

As Kear widened his inquiries, he tiptoed edgily around the possibility that Nancy might have been tangled up in an affair. When the suggestion was put to Georgia Mansbridge, she just gaped. Impossible, was her verdict; the Tittertons were utterly devoted to each other. Yes, Lewis worked long hours, but Nancy wasn't the type of woman to mind the isolation. On the contrary, it suited her ideally, giving her the time to work on that novel of which so much was expected. Even dinner parties were an unwelcome intrusion on her ascetic lifestyle; she had no interest in politics, fashion, or shopping and lived only for her husband and her literature. All of which left Kear scratching his head, as he struggled to fathom out who killed Nancy Titterton.

The next morning Gonzales did his best to fill in some of the gaps. He started his examination of Nancy Titterton's body at 10:30 A.M. and ended at 1:45 P.M. In an era when few autopsies took more than an hour, this was unusually lengthy, yet another indicator of the hierarchical nature of crime investigation, and the seriousness with which the authorities were treating this case. Gonzales found that the contusions above and below the left eye came not from some beating but were pressure marks caused by the weight of the head resting against the tub's plug hole. Swabs of the genital area confirmed that Nancy had been sexually assaulted. When Gonzales cut into the body and skull he found that the strangulation had caused a hemorrhage of the larynx and three slight internal hemorrhages of the scalp. Scrapings from beneath the fingernails were labeled and bagged and sent for analysis, along with samples from the bodily organs. Gonzales pored over every inch of Nancy's frail body and could find nothing to affect his original estimate of the time of death—an hour either side of 11:30 A.M.

Just a few blocks away, at Beekman Place, a battery of experts armed with microscopes, chemicals, measuring instruments, and special fingerprint cameras, were examining every square inch of the crime scene, all the furniture, rugs, walls, closets, doors and windows, even the fire escape that led down from the Tittertons' apartment. Never before had New York witnessed such a consolidated scientific assault on one crime scene. The twin bed nearest the bathroom was dismantled and taken to the laboratory along with the bed clothing. All these items would be subjected to the silver nitrate method of developing fingerprints, a technique that had featured prominently at the Hauptmann trial. This process—still in use today—works best on surfaces such as cloth or paper that do not respond well to conventional dusting powder. Say the test item is a piece of wood. Any fingerprint on its surface is most likely invisible. But because the body sweat inherent in fingerprints contains common salt, should this item be sprayed with a 10 percent solution of silver nitrate, then any salt present, under the action of the silver nitrate, becomes silver chloride, which is affected by light. When exposed to ultraviolet or even bright sunlight, the silver chloride darkens and the print emerges in its customary appearance of a series of black concentric lines against a white background, ready for the photographer and the classification expert.

Although the silver nitrate process was devised in the 1910s, its popularity is mainly credited to Dr. Erastus Mead Hudson, a New York physician, who first came to prominence in the Lindbergh kidnapping, with his claim to have recovered more than five hundred latent prints from the notorious ladder that conventional fingerprint testing had missed. (By the time Hudson was brought into the case, his contribution was virtually worthless, since so many people had handled the ladder.)

In the Titterton case, the silver nitrate test proved disappointing. Although fingerprints were lifted from the wooden bedstead, they were too smudged to be of any use. Better results were obtained from those items of clothing subjected to ultraviolet light scanning. This brought out several stains not visible to the naked eye.

As the investigation unfolded, a turf war broke out over just which official agency should be analyzing the samples of evidence. Although no one doubted the competence of the Police Research Laboratory technicians, pressure grew for the trace evidence to be analyzed by Alexander O. Gettler at the Office of the Chief Medical Examiner. Since his triumph in the Becker–Norkin case, the OCME's chief toxicologist had become recognized as the top forensic chemist on the East Coast. Credentials such as these made him the obvious choice to handle such a high-profile case. After some interdepartmental bickering, common sense prevailed and Gettler, aided by his assistant, Harry Swartz, began analyzing the body samples.

While test tubes bubbled and scientists huddled over microscopes, Kear pursued the routine work of crime detection. With a team now numbering fifty detectives under his command, he began by compiling a list of suspects. Since most murder victims are killed by people they know, Kear put Lewis Titterton's name at the top of the list, closely followed by Nancy's closest acquaintances. With the press hounding him on all sides, Kear, in off-the-record briefings with reporters, let slip that he had not entirely eliminated the secret affair angle. Nancy could still turn out to be the victim of a lover's quarrel gone wrong. Although not intended for publication, Kear's musings inevitably found their way on to the front pages, much to the fury of Nancy's family and friends. Besmirching her name in such a fashion was reprehensible, they said. No one was more devoted or faithful than Nancy Titterton; any suggestion to the contrary was a poisonous libel. The complaints became louder. Instead of peddling this muck, they raged, Kear should be investigating that mysterious prowler who'd recently been seen in other buildings along Beekman Place. In the latest alleged incident, the stranger had tried to force his way into one apartment, and only a well-aimed kick by the family maid had sent him packing. This maid, together with a clutch of Nancy's friends, now went to police headquarters to view mug shots of known sex offenders, voyeurs, and burglars, but a positive identification was not forthcoming.

The relentless media pressure forced Lyons to add yet another fifteen detectives to the investigation. This was now the biggest single homicide investigation in New York history. The main focus was directed toward tracking down the source of the scrap of cord found in the bathtub. Gettler's microscopic examination had identified it as made from low-grade Italian hemp and containing a small amount of jute. Various rope experts were called in to give their opinion. All agreed it was what the trade called "60 size," a five-ply cord with a diameter of one eighth of an inch. Immersion in water had caused the sample to swell to almost twice its original thickness. Now it was a question of tracking down the maker. Since one of the major rope manufacturers in the northeast was the Schlichter Jute Cordage Company in Philadelphia, a message was sent to the local police asking them to visit company officials to see if the twine had been made in their factory.

Just three days after she was murdered, Nancy Titterton was laid to rest. More than two hundred mourners filled the University Funeral Chapel on Lexington Avenue, while a further seven hundred lined the street outside. At Lewis's request, Nancy's wedding ring, which had been taken for forensic examination, was returned to him and buried with his deceased wife.

Every scientific twist and turn received front page coverage from a fascinated press. Readers were treated to full details of a test that Gettler had devised in 1921 to determine if someone had been alive when they were immersed in water. It worked by taking samples of blood from the left and right sides of the heart and comparing the plasma chloride levels therein. Gettler reasoned that if the person entered the water alive, then the water must cross the alveolar bed and reach the left heart, thereby causing hemodilution there and a lower chloride level when contrasted with right heart blood. This only applies if the drowning occurred in fresh water; in salt water drowning the reverse would apply. On this occasion, Gettler's formula showed thirty-five milligrams of salt less in the left heart than the right, suggesting that Nancy had been alive, though barely, when thrown in the bath and had inhaled water.

(Curiously, this contrasted with Gonzales's autopsy findings, which recorded no evidence of water in the lungs.)

Knowledge is never static, and subsequent research would cast doubt on this theory. It was discovered that, in practice, chloride undergoes radical changes after death. This means that Gettler's test, like every other test designed to ascertain if someone died from drowning, is not considered definitive, although some believe it can provide confirmatory evidence of drowning if the body is recovered and the tests performed within a few hours of death. The important element here is time. Because nonuniform and unpredictable changes in blood electrolytes always occur after death, the plasma chloride test loses effectiveness the longer the interval between death and recovery of the body.

Rather more definitively, Gettler was able to state he found no trace of alcohol in the body. Nor could he find any evidence to show that Nancy had been overcome by an attacker using ether or chloroform. The attack, in all its hideous brutality, had been carried out while the victim was fully conscious.

Each morning, Kear steeled himself for his daily grilling at the hands of a ravenous press, and humble pie was the only dish on the menu. "I regret to say that . . . in this case, clues are very scarce," uttered on the day of Nancy's funeral, was a typical quote. And there was further bad news two days later from Philadelphia; executives from Schlichter reported that the rope found in the bathtub had not originated from their factory. Kear's response was to widen the search for the rope manufacturer to other states.

Gettler continued analyzing the samples. On the skirt and bathrobe he found several strands of blond hair, all of which appeared to be from Nancy's head. What really caught his eye, though, was a single strand of hair that lay on the counterpane. To the unaided eye it looked as if it had been shed by Nancy, but the magnifying glass revealed a quite different picture. Barely a half inch long, the hair was white and strangely stiff. Carefully, Gettler removed the hair with tweezers and placed it under the microscope. After a few minutes' study, he decided it was most probably a horsehair, of the type used for stuffing furniture.

Immediately this refocused attention on the sofa that the Tittertons had sent to be repadded. Kear obtained a sample of horsehair from the couch, and when Gettler examined the two, side by side, he found them to be microscopically indistinguishable (not identical, because no one can state categorically that two fibers *are* exactly the same, only that they appear that way).

Kear ran a few suggestions past Gettler. For instance, the couch stood in the living room—was it possible for a single horsehair to blow along the corridor, past the kitchen and library, and into the bedroom? Gettler shook his head. Too heavy. No, something—or someone—had transported that hair into the bedroom. The likeliest mechanism, Gettler reckoned, was on someone's clothing; one of the officers, maybe. At a time when crime scene preservation was often slipshod and far less highly regarded than is nowadays the case, the possibility of innocent contamination by an investigating officer was an ever-present possibility. Despite this, Kear had doubts. Insofar as he could recall, the bedroom had been off limits to all but essential personnel; most of the activity had been in and around the bathroom. Gut instinct whispered to him that the answer lay elsewhere. A process of elimination left him with just the two furniture men. But their statements, corroborated by each other, showed that neither had entered the bedroom.

But what if one of them was lying?

Right from the outset, Kear had nursed serious misgivings about the skinny little guy who'd helped Theodore Kruger lug the sofa up to the Tittertons' apartment. There was something spooky about him; he had a kind of vacant semi-smirk that jarred on the nerves. Kear's suspicions were shared by everyone connected with the case, and these qualms soon hardened into something considerably more concrete when a background check showed that Kruger's twenty-four-year-old assistant was no stranger to the law.

John Fiorenza's problems had begun in his childhood. At age twelve—one year after his father died—the Brooklyn-born youngster had been arrested for stealing a bicycle and placed on probation. Two years later his mother married for a second time. Everyone agreed that Fiorenza's stepfather, Ignazio Cupani, did his best, but the boy shunned him with biblical intensity, retreating into a monastic silence when at home, communicating only through a series of nods and shakes of the head. The long-suffering Cupani later recalled that in eleven years he had only ever heard Fiorenza talk six or seven times. At school, Fiorenza was equally withdrawn, impervious to kindness or cajoling alike, and dropping out in the eighth grade. In 1932 the law caught up with him a second time, when he received another probationary term for stealing a car. Judicial leniency, however well intentioned, failed to straighten out his wayward personality. Quite the reverse. Fiorenza seemed to think he'd been given a license to steal. His next crime had a Samuel Beckett–like absurdity. For some reason, he broke into a store and stole two bass drums, a trombone, and several copies of sheet music. The haul totaled two hundred dollars, but it might as well have been a handful of dirt for all the good it did the bungling Fiorenza. With no idea why he stole the cumbersome musical instruments or how to dispose of them, he soon wound up in jail. And this time, as far as the courts were concerned, he'd run out of chances. On March 15, 1933, he was shipped off to the Elmira Correctional Facility. A year behind bars at the notorious ex–Civil War prison camp was reckoned to be punishment enough, and March 1934 saw him back out on the streets as a parolee. His liberty was brief. In July 1934 this criminal mastermind decided to steal another auto—without either noticing or caring that the chauffeur happened to be perched on the running board at the time—a violation of his parole conditions that saw him returned to Elmira. Upon his release, parole officers found him a job at Theodore Kruger's furniture store. Here, he swept floors, cleaned windows, ran errands, and paid close attention when the boss tried to teach him the skills and nuances of reupholstering furniture. From all accounts, he was a good, honest, reliable worker, even if Kruger did find Fiorenza's permanent and unwarranted grin utterly infuriating.

After digesting all this biographical detail, Kear ticked off some mental boxes: On the one hand, Fiorenza had a criminal record, was undeniably erratic, and mentally subnormal; in the plus column, recent evidence pointed to someone who had mended his ways, was engaged to be married to a young woman in the Bronx, and was holding down a steady job.

What eventually tipped the balance in Kear's mind was a prison psychiatric report on Fiorenza that had characterized him as "weak, emotional, given to self-pity and inadequate to meet emergency situations." Such a person, Kear reasoned, might easily topple over the brink into violence. By the same token, such a personality could be a sucker for flattery.

Crime solving can take many forms and now the investigation embarked on a radical step. Each afternoon, Lyons, Kear, and other high-ranking officers would convene and trade the latest developments with Gettler and Swartz. In these discussions, Fiorenza's name figured prominently, with everyone agreeing that he looked like the strongest suspect. It was decided that the best way to flush out Fiorenza—if he indeed was the killer—was through a subtle campaign of psychological warfare designed to target his vanity. Red herrings were deliberately planted in the press, professing that baffled investigators had never known a case plagued with so many blind alleys. One particularly cruel, though necessary device involved playing up the "secret lover" angle. Right from early on in the investigation Nancy Titterton's fidelity had never been in question, but Kear wanted Fiorenza to assume that investigators were actively pursuing some mystery paramour. Each day careworn detectives would call at Kruger's shop, to shoot the breeze with Fiorenza, tell him how stymied they were, and ask his opinion of the case.

All his life, the sallow-faced little man with the bony, scarred jaw had been a nobody. Suddenly he was the focus of attention. At first he was circumspect, suspicious even, but the unremitting flattery soon hit the mark, loosening his tongue and boosting his ego, sweeping him along on a tidal wave of suicidal overconfidence. The detectives played him like a hooked fish. In between comments about the weather and wisecracks about the Dodgers—wouldn't you know it, manager Casey Stengel was already downbeat about the Bums' chances in the upcoming season—they encouraged Fiorenza to theorize about the murder. Primed by the sensational newspaper reports, he jumped on the secret lover theory. The detectives dutifully logged his suggestions, all the while praising Fiorenza for his sharpness and inventiveness, contrasting it with their own stupidity. Then one would hotfoot it right away, ostensibly to follow up his brilliant lead. The next day the detectives would be back, glumly announcing another dead end, only to find Fiorenza ready for them. This time the surreal wasteland of his imagination had conjured up a mythical pots and pans salesman. Strong chance someone like that was the culprit, offered Fiorenza cockily. More awed expressions would follow as the officers berated themselves for being so dumb. "We'll be sure to look into that, Johnny," was their unvarying response. With his ego bloated like a football, and by now utterly convinced that the police had eliminated him from any list of potential suspects, Fiorenza grew sloppy. Unwittingly he let his guard slip, revealing details of the crime that the police were certain hadn't made it into the public domain.

And then there was that strange business about the phone call.

It was the emergency call made from the apartment just after the discovery of the body. When questioned, Theodore Kruger recalled that it was Fiorenza who'd phoned the police, and during the call he'd cried out, "There is a woman tied up in the bathroom." And yet, as far as Kruger knew, Fiorenza had never even looked in the bathroom, and he, sure as hell, hadn't told him that Nancy Titterton was tied up in the tub. So how had the young man known?

This inconsistency hadn't struck Kruger until the police quizzed him at length about the order of events on that fateful day. Even then, Kruger refused to buy in to the investigators' suspicions. Sure, he'd known all about Fiorenza's background when he'd hired him two years previously, but he was prepared to give the kid a chance. And in that time Fiorenza had not once let him down. "I trusted him with money," Kruger told the police. "He was good-natured and a hard worker. Sometimes he gave money to poor people."

In the meantime, while this war of nerves was being fought out in a Manhattan upholsterers, Gettler temporarily abandoned his laboratory at Bellevue and moved to a specially appointed laboratory at New York University, where the facilities were more sophisticated. By April 17, he had established that the rope contained istle, a brush fiber made from the *Agave lechuguilla* plant, commonly found in Mexico. Now it was a question of canvasing twenty-five rope manufacturers across three states and asking them to check their stocks to see if they had supplied the rope that figured in the death of Nancy Titterton. Responsibility for this time-consuming task was delegated to Detectives James F. Hayden and Frank T. Waldron.

Gettler's more advanced analysis of the rope paid off. Responding to a police circular, an executive of the Hanover Cordage Company of York, Pennsylvania, contacted the NYPD to say that his firm made rope using istle. Would it be possible to examine the actual sample? A detective immediately set off on the 185-mile journey to York, carrying with him that all-important length of swollen cord. As soon as technicians at the sprawling Hanover factory on North Street and Broadway saw the rope, they had no doubt that it had rolled off their machinery. Moreover, a check of their order book showed that several rolls had been delivered to a New York City wholesaler. When Hayden and Waldron called on this wholesaler and asked to examine company records they struck pay dirt: A single roll of this twine had been shipped to Theodore Kruger's Manhattan store just one day before the murder.

There was now enough evidence to take Fiorenza into custody. Suddenly, all those officers who had been so buddy-buddy before were now snapping around him like hungry jackals. The transformation totally unhinged him. Adding to his discomfiture was the fact that even before this latest development his boss had been questioned far more intensely about Fiorenza's whereabouts on the morning of April 10. And what Kruger had to say punched huge holes in Fiorenza's claimed alibi. Kruger recalled that Fiorenza had showed up for work late. He had called at 9 A.M. to say that he had to see his probation officer that morning and would be delayed getting to work. Kruger, a refreshingly enlightened employer for the time, said that he understood. He heard nothing more until around 11 A.M., when Fiorenza again phoned, to say that he was running late. Another hour or more passed before Fiorenza finally strolled into work. He was his usual vacuous self, the perma-grin unaffected by the blistering that Kruger gave him. But Kruger was a kindly soul, not the type to bear a grudge, and before long the two had applied themselves to the task of reupholstering the Titterton couch. That took until 4 P.M., at which time they loaded it into the truck and drove to Beekman Place.

When confronted by Kruger's statement, Fiorenza simply shrugged and stuck to his story: he had left home at 1601 Sixty-fifth Street, Brooklyn, and gone to his probation officer, after stopping off to see a couple of friends on the way. When he'd arrived at the probation office, he found it closed. To kill some time, he'd next tried to get into Judge John J. Freschi's court in the General Sessions Court Buildings, only to be turned away because the public gallery was too crowded. He'd hung around the lobby for a while, then called Kruger.

Immediately, the interviewing officers pounced—April 10 had been Good Friday, and this meant the General Sessions was closed.

Fiorenza's already shaky alibi was now in tatters and he knew it. "I was lying," he muttered after a long silence. "I was up around Forty-second Street and Times Square." At this point one of the interviewing detectives tossed the length of twine onto the table in front of Fiorenza and told how it had been traced to his place of work. Another surly silence followed. But after a long night in the cells, punctuated by several exhausting interviews, John Fiorenza finally ran out of lies.

He told how he and Kruger had picked up the couch on April 9, and during this visit he had somehow formed the extraordinary impression that Mrs. Titterton found him sexually desirable. All that night he had lain in bed, fantasizing about an assignation with the slimly attractive authoress in her upmarket apartment. By breakfast time his fevered imagination was close to bursting. He phoned Kruger and used the excuse of having to visit the probation office to explain his absence from work; then, after stuffing a fifty-two-inch length of the twine into his pocket, he had headed for Beekman Place.

He had arrived at Nancy's apartment some time after 10:30 A.M. She had been surprised to see him, because Kruger had suggested that the sofa wouldn't be finished until that afternoon. Despite her shock, she admitted Fiorenza anyway. Burbling some nonsense about finding an alternative site for the couch, Fiorenza maneuvered his way through the apartment. Nancy followed a pace or two behind, clutching some flimsy garment in her hand. When they reached the bedroom he suddenly whirled around, grabbed the garment from Nancy's hand and shoved it into her mouth, stifling any cry for help.

She struggled frantically and for a brief moment dislodged the gag just long enough to plead hysterically, "Please don't hurt me!" Fiorenza's response was to hurl her onto the bed, face against the counterpane, wrench the cord from his pocket and bind her wrists. In a blind sexual frenzy he tore at her clothing with such force that hooks and eyes were scattered like confetti on the bed and floor. Then he raped her.

Afterward, Nancy lay whimpering on the bed. In the next instant, Fiorenza made the irrevocable transition from rapist to sex killer. Grabbing the pajama top and dressing jacket that lay on the bed, he twisted them into a double-knotted noose around her slim neck. Then he began to pull tighter and tighter. At first his victim struggled feebly, then she fell limp.

He dragged her inert form—naked except for rolled-down stockings and a slip—into the bathroom and threw her facedown in the tub. His delirium fueled the ludicrous notion that he could somehow stage the scene to make it appear as if Nancy had drowned accidentally in the tub. Except he couldn't find the bath plug. He searched frantically. Every second only added to his panic. Eventually, he ran to the kitchen, grabbed a knife, ran back to the bathroom, and sliced the twine in two or three places, gathering up the pieces as he went. But in his rush he overlooked the telltale strand of twine that lay hidden beneath Nancy Titterton's violated body.

Aware that he and Kruger would be calling back at the apartment later that afternoon, he had deliberately left the door ajar as he left, driven by the misguided belief that if he were one of the people who'd found the body, it would help exclude him as a suspect.

After leaving the apartment, he had sauntered along Fiftieth Street until he passed an ash barrel. Here he ditched the pieces of twine used to tie Nancy. He stopped at a candy store on First Avenue to phone Kruger. This was at 11:00 A.M. Then he'd taken a languid stroll to work, arriving over an hour later, smiling like always, unconcerned and unruffled. When he and Kruger returned to the apartment that afternoon with the sofa, Fiorenza made sure it was his boss who found the body.

On April 21, ten days after the killing, Fiorenza was manhandled unceremoniously and very publicly back to Beekman Place, where, with the aid of a small detective who played the part of Nancy Titterton, he reenacted the strangling. With a police photographer snapping shots at every turn, Fiorenza walked everyone through the precise sequence of events that had led to Nancy's death, although he now claimed she was still breathing when he left.

When Fiorenza was formally charged with the murder of Nancy Titterton, Police Commissioner Lewis H. Valentine was generous with the credit. He hailed Gettler as the "the greatest toxicologist in the world." Assistant District Attorney William F. O'Rourke joined the chorus of praise, holding up the twine in front of reporters and saying, "This little piece of rope upset the supposed perfect crime." His boss, William C. Dodge, added the only cautious note, saying his department was holding back a few details, because "we don't want a repetition of the Vera Stretz case. We want a few tricks up our own sleeves that will surprise the defendant."

Jury selection for Fiorenza's trial began on May 19. His defense was two pronged; initially it hinged on the claim that Nancy had been the victim of the mysterious prowler who had terrorized the neighborhood recently, but when defense lawyers were unable to locate a single witness who had seen this probably apocryphal prowler, all hopes were then pinned on a plea of insanity.

This was always going to be a tough sell. For close to a century New York, like most states, had adhered to the M'Naghten Rule as its yardstick of mental competence. Based on an 1843 British murder trial in which the defendant was acquitted by virtue of insanity, the M'Naghten Rule held that someone could not be legally culpable for a crime if they were so deranged as to be unaware that what they were doing was wrong.* While no one disputed that Fiorenza was, in the words of his own counsel, "never quite normal"—even O'Rourke described him as "wacky"—he was clearly someone who fell outside the M'Naghten framework. By his own admission he had gone to the apartment determined to have sex with Nancy, and he had gone carrying a length of cord in case he needed to subdue her. When he left the apartment, all his subsequent actions were consistent with someone consciously trying to cover his tracks, fully aware of the illegality of his actions.

Throughout the trial Fiorenza remained cloaked in his invariable silence. Gonzales was the first witness and there wasn't a

---

* The M'Naghten Rule was not overturned in New York State until 1961.

flicker of emotion from the defendant as New York's chief medical examiner identified the knotted pajama top as the instrument of death. Extremely graphic photographs of the body in the tub and the various torn garments in the bedroom and bathroom prompted a similar torpor from the prisoner. Only when the piece of twine was produced did Fiorenza flinch, moistening his lips ever so slightly. He was smart enough to realize that this was the critical piece of evidence. Defense counsel Henry Klauber did his best, attacking Gonzales in a long convoluted cross-examination and drawing the witness into admitting that certain blood clots found in the body were technically consistent with causes other than strangulation. But it was a short-lived victory. When Dodge stood up on redirect, he didn't waste words. "But the discoloration in this case, Doctor, was caused by strangulation?" he asked Gonzales. "Exactly," was the emphatic reply.

Fiorenza's insanity plea fell some way short of sounding genuine. The final nail was driven into this particular coffin by Theodore Kruger. He testified how Fiorenza, accompanied by his mother, had come to the store and asked him to provide an alibi for the morning in question. When Kruger pointed out to Fiorenza that his time sheet for the day had not been stamped until 12:30 P.M., the little man had seemed crestfallen. Prosecutors turned to the jury. Did they need any more proof that Fiorenza was a sane person willfully trying to cover up his actions?

At the end of the day, all Fiorenza had left was familial loyalty. His mother, Theresa Cupani, took the stand and swore that "Johnny" was at home until 10:45 or 11:00 A.M. on Good Friday morning, which would have made it virtually impossible for him to get to Beekman Place in time to commit the murder and still be able to report to Kruger's upholstery shop at 12:30 P.M., as he did. After the murder, she said, there had been no change in his demeanor. "He was always quiet. He never speaks." She loudly refuted Kruger's allegation that she had gone to the store and attempted to arrange an alibi for him. Nor, she insisted, had Johnny ever mentioned being at the Criminal Courts Building on the morning in question. He had no need, because he was at home with her.

Dodge treated her gently. "Then why did you go with him to the Criminal Courts Building on April 20?"

Without thinking, Mrs. Cupani blurted out, "Because Mr. Kruger said to go and find out if he [had been] there." Too late she realized she had been trapped. Twisting her damp handkerchief this way and that, the poor woman lowered her head, sobbing silently. And then, mercifully, she was dismissed.

The jury received the case at 3:00 P.M. on May 26. After eleven hours of deliberations, their announcement that they were deadlocked received a harsh response from Judge Charles C. Nott Jr. He ordered them locked up for the night, with the instruction not to emerge until they had a verdict.

At just after 10:00 A.M. the next morning, the bleary-eyed jury staggered back into court with their verdict: guilty. All night they had argued over one thing: Fiorenza's sanity. While he was an inmate at Elmira, Fiorenza had been examined by a psychiatrist, Dr. James L. McCartney, who had concluded that Fiorenza should remain incarcerated as he was a "potential psychopathic paranoiac," highly likely to get into trouble again if released. Clearly several jurors had taken the view, early in the deliberations at least, that Fiorenza's mental confusion did contribute, in some small way, to the horrendous attack. But under the laws of the day, there can be little doubt that he was quite properly convicted.

His spell on death row was predictably uneventful: Appeal lodged, appeal denied, no great public clamor, gubernatorial clemency rejected. John Fiorenza's last few moments on this earth were just as silent as most of the others had been. On January 21, 1937, he was the second of four men to be put to death that night in Sing Sing's electric chair. He never said a word.

Although the Lindbergh kidnapping is widely regarded as the case that brought forensic science into the American mainstream and made the general public aware of the laboratory's capabilities, in terms of solid, scientific achievement it doesn't begin to compare with the investigation of Nancy Titterton's murder. Whereas the Lindbergh case was an example of far too many cooks spoiling the forensic broth—evidence was mishandled, jurisdictions over-lapped, egos clashed, and two years would elapse before Bruno Hauptmann, more through his own stupidity than any great feat of medico-legal detection, was run to ground—pure science solved the murder of Nancy Titterton in a matter of weeks. For Fiorenza it was the harshest possible lesson in modern criminalistics, one learned by thousands of murderers since. Had he been just a little more fastidious in his clearing up, then no matter how much suspicion fell on him, obtaining a conviction would have been devilishly difficult. As it was, one blunder—that single strand of twine—reinforced by Gettler's discovery of the horsehair, was enough to seal his fate.

There were plenty of congratulations flying round in the wake of this triumph. The police, quite rightly, were proud of the part they played. Hayden and Waldron, the two detectives who traced the twine, were both promoted and given pay raises; and while the plaudits heaped on Gonzales and Gettler were less noticeable, certainly in the paycheck department, they were equally warm. More important, this case highlighted the need for the city to get on with the task of appointing a permanent chief medical examiner. Six weeks after Fiorenza's execution, the Municipal Civil Service Commission did just that. Eighteen months of heel dragging came to an end with the announcement that an exam would be held to fill the vacant post, with the winner of that exam virtually certain to take Norris's job full time.

In the end it came down to a two-horse race between Gonzales and fellow deputy ME Dr. Manuel E. Marten, who was in charge of Brooklyn and Queens. In a three-part examination that rated the candidates according to their experience, mental ability, and record, Gonzales scored 94.75 percent, almost ten points clear of his rival. After such an emphatic victory, not even La Guardia could prevaricate any longer, and on July 21, 1937, Gonzales was sworn into office at a ceremony held at the Summer City Hall in College Point, Queens.

That same year also saw Gonzales's debut as an academic author. In association with two colleagues at the OCME—Morgan Vance and a promising newcomer named Milton Helpern—he published *Legal Medicine and Toxicology* (New York: Appleton-Century), a seven-hundred-page volume that would become the most authoritative textbook in its field (and *the* source for countless contemporary detective novelists; Raymond Chandler, for one, was an avid reader).

All this achievement did not go unrecognized by Gonzales's peers. In June 1938, he was elevated to the position of professor of forensic medicine at New York University. Lofty though these academic heights were, they formed just a tiny part of the Gonzales workload. First and foremost he was an administrator, and that meant paperwork, lots of it. His first annual report came in July 1938 and recorded that the OCME had investigated 16,313 deaths during the previous year, an increase of 499 over 1936. Like Norris before him, Gonzales was dismayed by the part played by alcohol in sudden death. Chemical analysis showed that 40 percent of auto deaths in New York were alcohol related, with a staggering 69 percent of these being pedestrians. These were depressing statistics.

On his more familiar home turf of crime fighting, Gonzales was able to lighten the gloom with one bright spot. At his request, the OCME had been provided with a small truck and driver in order that specimens from the various boroughs could be transported to the centrally located toxicological laboratory in the Pathological Building at Bellevue Hospital. This was an important development. Previously, delays in the transportation of organs—particularly in the middle of summer—meant that many specimens were too decomposed to provide useful data when analyzed. Gettler, in particular, had always harbored suspicions that some poisoners were literally getting away with murder because of this delay. The hope was that, now, this door had been slammed shut.

As always, the OCME investigated more than its share of bizarre deaths. Gonzales was forever advising his assistants on the need for constant vigilance, urging them to never accept anything at face value and to always see out corroborating evidence. He liked to talk of one utterly incredible case that occurred early in his career, back in the days of gaslight. It concerned a man driven by despair to attempt suicide. He began by slashing his wrists with a razor. Although he bled profusely, he lost patience before he lost consciousness and decided to turn the razor on his throat. This again was not quick enough for the would-be suicide, and with blood pumping from jugular and wrists, he struggled to a bureau, grabbed a revolver, and shot himself in the chest. Perhaps understandably in the circumstances, his aim was less than true. The bullet passed through his body, missed every vital organ, and succeeded only in adding to his frustration and agony. Still he clung unwillingly to life. In his misery, one last solution presented itself. He tore off his belt, knotted it around his neck, tied the other end to the old-fashioned gaslight chandelier and stepped off a chair. This time he succeeded. However, as the autopsy clearly showed, it wasn't the hanging that killed him, nor was it the slashed throat and wrists, and neither did the gunshot wound play any part in his death. No, he died from asphyxia. Apparently, when he stepped off the chair, his body weight tore the gas chandelier from its fixings. The exposed pipework was now able to flood the room with gas, and it was carbon monoxide that ultimately extinguished the man's life.

Of all the incumbents of the CME's post, Gonzales managed to keep the lowest profile. Two factors dictated this: first, as his first four years in office demonstrated, he was naturally reserved, quite unlike his flamboyant predecessor; second, on December 8, 1941, Japanese warplanes bombed Pearl Harbor.

Perspective is everything in politics; the interdepartmental sniping and personal backbiting that passes daily muster in peacetime takes on an entirely different hue when a nation is at war. Suddenly the criticism becomes more muted, the rivalries less severe, with no one wanting to run the risk of being branded as unpatriotic. With events in the Pacific and Europe suddenly taking center stage, the operations of the OCME were relegated to the inside pages. Not that Gonzales entirely escaped the upheaval. Following the havoc of Pearl Harbor, rumors raged that it was only a matter of time before the American mainland itself came under attack on both coasts from German and Japanese warplanes. However unlikely the reality—given the fact that the United States was many thousands of miles from its nearest enemy—the government, eager to reassure its citizens, realized that something needed to be done. In July 1942 it was announced that a special task force of volunteer medical examiners, under the leadership of Gonzales, had been formed to aid in the treatment and identification of victims of possible air raids. In the event, Gonzales's team was not called into action, but as a morale-boosting gesture it did no harm.

Largely insulated from public view, Gonzales went about his day-to-day work, investigating the victims of sudden death on the streets of New York. Since 1935 there had been a steady decline in the homicide rate, and with the outbreak of hostilities that number had fallen further still. Despite this, Gonzales's mortuary table remained a conveyor belt of domestic tragedy and his department was still performing feats of Holmesian investigation that even fiction's mightiest detective would have marveled over.

One forensic triumph every bit as remarkable as the Titterton case had its genesis on the morning of November 2, 1942, when Fridolph Trieman was exercising his German shepherd in a remote part of Central Park. As the dog disappeared into some tall grass, Trieman ran to keep up. Puffing and panting, he paused for breath, then stopped abruptly. Ahead of him, beneath the low hanging branches of a dogwood tree, lay the fully clothed body of a young woman. She looked ominously still.

At first the police were uncertain how the woman had died. Apart from a trace of blood at the nose and a faint welt around the neck, there were no other obvious signs of assault. It might even have been natural causes. Then a sleeve torn from the coat at the shoulder was found several feet from the body. This raised the prospect of some kind of struggle.

An autopsy carried out by Gonzales confirmed strangulation as the cause of death. Her larynx was fractured, but other than that there was no sign of injury, nor had she been raped. The fact that she had no handbag or money strongly suggested that this was a mugging gone tragically wrong—except the woman still wore a gold chain bearing a crucifix around her swollen neck. No self-respecting thief was going to leave that.

Later that same night, detectives Joseph Hackett and John Crosby of the Missing Persons Bureau identified the woman as Louise Almodovar, a twenty-year-old waitress and Sunday school teacher, who lived with her parents in the Bronx. They had reported her missing the previous day. According to the tearful parents, Louise's recent home life had been abusive and turbulent. Against their wishes, she had married Anibal Almodovar, a diminutive Puerto Rican ex-sailor, just five months earlier, only to leave him after a few weeks because of his insatiable womanizing.

When tracked down and told of his wife's fate, the twenty-one-year-old Almodovar just shrugged. She had made his life hell, he said. The bitch even had the nerve to beat up one of his girlfriends and swear at another! Good riddance, was his verdict, though he vehemently denied any involvement in her death. And the facts seemed to bear him out. According to Gonzales, Louise had met her death most probably between 9:00 and 10:00 P.M. on the night of November 1, at which time Almodovar had been carousing in a dance hall called the Rumba Palace with the very woman whom Louise had attacked. Furthermore, there were dozens of other witnesses who could testify to his presence. In the face of such an ironclad alibi, detectives understandably began widening their search for suspects, until Louise's parents produced several threatening letters that Almodovar had written to their daughter. The bile that dripped off every page convinced detectives to hold the amorous former seaman as a material witness.

Still, they couldn't get past that seemingly impregnable alibi. Only when detectives visited the dance hall, just a few hundred yards from the murder scene, did they realize that it would have been possible for Almodovar to have sneaked unnoticed out of a back door, gone to Central Park where he might have previously arranged to meet his wife, killed her, and then crept back into the Rumba Palace without anyone being the wiser. It was theoretically possible, nothing more. Without a scrap of solid evidence against Almodovar, he was released.

Given the absence of any alternative suspects, this was one of those cases that looked destined for the "Unsolved" cabinet, until Gettler had a flash of inspiration. More out of curiosity than any-thing else, he happened to glance at the crime scene photographs. He noticed that the body was lying in some very tall grass. This set him thinking. At the time of Almodovar's arrest, his clothes had been given to Gettler for analysis, and in the trouser cuffs and jacket pockets, he had found some tiny grass seeds. Gettler now sent the crime scene photographs off to be enlarged. When they came back, this higher magnification allowed him not only to iden-tify the individual strain of grass but also to declare it identical to the seeds found in Almodovar's clothing. When confronted with this evidence, Almodovar blustered that he had not visited Central Park for over two years. Any seeds in his pockets, he said, must have been picked up on a recent visit to Tremont Park in the Bronx.

Gettler decided to test this story. He forwarded the seeds to Joseph J. Copeland, formerly professor of botany and biology at City College, and a recent addition to the U.S. Air Force. It didn't take Copeland long to identify the grasses in question—*Plantago lanceolata, Panicum dichotomiflorum, Eleusine indica*—all were exceptionally rare and grew only at two spots on Long Island and three places in Westchester County. The only place in New York City where such grass occurred was Central Park. Moreover, it could be further isolated to the very section were Louise's body had been found.

Almodovar panicked, suddenly recalling a walk he had taken in Central Park two months previously, in early September. Copeland shook his head. The grass in question was a late bloomer, mid-October at the earliest, therefore Almodovar could not possibly have picked up the seeds in September. But on November 1 . . . ?

After nearly two months of parrying questions, Almodovar was utterly floored by Copeland's intervention. On December 23, he broke down and confessed. He had arranged to meet his wife in

Central Park on the night of November 1; they had quarreled again, and he had killed her in a fit of rage. Later in court, he recanted this confession, saying it had been beaten out of him in the interviewing room. But the jury did not believe a word and after just three minutes' deliberation, they found him guilty of first-degree murder. When sentence of death was passed, Almodovar, despite being shackled from head to toe, fought like a madman. No fewer than nine guards were needed to restrain him. Howling demonically, he was dragged off to Sing Sing. Six months later, on September 16, 1943, he died in the electric chair.

While the OCME kept churning out investigative miracles, La Guardia was still threatening to deliver that elusive Institute of Forensic Medicine he'd been promising for years. The mayor's dream was for a building near Bellevue, with its own morgue, laboratory, dissection room, lecture halls, and a chemical division, a regular clearinghouse for all matters pertaining to medical jurisprudence. Gonzales adopted his customarily laconic "Okay, we'll wait and see" attitude and simply got on with his job.

Although the war had initially seen a decrease in the number of murders, by 1945 they were on the rise again, and there was something else, something Gonzales hadn't seen before: a sudden spike in the number of deaths attributable to sleeping tablets. Many were suicides, some accidental, most were preventable, thought Gonzales. He blamed the increase on a new and thriving black market in prescription drugs. In the first half of 1945 he had recorded forty-seven deaths, already more than he had seen throughout the entire year of 1944. By 1948 the numbers had doubled, reaching such a pitch that in September 1949 a police sting netted eight pharmacists for peddling under-the-counter sleeping tablets. Most of the druggists bought their pills in Pennsylvania, which had no restrictions on the sale of barbiturates, paying the wholesale rate of nine dollars for a thousand tablets, later selling them in New York at a huge profit.

Gonzales's caseload was on a steep upward curve. By 1949 the OCME was investigating eighteen thousand deaths a year, of which some five thousand were violent. More ominously, each year the OCME was uncovering between thirty and forty deaths that general practitioners had reported as nonsuspicious but which chemical tests showed had involved violence or poison.

It was this toxicological upsurge that really exercised Gonzales, and more especially Gettler. The newer synthetic drugs were resisting detection by old methods, and Gettler pleaded for more funding to buy the latest equipment. Gonzales lobbied hard. In April 1949, he was able to announce that twenty-five thousand dollars had been set aside for the purchase of ultraviolet and infrared spectrophotometers designed to help detect synthetics and do more precision work on alkaloids, barbiturates, and organic drugs of any kind. All this new technology was installed in the Pathological Building at Bellevue Hospital.

Around him, Gonzales had amassed a formidable team of scientists and pathologists. There was Gettler, of course, who headed up the chemical and toxicology lab, and Dr. Alexander E. Wiener, a specialist in serology. Dr. Charles Umberger took care of spectrography and microscopy. The pathology side was equally distinguished. Dr. Morgan Vance was the Deputy CME in charge of Manhattan, the Bronx, and Richmond. In Brooklyn and Queens, it was Gonzales's longtime colleague, Dr. M. Edward Marten, who held sway. Responsibility for the city morgue in Manhattan resided in the more than capable hands of Dr. Milton Helpern.

It had been thirty years since the OCME was founded, and in that time it had grown enormously in size, skill, and influence to become the preeminent forensic facility in the world. Just about the only factor that hadn't kept pace was the age-old problem of funding. Gonzales was expected to run the OCME, with its seventy-seven-strong staff, all on an annual budget of just $321,165.

And there were other concerns. In 1948 Gonzales reached the age of seventy, the mandatory retirement age for his position. A special dispensation from the mayor, William O'Dwyer, had granted him a two-year extension, and in 1950 that extension had been renewed. When the favor was repeated for a third time in 1952, inevitably it triggered a certain restlessness among some of the younger staff. Complaints, whispered at first, then much louder, began to circulate that it was time for Gonzales to step aside. Coincidentally it was around this time that inflammatory articles began appearing in the press, alleging mismanagement and even fraud at the Office of the Chief Medical Examiner.

The problems came to light following the death of ten-year-old Roy Behanan at Kew Gardens General Hospital in Queens following a routine minor operation on April 4, 1952. Cause of death was attributed to an adverse reaction to the anesthetic used, sodium pentothal. This didn't satisfy Roy's father, K. T. Behanan, an Indian employee at the UN secretariat, who demanded access to the hospital records. What he found led to two doctors being charged with manslaughter (they were eventually cleared). More disturbingly for the OCME, in delving through the records, Behanan discovered that the assistant ME for Queens, Dr. Jacob Werne, appeared, literally, to have developed a split personality. According to simultaneous reports signed by Werne, he had performed autopsies at two different hospitals at the same date and time.

When Gonzales called in Werne and asked for an explanation, the veteran assistant shamefacedly admitted that owing to pressure of work, he had taken to signing death certificates without actually conducting an autopsy. Werne's wife, Dr. Irene Garrow, also a pathologist who had acted as assisting CME, tried to fend off media hostility by saying that her husband had performed the "crucial" parts of the autopsies at both hospitals but that he had delegated the "routine" beginning or end of the autopsy to other, junior pathologists.

Although Gonzales had some sympathy for Werne—he realized the crushing burden that each of his assistants was expected to bear—he could not countenance or tolerate such grave dereliction of duty. He issued a final warning. Werne had reached the apex of his career when he gave evidence at the 1950 trial of the notorious "Lonely Hearts" killers, Raymond Fernandez and Martha Beck, but since that time he had begun cutting corners. The press wouldn't let go. They ran stories that as many as fourteen other cases that Werne had signed off on were being investigated for impropriety. On November 5, 1953, Gonzales decided to pull the plug; he summoned Werne and demanded his resignation. Werne, a man of immense integrity who had temporarily buckled under pressure of work, cleared his desk and left.

This incident had hit Gonzales hard. He was now seventy-six years old and already had received three two-year extensions over the mandatory retirement age. The murmurings from those below had become too loud to ignore. In February 1954, he called a press conference and announced his retirement, saying, "I think that's enough."

The following month, a Queens grand jury delivered what should have been the last word on the Werne affair. It found that Werne had "consistently and flagrantly disregarded legal requirements for the conduct of autopsies, despite warnings from Dr. Gonzales." Werne might have been slipshod, the grand jury decided, but in the absence of unlawful intent, it decided that remedial rather than criminal action was required. So far as Werne was concerned, the verdict came as scant relief. After leaving the OCME he had signed on as a lieutenant colonel at the medical laboratory of the Army's Chemical Corps Arsenal at Edgewood, Maryland, and at the Rocky Mountain Arsenal at Denver, Colorado, where he directed research on gases and diseases. But everywhere he went, the black dog of depression was his constant and unwelcome companion. On April 14, 1955, while on leave from the army, he took the cord from a bathroom robe, tied it to the hinge of the bedroom door at his home in Jamaica, Queens, and hanged himself. He was age forty-nine.

The following day, a twenty-seven-year-old former aide of Werne's, named Robert Mincey, was found unconscious by his wife on the kitchen floor of their Queens home, having swallowed a handful of sleeping tablets with all the gas jets on the stove open. Fortunately, he was revived in hospital and later discharged. Mincey's background was checkered. In 1950, soon after he became a lab assistant to Werne, the State of Georgia sought to extradite him as a fugitive from justice. He had apparently escaped from the Atlanta prison farm after serving part of a one-year sentence for grand larceny. Werne not only stood bail for Mincey, but he also paid for a lawyer, and the extradition attempt failed. Mincey repaid Werne with unswerving loyalty. The Werne tragedy undoubtedly cast a wholly undeserved pall over the OCME in the final years of Gonzales's stewardship. During his nineteen-year tenure, he had built on the bedrock laid by Norris and made the OCME the technological and scientific envy of the world. Successes such as the Titterton and Almodovar cases are the reason why many refer to this as the Golden Age for forensic science in America. Gonzales had much to be proud of when he officially left office on May 1, 1954, and in his wake, there was none of the bureaucratic shilly-shallying that had marred his own accession. This time the crown prince had already been anointed.

THREE

A TOWERING PRESENCE

"When the recent history of legal medicine comes to be written . . . the name of Milton Helpern will tower above those of his fellows." So wrote the celebrated British pathologist Professor Keith Simpson about the man who took over as the chief medical examiner on April 19, 1954. This was no empty platitude. Milton Helpern, a rumpled bear of a man, was a colossus in the field of forensic science. Simpson might have performed more autopsies than anyone else in history—well over one hundred thousand by his own calculation—but he knew that when it came to ferreting out and cataloging homicide in all its infinite variety, the tailor's son from East Harlem was in a league apart.

Helpern's origins were as blue collar as it gets. His father, Moses, cut cloth for ten hours a day, six days a week, at a factory in Lower Manhattan's garment district. It was a tough life, but no tougher than that endured by millions of others at the dawn of the twentieth century, and it allowed Moses and his wife, Bertha, to raise four boys and a girl in a tenement house on 114th Street. This was where Milton, the middle of the five children, was born on April 17, 1902. When asked later about his childhood, he would shrug and say it was nothing out of the ordinary, just a good, solid working-class upbringing. Similarly, at school early on his grades were unremarkable, with nothing to single out the youngster from the pack. But all that changed in his teens. Science was the key that unlocked Helpern's future. His interest had been kindled in an offbeat way; around age twelve he became fascinated by the activity and habits of fruit flies, and after they died, he often stored them in the family icebox for future study. Hand in hand with this avocation went a love of photography. It became his lifelong passion. He learned how to convert the bathroom into a photographic darkroom and was soon producing his own black-and-white prints. As his grades improved and Helpern neared the end of his time at Townsend High School, he weighed his options. In one respect, he was extraordinarily fortunate. Had he been born just a couple of years earlier, he would probably have been shipped off to the killing fields of western Europe where the armies of the world were blowing each other to bits with technological relish. As it was, just a month or so before the Armistice was signed, the sixteen-year-old Helpern entered City College, where he majored in biology. Early on, an unsettling experience while observing an operation at Roosevelt Hospital, with its smells of ether and disinfectant, and the quick, slicing scalpel of the surgeon, proved altogether too much for the young intern and he left hurriedly, convinced he was not cut out for the medical life. (This queasiness was not unique to Helpern. Keith Simpson freely confessed that he had no stomach for the traumas of the living, hence his devotion to forensic pathology). For the remainder of his time at City College, Helpern's career aspirations were hazy, so much so that when

But with job opportunities looking bleak and a Civil Service examination for the post of assistant medical examiner in the pipeline, a colleague urged Helpern to apply. It wasn't a position that held any great appeal—Helpern still harbored dreams that the clinical post would be revived—but when it became quite clear that this had indeed been abandoned, Helpern swallowed his pride and sat the exam. He passed and on April 15, 1931, joined Norris's staff as assistant medical examiner.

With the ink hardly dry on his contract, Helpern received a body blow. Budget cuts at the OCME led to his starting salary of forty-one hundred dollars being slashed to thirty-eight hundred dollars, and the following year it was cut another two hundred dollars. Like just about everyone else on the staff, he wouldn't have survived without handouts from Norris.

Helpern repaid his boss's generosity by throwing himself headlong into a hectic schedule, seven days a week at the pace Norris set for himself. He soon learned that what the job lacked in salary, it more than made up for in variety and surprise. Even before taking this position, he had received firsthand experience of just how quirky the medical life can sometimes be. In the aftermath of the 1929 stock market crash, the national suicide rate doubled. Lives ruined became lives lost, as victims of the financial carnage opted for self-immolation. Stepping out of hotel windows was a popular option. On May 7, 1930, a Bronx resident, Charles Mayer, added his name to the tragic roll call. He had checked into a sixteenth-floor room at the Governor Clinton Hotel on Seventh Avenue. After writing a brief note, he opened the window and jumped. His body was discovered by hotel employees as it lay on a fifth-floor extension. The contents of the note gave a contact address for Mayer's brother. Then came a strange codicil. Mayer requested that if his body was sent to Bellevue Hospital, then he wished for

Dr. Milton Helpern, an intern at the time, to be notified. When told this, Helpern just scratched his head. He neither knew nor recognized Charles Mayer. Why Mayer had singled out the rookie intern for this unusual request was a mystery that would baffle Helpern for the rest of his life.

Another mystery that Helpern *did* solve was the source of a malaria outbreak that suddenly hit New York City a couple of years after he joined the OCME. Surprisingly, malaria has been a recurring problem in the United States throughout most of its history,* but the strain that struck down fourteen people in December 1933 was of a type rarely seen in latitudes as far north as New York. Nine of those victims died and found their way to Helpern's mortuary table. Judging from the victims' generally poor physical condition, and the needle tracks on the arms, Helpern suspected that all had been drug addicts. This was confirmed by narcotics officers. They also told him something interesting. In recent weeks the strength of street heroin had declined significantly. For desperate addicts who craved the same high as before, this meant abandoning their pipes and reaching for the hypodermic. Helpern knew he was on to something. Sure enough, all fourteen victims had mainlined from the same needle. From this, Helpern deduced that one of the junkies must have been carrying the malaria parasite, which was then transmitted to the others. Thanks to Helpern, and prompt treatment with quinine, New York's mysterious malaria outbreak was nipped in the bud.

Medical breakthroughs such as this did not go unnoticed, and in January 1935 Helpern was invited to join the New York University faculty as lecturer in forensic medicine. That same year he investigated a case that would have resonance for the OCME

---

* As recently as September 2002 two boys in Virginia contracted the disease from a mosquito-ridden pool near their homes, the first such case in the United States for two decades.

almost four decades later.* At about 5:00 A.M. on October 29, a twenty-six-year-old meat cutter named Theodore Plona was found sprawled in the hallway at 501 West Fortieth Street, a tenement building, where he lived with his wife, Theresa. An ambulance surgeon called to the scene diagnosed a possible fractured skull, with many other bruises and lacerations. He also thought that Plona had been drinking heavily. When the unconscious man's trouser pockets were turned inside out, the only possession on his person was the latchkey that let him into the hallway. From this the police concluded that he had been set upon by a gang of hoodlums, beaten and robbed. Plano died at 11:04 A.M. without regaining consciousness. Only when Helpern performed an autopsy did the true cause of death come to light: one small caliber bullet in the victim's head, another in his back. As we shall see elsewhere, bullet wounds can be extraordinarily tricky to find, especially if the gun used is a low-power weapon that doesn't leave any exit wound. On this occasion, Helpern had nothing but sympathy for the hard-pressed ambulance surgeon. In all the blood and the chaos, two tiny bullet wounds were easy to miss because they were so well concealed. Helpern's discovery was the only ray of light in this otherwise murky case. The killer was never caught.

At the other end of the social spectrum, just two weeks later, Helpern became involved in the first major case of his career, when he autopsied Fritz Gebhardt, who had been shot by his lover, Vera Stretz (see chapter 2). When Stretz stood trial for murder the following spring and Helpern took the stand, he gave the jury an early indication of the lucidity and straightforwardness that would impress courtrooms for decades to come. There were no highfalutin medical phrases, no jargon, no self-aggrandizing attempts to impress, just simple easy-to-understand explanations of the issues

---

* See chapter 4 and the death of Laura Carpi.

involved. He also sent a stark and unequivocal message about his independence. One newspaper noted peevishly: "Although called by the State, Doctor Helpern failed to go as far as the prosecution wished." This single sentence summed up the Helpern credo: a point-blank refusal to embellish the facts, no matter how important the trial or how great the pressure. Unlike some medical examiners, he didn't see himself as an arm of the judiciary or a prosecution pawn; he was purely a man of science, there to give his opinion on the evidence as he saw it.

In following this strategy, Helpern was merely echoing the maxims of his new boss. Dr. Thomas Gonzales had no doubts about his young assistant's ability. Indeed, it was Helpern who provided much of the input—and virtually all of the photographs—for their joint work, *Legal Medicine and Toxicology*, the epic reference book that Helpern continued to edit right into the 1950s.

And Helpern certainly had no shortage of unusual case material on which to draw. For instance, in 1941, he had to deal with the case of The Man Who Strangled Himself. Mehment Ali Yukselen had been the Turkish consul general in New York City for four years and for most of that time he had suffered from a painful heart condition. As the condition worsened, his depression grew blacker. Around 5:00 A.M. on the morning of September 21, his wife, in an adjacent bedroom, heard him stirring rather noisily but thought no more about it. When Yukselen had not appeared by lunchtime, his wife and a consul employee broke down the door. They found Yukselen lying in bed. Around his neck were two ties, knotted together. With these he had slowly garroted himself to death. On a night table next to the bed lay a note. It gave the address of a priest and said, "Let him bury me in a very simple way with the money which was in the pocket of the suit I wore yesterday." Detectives found $401 in the pocket. When skeptical reporters quizzed Helpern over the bizarre nature of Yukselen's demise, he told them it was entirely possible for someone to choke himself to death in such a manner, particularly if he had a weak heart.

Just a few short months later, the United States was at war. Two events stood out for Helpern during this period: In 1943 he was promoted to deputy chief medical examiner; then, as part of the war effort, he was posted to England to act as a civilian consultant to the Royal Air Force. Apparently his biggest concern about this posting, which was in the depths of winter, was a worry over how to keep warm in that notoriously cold country. Consultation with a fellow forensic scientist, Dr. Sydney Kaye, led to Helpern being kitted out in long johns and heavyweight military khakis.

The New York that Helpern returned to at war's end was confident and bursting with triumph, but the battles on its own streets were just as bloody as before, and just as peculiar. Probably the most bizarre case that Helpern ever investigated—he called it "one of the most unusual in medical history"—began on a hot August night in 1946, when Raul Alvarez, a twenty-two-year-old factory worker, stormed into a bar and grill on Lexington Avenue, determined to settle a long-running feud once and for all. The object of his ire was the bartender, Basilio Guadalupe. Word had reached Alvarez that Guadalupe had been sneaking dates with his girl behind his back. Once inside the bar, Alvarez squared up to his rival, turning the air blue with a long string of insults. What happened next was always in dispute. According to Guadalupe, the enraged Alvarez pulled a knife and lunged forward. Guadalupe, fearing for his life, grabbed an ice pick from behind the bar. A single swipe with the ice pick caught Alvarez in the back. He drew away, more startled than hurt, but the incident did bring him to his senses. He scoffed at the wound, insisting it was nothing more than a scratch and, as if to demonstrate his toughness, swaggered from the bar.

The next day he went to work. And the day after that. In fact,

Alvarez carried on working, right through Thanksgiving, the Christmas holiday, and into the new year. Only in February 1947 did he begin to suffer any serious discomfort in his back. Finally, the pain became so severe that he went to Harlem Hospital. An X-ray revealed the problem: The ice pick wound had been three inches deep and had passed through the spine, to penetrate the heart and mitral valve. Once there, a fragment from the ice pick tip had broken off and lodged in the heart. It was this fragment that was causing the pain. To make matters worse, an infection had now set in. When Alvarez's condition suddenly deteriorated in early April, he underwent an emergency operation to remove the ice pick tip from his heart. Sadly, the operation failed. On April 3, 1947, eight months after the barroom brawl, Alvarez died.

Helpern had never seen anything like it. As he told the court, when Guadalupe stood accused of fatally stabbing Alvarez, the dead man had been living on "borrowed time" for eight months. If the tip had been discovered any earlier, and an attempt made to remove it, he said, the outcome would have been exactly the same, for the point had actually sealed the wound's opening. Once the tip was removed, death was inevitable. The court didn't really know what to make of all this. Was Guadalupe guilty of murder or not? After much judicial head shaking, Guadalupe's uncorroborated insistence that he had acted in self-defense, combined with the extraordinary medical circumstances, resulted in the bartender receiving a prison sentence of five to ten years for manslaughter.

The postwar boom that America enjoyed brought many modern conveniences to the average household, but there were dangers as well. When Mrs. Mercedes Gomez de Barry contacted her building superintendent on Saturday, November 18, 1950, and told him her gas refrigerator was not working properly, he immediately called an independent company to fix it. It was Monday morning before the service engineer arrived at the apartment at 310 East

Fifty-fifth Street. Tragically, the thirty-nine-year-old Mrs. de Barry lay dead on the floor. Helpern rushed to the scene. Her pinkish skin and the bright cherry color of her blood left no doubt as to the cause of death: Mrs. de Barry had been poisoned by carbon monoxide leaking from her defective gas refrigerator. Helpern was incandescent; this was the seventeenth such death investigated by the OCME this year alone. Most of the deaths had occurred in colder weather, when users were reluctant to leave windows open to provide the recommended and essential level of ventilation. Helpern wanted the service company charged with criminal negligence. That didn't happen, and it would take another decade of vociferous campaigning on Helpern's part before the city's Board of Health issued restrictions on these potentially lethal devices. (As recently as 1998, the U.S. Consumer Product Safety Commission was warning consumers to stop using gas refrigerators manufactured between 1933 and 1957, owing to the risk of carbon monoxide leakage in deadly quantities.)

Helpern's headline-making campaign against the dangers of gas refrigerators, allied to his commanding presence on the witness stand, ensured that his name remained firmly in the public eye. He also made giant strides on the academic front, adding a lectureship at Cornell Medical College to the one he already held at New York University. By the early 1950s his reputation also began to spread abroad, and as Gonzales edged ever nearer retirement, it became obvious that Helpern's name would figure prominently in any contest when the top job became vacant. But nobody was prepared for what came next.

Astonishingly, and in flagrant violation of the legislation that established the OCME, on April 15, 1954, Mayor Robert F. Wagner announced that Helpern would take over from Gonzales. There would be no Civil Service examination, no open competition, just the rubber-stamped recommendation of City Administrator

Dr. Luther Gulick, who said that leading authorities in the field of forensic science agreed that Helpern was the best qualified man for the post. Although no one seriously disputed Gulick's choice on a professional level—Helpern stood head and shoulders above all his rivals—the unilateral and arbitrary nature of his decision making harked back to the bad old days of cronyism and favors.

The department that Helpern took over was racked by turmoil. The press had been subjecting the OCME to death by a thousand cuts, and first on the new boss's agenda was a honeymoon period with the fourth estate. Helpern was shrewd. Like Norris, he understood the importance of the media and had seen the way they toppled his predecessor. Determined to get the press on his side, Helpern launched a compelling charm offensive. Newspaper readers soon became used to his craggy face, with its shock of iron-gray hair, accompanying a string of complimentary articles about his department. They learned that being a good medical examiner wasn't just about microscopes and test tubes, sometimes a good ME needed to follow his intuition. There was the time, for instance, when Helpern had been called to a crime scene and, after studying the body closely for a while, suddenly turned it over and ran his hands down the back. Police officers present gaped in open amazement as Helpern, after asking if anyone had a nail file, then made a little X in the skin, and out popped a small bullet. Experience, chuckled Helpern; so far as the astonished onlookers (and the readers) were concerned, it looked more like magic.

Less than a year after taking office, Helpern married for the second time. (His first wife, Ruth, had died of a rheumatic heart condition in January 1953.) This time around Helpern got more than just a spouse. Beatrice Helpern would become his personal secretary at the OCME and remain by his side for the duration of his tenure. "Often secretaries take a job to marry the boss," Helpern joked. "My wife married the boss to become his secretary." Only once, though, did Beatrice's fascination for the job extend to actually accompanying her husband on a field trip to examine a newly found body. It was especially gruesome and delivered the kind of sensory overload that her husband coped with on a daily basis. For Beatrice it was one stomach-churning spectacle too far, and thereafter she resolutely refused to leave the relative comfort and safety of the office.

And finally it was beginning to look as if that office was on the verge of getting a whole lot better. For decades the OCME had lobbied for its own dedicated facility. The promises from City Hall had been lavish, the reality notably barren. But in August 1956, when Helpern put in a request for $2,850,000 for work to begin on a new office building, morgue and laboratory adjacent to Bellevue Hospital, he did so with a newfound air of confidence that this time the department would not be denied.

Before that could come to fruition, however, Helpern received a nasty reminder of the need for constant vigilance on his own watch. Dr. Alfred L. Shapiro had first started doing work for the OCME in 1952, and like many of the more peripheral staff members, the Brooklyn assistant ME had supplemented his meager city income by means of a private practice. Helpern had no quibble with this; so long as the OCME job was done properly, then a spot of moonlighting was perfectly acceptable. But in 1957, whispers began to filter through that Shapiro was shading the system. Reportedly, in April of that year, while on sick leave from the city, the assistant ME had been treating patients privately. When the abuse was repeated in mid-June, Helpern exploded. Shapiro, forced on the defensive, claimed that he had suffered a relapse of hepatitis after working seventy-two hours straight from June 14 to 17. Helpern checked the claim and found that during this period

Shapiro had handled twenty-seven cases, mostly by phone, and only two entailed much work. On June 22 Shapiro produced a letter from his doctor advising him "to rest as much as possible." Coincidentally, this letter was dated one day after Helpern had filed charges against Shapiro, alleging failure to respond promptly to three deaths, two counts of having failed to complete autopsy reports, and failure to answer subpoenas to testify in criminal cases. For the first time in its history, a member of the OCME was charged with misconduct.

The hearing was held on August 28, 1957, in Helpern's office at the Department of Health and Mental Hygiene at 125 Worth Street, with Helpern presiding. Shapiro tried to turn the tables on Helpern by making *him* the target of the inquiry. It had been Helpern's brutal insensitivity, claimed Shapiro, that sparked this crisis. When he had gone to Helpern and requested sick leave, Helpern had turned him down flat. Despite being laid low by a debilitating illness, Shapiro had bravely soldiered on, fulfilling his duties to the best of his ability. It was the kind of performance that impressed no one save the teller. A decided frostiness filled the room. Shapiro could sense it hadn't gone well. In his desperation to regain the initiative, even before the commission announced its finding, he filed a twenty-five-thousand-dollar suit against the city and Helpern for having caused his illness. When the inevitable happened and Shapiro was axed, he began a long, protracted appeal process that dragged on until October 1958, at which time his petition to be reinstated was thrown out by the courts. The lawsuit was also dismissed.

Two rather happier departures from the OCME were announced on January 1, 1959. Dr. Alexander O. Gettler, the city toxicologist, and Dr. Benjamin Vance were both age seventy-five, and between them they had notched-up eighty years of service to the Office of the Chief Medical Examiner. Gettler had been there right at the beginning in 1918 and had progressed to become, arguably, the foremost forensic chemist in the world, featuring in many of the nation's most spectacular poison murder cases. Vance was less well known to the newspaper-reading public, but since joining the OCME in 1920, he had become one of its foremost academics, coauthoring with Gonzales and Helpern *Legal Medicine and Toxicology*. His particular expertise was in hair and fibers, and at the time of retirement he was the deputy chief medical examiner. Both were badly missed by Helpern, who said they had brought "great esteem and praise to this office [OCME]."

By this stage of his career, although Helpern was virtually unassailable in the New York courtroom, peering over his Benjamin Franklin half-moon spectacles, delivering opinions in a rich, creamy voice as avuncular as it was authoritative, there was one criticism he could not shake off: the snide accusation that he was "a prosecution man." Critics who complained that Helpern rarely testified for the defense were usually missing half the picture. What they failed to realize was that most of Helpern's "defense work" was done behind the scenes. As one district attorney put it, if, after studying the evidence, Helpern decided there was no homicide, only a fool would dare take the case to court.

A prime example of Helpern's independence and supreme authority came one time when a man called the police and confessed to killing the woman with whom he lived. When the police arrived, they found the man blind drunk and a woman dead in bed. Racked by remorse and almost incoherent with grief, the man described how they had been drinking heavily, then started fighting. It had ended with him wrapping his hands around her throat and squeezing. The case seemed open and shut. The man was charged with murder and arraigned in court the next morning. That afternoon, Helpern got to see the body. He immediately reached for the phone. The woman had died of natural causes, he told incredulous detectives, cirrhosis of the liver, there was absolutely no sign of strangulation. Helpern's intervention led to the case being thrown out. Despite this, the man continued to insist that he was a murderer. He never got over the grief. Two weeks later, he killed himself.

Because of the reasons stated, Helpern's appearances for the defense were rare events. For the most part they occurred outside of New York. The most controversial of these came in 1959, when defense lawyers in Boston asked him to review the medico-legal findings in a sensational headline-making case that had locals agog. What Helpern found as he delved through the papers offended every fiber of decency and justice in his body. But that didn't surprise him. He'd been down this particular road before.

CASE FILE:
Willem van Rie (1959)

During the last ice age, when huge glaciers engulfed New England, a sliver of rock was carved off what is now the Massachusetts coastline and dumped in the ocean, with just its uppermost edge peeking above the icy waters. Archaeological evidence suggests that the tiny island was first inhabited more than one thousand years ago, its settlers drawn by the abundant aquatic life and shellfish. When early European colonists arrived it struck them that the island, which consisted of two glacial drumlins connected by a single spit, resembled a pair of eyeglasses, and before long it became known as Spectacle Island. Standing four miles south of the modern-day Boston dockside and buffeted by constantly swirling tides and currents, Spectacle Island has enjoyed a colorful history. In 1729 it was commandeered as a quarantine station for Irish immigrants, a holding area to see if any exhibited signs of the dreaded smallpox. By the early nineteenth century the immigrants and the pox-watchers were gone and someone had the bright idea of converting the ninety-seven-acre outcrop into a summer resort. Two clapboard hotels appeared almost overnight and were soon catering to regular boatloads of holidaymakers from Boston and the surrounding areas. It's fair to say that the island's relative isolation from the mainland did encourage a certain moral laxity among the visitors, one that the hoteliers were quick to capitalize on. For a few years Spectacle Island was wide open, bursting to the seams with illegal gaming tables, cheap plentiful booze, and reputedly the highest concentration of hookers in New England. There was something for every appetite and every pocketbook. The party lasted until 1857, when outraged Bostonians, sick of seeing all that disposable income going offshore, dispatched a squad of police officers to stamp out the illicit revelry. As soon as the hotels shut down, the visitors dried up, and the island resumed a humdrum path. First came a rendering plant for dead horses and cattle, followed by a garbage recycling facility, then a landfill for the city across the bay. This latter use proved so successful that by the time Boston had finished dumping its waste, Spectacle Island had gained an extra eight acres in area, mostly along the spit, so that its resemblance to the eponymous eyewear had all but vanished. The dumping ended in 1959. Coincidentally, that year marked the discovery of yet another kind of detritus on the island's shoreline.

The young woman's body was found in the early hours of September 19, 1959, by a passing tugboat captain. She was badly bruised and clad only in gray Bermuda shorts and blue slippers. Judging from her condition, she had not been in the sea for long, as there was none of the grotesque bloating or marine depredation that generally accompanies long immersion in water. Putting a name to the corpse took only a few hours. Late the previous evening, local coast guards had received a radio message from the *Utrecht*, an

8,346-ton freighter en route from Boston to New York, that one of its passengers was missing, feared overboard. From the description, there could be little doubt that Lynn Kauffman had been found.

The twenty-three-year-old had definitely been aboard the *Utrecht* at 6:15 P.M. the previous evening, when the steamer slipped its moorings at Commonwealth Pier in South Boston, then cleared the harbor, before speeding up to sixteen knots on a course for the Cape Cod Canal. But by 9:00 P.M., it was evident that Lynn Kauffman had vanished.

The *Utrecht* was not some modern-style cruise ship but rather a working freighter that transported cargo from one part of the globe to another. Like many tramp steamers of the period, it also offered a few cabins to passengers, who got to see the world at an unhurried pace, while receiving a level of personal attention from the crew and stewards that only the most expensive liners could hope to match. For Lynn Kauffman, the voyage had been a glorious opportunity to expand her personal horizons, the well-deserved reward for much hard work. Three years previously she had entered Washington University in St. Louis to study the Far East. One of her tutors was Dr. Stanley Spector, a professor of oriental studies, and he had quickly realized Lynn's potential ("a brilliant student of the orient," was his later assessment). A bond grew up between them, with Lynn first becoming his secretary and research assistant, then moving into the family home in a St. Louis suburb called Clayton. It was a great arrangement for everyone concerned. Spector's wife, Juanita, and their two children, Stephanie and Jon, warmly welcomed Lynn into their family.

Despite her tender years, Lynn had already packed a fair chunk of life experience into her résumé. She came from a comfortable background—her father was a well-to-do Chicago businessman— and after attending private school, she won a place at prestigious

Smith College in Massachusetts, one of the so-called Seven Sisters of the Ivy League. It was on a home visit that she met and later married Arthur B. Tucker, who was stationed in Chicago with the army. When he was assigned briefly to Alaska, Lynn went with him. Shortly after this, Tucker received his military discharge and the couple moved to St. Louis, where he qualified as a lawyer, and Lynn resumed her academic studies. But the marriage soon foundered, and in 1956, while Lynn was still a junior at Washington University, she joined the ranks of the freshly divorced. She was just twenty years of age. Curiously, despite the divorce and reverting to her maiden name, Lynn always insisted on being called *Mrs.* Kauffman.

Moving in with the Spectors brought Lynn a whole raft of job benefits, not the least of which was a chance to see the world. In the course of his work, the forty-five-year-old Spector frequently traveled abroad, and the summer of 1959 saw him undertake a lengthy research program in Asia. It was a great chance for his family to do some sightseeing, and Lynn, too, went along. The trip went well and the family booked return passages to the United States on the *Utrecht*. But, when the ship left Singapore on August 5 and chugged out into the Main Strait, the professor was not on board. He still had plenty on his academic plate in Singapore and elsewhere. Eight days later Spector flew out of Singapore to continue his research studies, first in New Delhi, then on to Tashkent, Moscow, and Prague. In Prague he suffered a serious knee injury. Unable to get the medical attention that he required in communist Czechoslovakia, he decided to cut short the European leg of his tour, and on August 26 he flew back to St. Louis.

While Spector crisscrossed Eurasia by plane, the *Utrecht* steamed steadily northwest across the Indian Ocean, with its cargo of sugar, on a course for the Red Sea. Although the languid lifestyle of a passenger on a tramp steamer had many pluses, there were drawbacks.

Unlike cruise liners, the ship's itinerary was not designed to thrill tourists. The *Utrecht* was first and foremost a working vessel and that meant taking the most direct route at the most economical speed and avoiding unnecessary stopovers. This mandated long stretches at sea, with little else for passengers to do except read or take the sun. And the one commodity you can guarantee in the Red Sea in the middle of August is blistering sunshine. A sultry tropical ennui settled over the steamer as it nudged toward the Suez Canal. The ship carried just nine passengers. Besides the Spectors and Lynn, there was a fifteen-year-old Chinese boy named Lee You Kah, whom the Spectors hoped to adopt, and one other family, an army sergeant named Arden Brown, his wife, and two children.

One way of filling up the hours, Lynn found, was by practicing her Mandarin on the largely Chinese crew. At night, over the dinner table, it was conversation of a different stripe. Lynn's natural vivacity always shone through. She was attractive and knew it. Her close-cropped brown hair framed an oval face that sparkled when she smiled, which was often, and although barely five feet two inches tall, and rather less than one hundred pounds, she exuded a natural effervescence that seemed to fill every room she entered. This ebullience was even reflected in her correspondence. At the northern end of the Suez Canal, when the *Utrecht* docked at Port Said, Egypt, she mailed a long, happy letter to Spector, saying how much she was looking forward to returning to St. Louis and working with him on his latest book.

But as the ship trudged its way westward through the Mediterranean, Lynn's sparkle seemed to fade. Perhaps this was only to be expected. Hour after interminable hour on the long, flat sea, with little in the way of diversion, can sour the sweetest disposition. By the time the ship cleared Gibraltar, the voyage had already lasted for well over a month, and there was still that last featureless slog across the Atlantic to overcome.

Even so, no one had been prepared for such a marked deterioration in Lynn's mood. From being the life and soul of the ship, she had slumped into a moody torpor so bad that when the *Utrecht* finally docked in Boston on September 18, she refused to come out of her cabin. At 12:55 P.M. Juanita Spector knocked, to see if she was coming down for lunch. Lynn opened the door an inch or two, looking utterly miserable. No lunch today, was the response. She wanted to lie down. Rotten headache, you know.

As that evening was the last night of a voyage that had begun forty-four days earlier in Singapore, Lynn, together with all the other passengers, was invited to dine with the captain in the lounge at 7:00 P.M. Five minutes beforehand, Juanita again knocked at Lynn's cabin door. From behind the door, which this time remained firmly closed, Lynn cried out in a broken voice that she was still not hungry and would not be attending the meal. When Juanita reached the captain's table and passed on this news, the ship's second steward, Lubertus van Dorp, excused himself and went to investigate. It was 7:05 P.M. when he reached Lynn's cabin. Again she refused to open the door, insisting that she would be fine if everyone just left her alone. Beneath the muffled protestations, van Dorp thought he detected a sound of sobbing. He, too, then returned to the party.

About nine o'clock, the chief purser, Andreas P. van Oosten, became worried enough to intervene personally. He knocked at Lynn's door and got no answer. When he tried the door, he found it wedged tight but unlocked. He shouldered his way in. The cabin was empty and both portholes were wide open. Immediately he raised the alarm.

The ship was searched from bow to stern. Nothing. As a last resort, Captain Albert de Bruijn ordered an emergency lifeboat drill. The ship's whistle blasted. This was the signal for everyone on board—passengers and crew alike—to proceed to a designated spot. Had Lynn been in someone else's cabin, this should have flushed her out. Still, she remained resolutely missing.

Even though a high rail on the deck outside the companionway that led to Lynn's interior cabin reduced the likelihood of anyone's falling overboard accidentally, Captain de Bruijn feared the worst. He was especially alarmed by the two open portholes. At midnight, he ordered the radio officer to send a message to the Boston and New York coast guards, informing them of a passenger missing, feared overboard. As a precaution, he ordered that Lynn's cabin be locked, until such time as the authorities could investigate the disappearance.

As we have already seen, the search for Lynn Kauffman was over in a matter of hours. A message radioed back to the ship allowed the *Utrecht* to continue its short somber voyage to New York, docking at Pier 1, Bush Terminal in Brooklyn at 1:00 P.M. on September 20. Police met the vessel when it tied up and immediately sealed Lynn's cabin. For three hours they questioned the twelve officers, the crew, and the other passengers, without uncovering a single clue as to how Lynn ended up in the water.

Although a Boston detective, Captain Joseph B. Fallon, was putatively in charge of what was already shaping up to be a tricky investigation, he and his New York counterparts agreed to coordinate their efforts through the U.S. Coast Guard. With this arrangement in hand, Fallon and two subordinates headed to New York to conduct their own interviews of the crew.

In a strange quirk of fate, Dr. Stanley Spector was actually decorating Lynn's room at his St. Louis home, in anticipation of her arrival, when he received the telephone call. Dropping everything, he caught a flight to Boston, and to him fell the grim task of identifying his young assistant's body.

An autopsy had already been carried out by the Boston medical examiner, Dr. Michael A. Luongo, and his findings would turn the investigation on its head. Even though he recorded the cause of death as drowning, the scale of injuries to the head, brain, and body left him in no doubt that Lynn had been beaten severely at some time immediately prior to death, probably to the point of unconsciousness. If this were true, it drastically diminished the chances of her having fallen overboard accidentally. Luongo was in no doubt: Lynn Kauffman had met her "death by violence."

Cross-purposes seemed to be the order of the day, with Luongo saying one thing, and Fallon another. Although the detective initially went on the record with his belief that the death had been accidental, now he told a press conference, "We have not ruled out suicide." In a sidebar, he added that "the injuries Mrs. Kauffman suffered could have been caused by a fall from the vessel." Noticeably absent from Fallon's press briefing was any mention of murder. And certainly there was nothing on board the *Utrecht* to indicate foul play. Lynn's compact eight-by-ten-foot cabin was immaculate, with no sign of a struggle having taken place. A search of her foot locker revealed some Chinese, Indonesian, and English manuscripts, while a bittersweet reminder of that last missed dinner engagement came in the form of an unworn cocktail dress hanging from a clothes hook.

As Fallon struggled to keep the investigation on an even keel, a flock of federal narcotics agents began swarming all over the ship, after receiving a tip-off that Mrs. Kauffman had been murdered after stumbling on evidence of a drug-smuggling ring. Fallon's protests were brushed aside. Only after the gung-ho agents had fruitlessly interviewed every crew member and wasted hours of valuable time did they accept what Fallon had told them all along: forget it, you've been sent on a wild goose chase.

The confusion only worsened as doubts began to emerge about what exact route the *Utrecht* had taken on the night in question. According to the ship's log, Spectacle Island was rounded at 6:45 P.M.

Another twenty minutes passed before van Dorp went to Lynn's cabin and spoke to her through the door. So far as anyone knew he was the last person to speak to Lynn, by which time the *Utrecht* would have steamed several miles past Spectacle Island. However, drawing on a report by the U.S. Coast and Geodetic Survey on the prevailing winds and currents at the time of Lynn's disappearance, Captain James J. Crowley, harbor master for the Boston police, said that for the body to have washed up on Spectacle Island, it must have gone into the water within six hundred yards of the shoreline. Any further away, and the body would have been washed out to sea, most probably to be lost forever.

Although ocean currents can never be entirely predictable when talking about the disposition of a single object, this finding—if accurate, which Fallon doubted—clearly raised several possibilities: (1) the ship's log was incorrect, (2) several people had been mistaken about the time, or (3) the voice heard was not that of Lynn Kauffman.

Despite these anomalies, four days into the inquiry, Fallon was still repeating his mantra that Lynn's death was "either an accident or suicide." He returned to Boston with three trunks impounded from Lynn's cabin, intending to study the papers and manuscripts contained therein to see if they provided any evidence to support the idea of suicide.

Three days later everything had changed. Fallon was back in New York, in hot pursuit of a case he now declared to be "wide open." Close study of Lynn's papers had made it apparent that some passengers and crew on board the *Utrecht* had been highly economical with the truth. In fact, this was beginning to sound very much like one of those Agatha Christie murder mysteries, where almost every character might be a suspect.

*   *   *

For many older Bostonians the death of Lynn Kauffman had resurrected memories of Starr Faithfull, the twenty-five-year-old New York socialite whose drowned body had washed up on Long Beach, Long Island, in June 1931. Murky hints that ex-Boston mayor Andrew Peters was somehow involved in her death only added spice to an already juicy saga of sex and intrigue. According to the scandalmongers, several years earlier the horny Peters had coughed up thousands of dollars in blackmail to bury allegations that he had seduced Starr while she was still a juvenile. It was one of those stories with plenty of gossip and precious few facts, and in the end, Starr's death—like much of her life—remained a mystery, without any firm evidence to say if it was an accident, suicide, or murder. Many now wondered if the death of Lynn Kauffman was destined for a similarly ambiguous conclusion.

Fallon had no intention of allowing this case to slide. But he was cagey. On his return to New York, all he would tell reporters was that forty-eight hours before her death, "[Lynn] was in a very depressed state after receiving certain information." But the reporters had also been digging, and they wanted clarification about an alleged spat between Lynn and Mrs. Spector on September 17, the night before Lynn's disappearance. It had reportedly begun while the ship was still docked in Halifax, Nova Scotia, at a party to celebrate Mrs. Spector's birthday. Allegedly, Juanita had confronted Lynn with news that she was no longer welcome at their St. Louis home, triggering a sharp argument that spilled over into the following day, as the *Utrecht* entered Boston Harbor. Had this rejection been the catalyst for Lynn's suicide? Clearly Fallon hadn't excluded the possibility, going on record as saying that Lynn "had received some distressing news that day, which would have affected her life profoundly." So, had she been kicked out of the Spector household?

When phoned by reporters, Stanley Spector hotly denied any

such thing, adding that even if his wife had said this, it would hardly have driven Lynn to suicide. "Lynn was an intelligent girl. She would at least have waited twelve hours to ask me what I thought about it." Spector did offer one clue as to how this rumor might have got started. While in Singapore, the family had discussed the possibility of Lynn's moving to another apartment when they returned to St. Louis, because young Lee was joining the household. Apparently the potentially divisive issue had surfaced again at the start of the voyage, but it was all settled amicably, Spector told the reporters, with Juanita's agreeing that Lynn should continue to live with them.

At this point Spector handed the phone to his wife. She recalled that on the day of her (Mrs. Spector's) birthday, Lynn had gone ashore in Halifax and purchased several presents, including a bathrobe, and that relations between the two had been nothing but harmonious.

Neither clarification poured much water on the flames of speculation, which by now were raging like an inferno. What else, reporters conjectured, might have caused the alleged rift between Lynn and her employer's wife? Might it center on that other rumor, the one about a shipboard romance? Maybe Mrs. Spector had disapproved of Lynn's reported affair with one particular young officer?

This story had also reached Fallon's ear. The first inkling had come when he'd examined Lynn's cabin and found a neatly pressed uniform belonging to Willem van Rie, the ship's slimly built thirty-year-old radio officer who had broadcast the message of Lynn's disappearance to the outside world. At the time Fallon had played down the significance of this discovery, after hearing that during the long voyage, as a means of alleviating the boredom, Lynn and Mrs. Spector had volunteered to mend and press clothes for all the officers, several of whom availed themselves of this generosity.

Juanita Spector continued to stir the pot of intrigue. In a revised statement she now said that at 6:05 P.M. on September 18—while the *Utrecht* was still moored in Boston—she had been in her stateroom and heard a voice coming from the adjoining cabin, which was Lynn's. "Nita, Nita," the voice had cried through the steel bulkhead that separated the two cabins. "What do you want?" Mrs. Spector had asked. On getting no reply, she had wondered if the incident had been a figment of her imagination. Interestingly, she now claimed that the voice she heard at 6:55 P.M.—which she'd earlier said belonged to Lynn—was actually so muffled as to be unidentifiable.

Fallon watched all these developments with a disdainful eye. He had already sidelined the harbor master's assertion that Lynn's body must have been in the water at the time when two persons claimed to have spoken to her, dismissing the report as "just a theory." And he refused to be budged from his belief that Lynn's death had been a suicide. He based this on careful questioning of the crew. Between the hours of 6:00 and 8:00 P.M. it appeared as if each crew member, from the captain on down, had been under surveillance by someone else, and none had the opportunity to commit the murder—if murder it was.

Behind the scenes, though, a bitter dispute had erupted over the circumstances of Lynn Kauffman's death. Luongo was emphatic that she had been beaten half to death by someone's fists before being thrown into the water; Fallon could find no evidence to support that theory. He took the view that Lynn, after feeling ill all day, might have gone to the rail of the ship for some fresh air, fainted, and fallen overboard. When Fallon stuck to the suicide/accident scenario, Luongo dug in his heels and refused to sign a death certificate. Ten days after the discovery of Lynn's body, Fallon was still insisting that this was no homicide.

On the eleventh day he charged Willem van Rie with murder.

*   *   *

The change of heart had come about after Fallon had suddenly flown down to New York and boarded the *Utrecht*. Originally the ship had been scheduled to sail for Philadelphia, but because two hurricanes, "Gracie" and "Hannah," were chasing each other up the eastern seaboard, de Bruijn decided to ride out the weather. Gracie had already made landfall in the Carolinas on September 29, and Hannah was expected to do likewise a day or so later. De Bruijn opted for caution.

This delay allowed Fallon, under orders from his superiors, to arrest the handsome radio officer, and whisk him off to a Brooklyn precinct station where for the next fifteen hours he was grilled nonstop. Van Rie later claimed that being forced to speak in English had placed him at a disadvantage and that in his confusion he had been bullied into giving a damaging statement.

Van Rie, the son of a Roman Catholic school headmaster, had been on board the *Utrecht* for a little over a year. Although he had a wife back in Holland, like many a naval man before and since, he was not averse to the chance assignation, and when, a few days out of Singapore, Lynn had asked him if he liked sleeping alone, he had replied, "Not necessarily." Van Rie wasn't about to pass up the chance of bedding the delectable Lynn, and thereafter they visited each other regularly in their cabins. As he put it to the interviewing officers, "I don't go looking for romance, but when it comes my way, I don't turn it down!"

The interrogating officers noted every word, as the questioning dragged on deep into the night and the next morning. By 6:00 A.M., van Rie was exhausted and at his wits' end. Finally, he caved in and blurted out what those present later described as a confession. What had started life as a pleasant tropical diversion, he said, had assumed matrimonial proportions in Lynn's eyes. For his part, van

Rie was ready to move on and had made it plain that New York would mark the end of the affair. But Lynn wasn't about to relinquish her dreams of permanently capturing the handsome naval officer. In his statement, van Rie said that about seven o'clock on the evening that Lynn vanished, he went to her cabin to ask why she was sick.

"Are you pregnant?" he asked.

"What would you care if I were?" she is supposed to have replied.

Listening to van Rie's story made Fallon's blood boil. For more than a week, he'd been lied to, deceived, and given the runaround by everyone on board the *Utrecht*. Now it was payback time. He turned viciously on the young Dutchman, yelling that he'd tried to dump Lynn, then started hitting her when she wouldn't go quietly. Van Rie reeled under the onslaught. He said only that Lynn had become very angry and had started swinging punches at him. To defend himself, he had lashed out in return.

Fallon was having none of it. He bored in like an enraged bull. And then you beat her unconscious and pushed her body out through the porthole. Isn't that what happened?

No! No! No! Van Rie protested. When he'd left the cabin—at a few minutes before 7:00 P.M.—Lynn had been deeply upset but very much alive. What happened thereafter was a mystery to him. All he could imagine was that in a fit of remorse or depression she had taken her own life. He swore that he had no knowledge of how she came to be in the water.

As damaging as these remarks may sound, it is important to note that we only have the interviewing officers' assurances that they were ever spoken. At no time did van Rie sign a statement admitting that he had beaten Lynn, and he retracted his alleged oral admission at the first opportunity, protesting that he had been bullied and tricked into making statements that weren't true. He claimed, rather weakly, that he had been victimized because his uniform had been in Lynn's cabin, because of discrepancies in the ship's log that recorded his attendance in the radio room at a time when he was actually absent, and because his weather report to the bridge had been late on the evening that Lynn vanished. One point in van Rie's favor was the prominently displayed photograph of his wife that stood in his cabin. This put a big dent in Fallon's suspicion that van Rie had duped Lynn into bed by claiming he was unmarried.

The deeper that Fallon dug, the more furious he became. It transpired that the supposedly clandestine affair had been anything but: the captain knew, Mrs. Spector knew, the purser knew, as did just about everyone on board the claustrophobic little freighter. How much lighter Fallon's investigative burden might have been had everyone come clean right at the outset. There can be little doubt that this collective reticence served only to harden attitudes to the handsome officer from Holland.

Even so, van Rie's earlier lack of candor was hugely damaging, and the district attorney's office now went gunning for him with both barrels. It became an article of faith with them that in order to get rid of an unwanted and troublesome lover, he had beaten Lynn senseless, then shoved her body out through a cabin porthole, leaving her to drown in the ship's wake.

Curiously enough, a remarkably similar incident had happened on a ship sailing from South Africa to England twelve years previously. In a case widely covered by the American press, an English room steward named James Camb had been charged with murdering Eileen "Gay" Gibson, an actress, in her cabin. Camb claimed that while he and Gay were engaged in sexual intercourse she had suffered some kind of fit and died. Panic stricken, he lost his head and pushed her lifeless body out through the porthole. The jury preferred the prosecution's version: this had Camb forcing his attentions on Gay, becoming enraged when she refused him, then raping and strangling her. In March 1948 Camb was convicted of murder and sentenced to death. He avoided the gallows by the skin of his teeth. At the time, a heated debate regarding the abolition of capital punishment was exercising the politicians of the land, and in the circumstance it was thought proper to reprieve Camb. He served a life sentence instead.

If found guilty, van Rie could expect no similar mercy. On October 5, 1959, a grand jury, after digesting the explicit contents of Lynn's diary and listening to the prosecution's case, returned an indictment of first-degree murder against van Rie, and in Massachusetts that could mean the electric chair.* The next day a warrant was delivered to New York, where van Rie had been held on a technical charge of being a fugitive from Massachusetts' justice, and he was returned to Boston.

Like all shipping lines, Royal Rotterdam Lloyd, the company that operated the *Utrecht*, was sharply attuned to any whiff of bad publicity, not to mention the specter of an expensive civil suit should van Rie be found guilty. Desperate to put the very best face possible on events, the company hired a solid defense team for its employee. On October 7, van Rie's lawyers filed a motion for permission to view the dead body, only to be told that on the very day that the defendant was being returned to Boston Lynn Kauffman had been cremated. It seemed a curious accident of timing. When defense attorney Samuel Silverman complained that the body had been "rushed to cremation," he was told that approximately fifty color photographs had been taken of the body and that these, plus the medical examiner's autopsy report, would be made available to the defense. Because

---

* Although Massachusetts had not executed anyone since 1947, the death penalty remained on the statute book and would do so until 1984, when it was abolished.

Luongo showed no signs of altering his view that Lynn had been murdered, the defense team went hunting for an expert of their own. Their search began and ended with Milton Helpern.

Since the death of the legendary Sir Bernard Spilsbury in London just over a decade earlier, Helpern had assumed the mantle of the best-known pathologist in the world. A great internationalist, he traveled the world, attending conferences, lecturing, and spreading the gospel of science-led crime investigation wherever he went. Because New York City had more murders per square mile than any other stretch of real estate on earth, Helpern's views on what did or did not constitute homicide were always worth canvasing. When contacted by counsel for Royal Rotterdam, he agreed to review the case notes and photographs.

He did so with a considerable sense of foreboding. As the crow flies, Boston might only be a couple of hundred miles or so from Manhattan, but to Helpern's way of thinking, when it came to justice, the difference between New York and New England could be measured in centuries, not miles. In 1944 he had traveled to Boston to testify at the trial of John Franklin Noxon, a forty-eight-year-old lawyer charged with murdering his mentally subnormal son. The infant had been electrocuted by a frayed extension cord. Helpern thought it nothing more than a ghastly accident—even the state's medical examiner, Dr. Alan Moritz, was by no means convinced that murder had been done—but that didn't prevent the state prosecutors from pursuing Noxon with a Salem-like ferocity that appalled Helpern. He could scarcely believe the splenetic level of animosity directed at the defendant and the stuffy, moralistic tone that pervaded the proceedings. Despite this, Helpern was still utterly incredulous when the jury came back with a guilty verdict.*

---

* In 1946, just days before his date with the electric chair, Noxon was reprieved. Astonishingly enough, two years later he was paroled.

The trial/witch hunt left a bad taste in his mouth that lingered for the rest of his life, as did his contempt for what he sourly termed "New England justice!" So, perhaps partly motivated by an unconscious desire to settle an old score, Helpern agreed to testify for the defense.

He knew Luongo by reputation only but held him in the highest regard. Just the previous year, the Suffolk County Medical Examiner had been one of the first medico-legal experts to be board certified in forensic pathology when it became recognized as a separate medical specialty. And certainly Helpern could find nothing to fault in Luongo's autopsy. It was thorough and exhaustive and there were undisputed signs of drowning as the cause of death. So far, so good. It was the bruising that worried Helpern. There was a subarachnoid hemorrhage—bleeding between the middle membrane covering the brain and the brain itself—but Helpern had no idea whether this occurred ante- or post-mortem. The photographs showed superficial abrasions and bruises from head to toe, virtually all of which were confined to the left side. Helpern could see contusions on the left forehead, left cheek, and chin. This bruising continued onto the left shoulder, chest, inner and outer left thigh, as well as the shin.

When Helpern set the photographs to one side, he was frankly puzzled. Given the kind of frenzied attack—with its punching and kicking—that Luongo had advanced, he found it hard to imagine all the injuries being restricted to just one side of the body. In his experience, Lynn Kauffman would have been black and blue from top to bottom. On the other hand, this distinctive pattern of bruising was exactly what Helpern would expect to find if someone had fallen from a great height and landed on one side. No one disputed that Lynn had either jumped or was thrown into the water from a ship steaming along at sixteen knots. That meant that from a height of forty feet she would have been traveling at almost

35 mph when she hit the water. At that speed, water can be as hard as rock.

Helpern spotted a further complication. The photographs showed that just below Lynn's porthole, a folded gangplank protruded from the side of the ship. Maintenance on board ship is an ongoing process. If some rust needs removing from the hull or a spot of paintwork is required, then when the ship is docked crew members will often carry out the necessary work while suspended on a gangplank. When not in use, these gangplanks are lashed to the ship's side. If Lynn did throw herself from her cabin porthole, she could well have struck this gangplank before plunging into the water. Certainly this would explain why her injuries were overwhelmingly confined to one side of the body. The other, minor marks that Helpern saw might easily have resulted from being buffeted among the rocks on Spectacle Island. So far as Helpern was concerned, the picture was clear: the injuries on Lynn Kauffman's body were far more consistent with a fall from a great height than with a murderous assault.

Helpern wasn't the first person to come up with this theory. Fallon, too, subscribed to this view, and he'd said as much to his superiors. Initially the Boston PD had backed Fallon's version of events—he was, after all, a highly experienced homicide detective—but Luongo had gone above their heads to the Suffolk County DA's office. To hear Luongo tell it, Lynn had "died of drowning after violence. She had been so badly kicked and pummeled that she was incapable of moving voluntarily into the water." The injuries to the left side of her face, said Luongo, had definitely been caused by someone's fist.

Helpern thought this was utter nonsense. No one in the world had seen more victims of violent death than himself, and he defied anyone to look at a bruised and battered body and state categorically *how* those injuries had been sustained. There was no disputing that Lynn had suffered some kind of head injury, and, yes, there were widespread marks down her left side, but Helpern couldn't see a single scrap of evidence to prove *how* these injuries had been inflicted. He certainly wasn't ruling out the possibility that Lynn Kauffman might have been beaten up before being tossed into the water, and if someone had seen van Rie throw Lynn overboard, then that would have been case closed. But without any such witness to the alleged assault, Helpern could scarcely believe this case was going to court.

And then it got uglier. Word came through to Helpern that Luongo was prepared to testify that the injuries were inflicted *in the cabin*, that Lynn was assaulted *in the cabin*, that she was rendered unconscious *in the cabin*, and that thereafter, she had been pushed, unconscious, through the porthole and into the water. This was staggering. With the Suffolk County D.A.'s office straining at the leash to act on Luongo's conclusion, once again Helpern was forced to the unsavory conclusion that the Commonwealth of Massachusetts was out to "get" the defendant come "hell or high water."

They began on February 11, 1960, by giving the trial jury a brief voyage from Commonwealth Pier 5 in Boston Harbor, out to Spectacle Island and back again, a rough and uncomfortable round-trip of approximately eight miles in the gusty prevailing wind. It's difficult to gauge what purpose this could have served to twelve landlubbers unaccustomed to the vagaries of tides and currents, but it did set the scene nicely for an all-out assault on van Rie's morals and murderous intentions. He was portrayed as a scheming, heartless lothario who had posed as a single man in order to lure Lynn into his bed, then made a "last and fatal visit" to Lynn's cabin as the *Utrecht* was leaving Boston Harbor. Believing

Lynn to be pregnant—the autopsy showed that she wasn't—van Rie had killed her to prevent his duplicity ruining his eighteen-month marriage.

Quite what Nella van Rie, the defendant's wife, who had traveled over from the Netherlands and sat in court, made of all this is unknown, but throughout the trial she remained steadfastly loyal to her beleaguered husband as details of his transgressions were paraded before a drooling media. Confirmation that van Rie *had* conducted a shipboard romance with the dead woman came from Captain de Bruijn, who said that the radio officer had made no secret of the affair; indeed, it was common knowledge on the ship. Far more damaging to the defendant was de Bruijn's claim that van Rie confessed to having had an argument with Lynn on the night of her disappearance.

This point was reinforced by Fallon when he gave evidence. Insisting that the interview with van Rie, while lengthy and robust, had been conducted fairly, Fallon was forced to backtrack when he conceded that van Rie had mentioned the fight only after being told that Lynn had committed suicide. The defense seized on this hungrily. After all, if van Rie had murdered Lynn, why mention the fight at all? It didn't make any sense.

Then came the prosecution's star witness, Dr. Michael A. Luongo. Like most veteran expert witnesses, he was comfortable on the stand and gave his evidence with practiced ease. "The cause of death was drowning, following the inflicting of multiple blunt-force injuries," said the pathologist. He then proceeded to draw a murderous picture for the jury. In this, he had van Rie becoming so enraged by Lynn that he struck her with his fists until she fell to the ground; then he knelt on her chest and continued pummeling her. Unable to control his fury, he then stamped on her and battered her from one side of the cabin to the other. Finally, with Lynn unconscious at his feet, he picked her up and shoved her through a porthole. Being senseless from her wounds she would have drowned in a matter of minutes at most.

Assistant DA John F. McAuliffe then asked the critical question: "In your opinion was the deceased, Lynn Kauffman, capable of performing a voluntary or purposeful act [after the injuries were sustained]?"

"No, sir," said Luongo. "A person would be unconscious and incapable of performing a purposeful act." The bruises and abrasions, he maintained, were consistent with his theory. All the injuries, he said, were caused before the brain hemorrhages that led to death—a conclusion that Helpern found breathtaking. Throughout his long career, Helpern continually warned his students about the dangers of being led by overzealous advocates. "The law demands more than medicine can honestly give" was one of his favorite aphorisms. He understood the desire of courts, which prefer to deal in absolutes, black and white. But Helpern knew that medicine was made up of an infinite number of shades of gray. Once, in a case where an opposing lawyer was pushing hard for Helpern to add his weight to a previously expressed opinion that Helpern thought was medically unjustifiable, Helpern crushed the attorney by saying, "I refuse to play God. If your doctor wants to assume that role, he is perfectly entitled to attempt it." Here, Helpern felt Luongo had fallen headlong into that selfsame trap.

Defense attorney Walter Powers Jr. verbalized Helpern's skepticism. He asked Luongo if such injuries could have been sustained if the body had fallen forty feet into the water, perhaps striking the ship's side or a gangplank lashed beneath her porthole. In most cases, Luongo agreed it was possible, but in this instance the severity of the chest and head injuries he saw on Lynn's body could hardly have resulted from a single fall.

Right from day one of the trial the prosecution kept dropping heavy hints that Dr. Alan R. Moritz, former professor of pathology at Harvard and now teaching at Western Reserve University in Cleveland, would be flying in to testify in support of Luongo. This was shrewd psychology. The prosecution team was only too aware of the impact that the magic name "Harvard" would have in the Boston area. Moritz's opinion, they confidently predicted, would be the final word on the death of Lynn Kauffman.

Such threats didn't faze Helpern. Twenty-five years of court-room skirmishes, fencing with lawyers, parrying their blows and feints, had left him battle hardened and tougher than steel. No one in America, not even some fancy Ivy League academic, had Helpern's breadth of knowledge about how and why human beings take their leave of the mortal coil. He was confident he could counter any-thing that Moritz might throw at him.

In the end, Moritz didn't show. This shouldn't have come as any surprise to the prosecution had they bothered to read a paper entitled "Classical Mistakes in Forensic Pathology," published by Moritz just a few years earlier. In this, Moritz questioned the prac-tice of substituting intuition for scientifically defensible interpreta-tion, writing, "He [the pathologist] may be highly esteemed by the police and by prosecuting counsel because he is an emphatic and impressive witness. His prestige, together with exclusive access to original evidence, places him in an exceedingly powerful position in the courtroom." Moritz concluded by arguing that the stakes in forensic pathology are too high to deal in anything other than cold, hard facts.

Instead the prosecution had to make do with Rhode Island pathologist Dr. Arthur O'Dea, who supported Luongo, insisting that Lynn had been kicked, stomped on, and rendered uncon-scious, to the point where she couldn't possibly have moved after the assault and must have been thrown overboard.

When the defense opened its case, rather than throw Helpern into the fray immediately counsel began instead by attacking a key factor in the state's case: the fact that van Rie's clothes were found in Lynn's cabin, proof positive, according to the state, that he had been sleeping with her. To diminish the impact of these findings, Second Officer Johannes van Brummelen took the stand. His wool socks and a blue sweater had also been found in Lynn's cabin and were the result of nothing more incriminating than a desire by Lynn to keep warm. Ever since the *Utrecht* had entered the northern Atlantic, she had complained continually of feeling cold, prompting van Brummelen to lend her his clothes. He further aided the defendant's cause by stating that van Rie was in the wheel house at about 7:25 P.M., during the period when the state said that Lynn was beaten insensible and thrown overboard.

Next up was Willem van Rie. In a self-assured voice tinged with only the barest hint of an accent, he emphatically denied any involvement in the death of Lynn Kauffman. The damaging statement, he said, had been made after being "scolded and pounded at" for nearly fifteen hours in a Brooklyn police precinct station. He claimed that he had been urged to "make a false statement" by a policeman, though, significantly, he was unable to either name or identify this officer. He also denied ever having given Lynn the impression that he was single, citing the photograph of his wife in his cabin as evidence of his candor.

Most observers were impressed by van Rie's coolness on the stand. Clearly he wasn't someone easily rattled or lacking in confidence to judge from his surprise decision to offer yet another version of that day's events. He now claimed that the last time he actually *saw* Lynn was about 8:00 A.M. on September 18, in the ship's lounge in the presence of U.S. immigration and public health inspectors, customary procedure whenever a ship arrived from a foreign country, in this case Canada. For the first time he mentioned that, around midday, he had spoken to Lynn, though only through an open porthole in her cabin. At that time she complained of feeling "terrible." When he asked if she needed anything, she had said no. He swore that he neither saw nor spoke to her again.

Under cross-examination, van Rie fared less well. He admitted that Lynn had visited his cabin "seven or eight times" during the voyage, and that he had lied to both the New York and the Boston police about this affair. When asked about testimony against him, all he could say was that Mrs. Spector and the captain had "inaccuracies" in their evidence. Similarly, he accused van Oosten, the ship's purser, Fallon, and Brooklyn police captain William Whalen of lying about whether he had discussed with them the difference between murder and manslaughter.

McAuliffe sneered his disdain. "You beat this girl into submission and dumped her overboard."

"No," was van Rie's measured reply. And then he left the stand.

In a shrewd move, the defense had kept Helpern until near the end, judging that his would be the freshest medico-legal testimony in the jury's collective consciousness as they began their deliberations. Helpern's great forte was simplicity. He never made the mistake of trying to sound clever. When Winston Churchill wrote, "Broadly speaking, the short words are the best, and the old words best of all," he could well have been describing Helpern's courtroom technique. Better than most—certainly at that time—Helpern understood that for the most part juries comprised people with only the faintest grasp of science and that the best way of getting his point across was by delivering it in the clearest terms possible. He began by saying it was perfectly possible for Lynn Kauffman to have fallen or jumped overboard of her own accord.

"Could she have been pushed?" he was asked.

"Yes, sure she could—but you have to prove that some other way; you can't tell that from an autopsy." He went on, "In my opinion, her injuries were not due to an assault by a fist or a foot or by punching, kicking or mauling." Instead, he stated his belief that her injuries were caused by falling forty feet into the waters of Boston Harbor, after which she drowned.

McAuliffe didn't care for this one little bit. "You did not exclude the deceased's being thrown into the water, did you?"

"I did not mean to imply that I knew how the fall took place."

This was McAuliffe's cue to go through each of the bruises individually, asking whether it could have been caused by a blow from a fist or a kick. Naturally, each one could, but Helpern was far too wily to be suckered in by that sort of advocacy. When it came to deflecting a crafty cross-examination, he was peerless. Unlike many witnesses, he didn't allow himself to be coaxed and cajoled into an injudicious comment and would often turn the tables on his inquisitor by saying something along the lines of, "If what you are trying to ask is . . . ," before steering the subject back to the matter in hand. His battle with McAuliffe provided a supreme example of this singular technique.

"If you've ever seen a body falling," he told McAuliffe, "you'll know there's a lot of action. It doesn't fall like a statue. A body falling forty feet is going over thirty miles an hour. The body is folded, the limbs are flexed, the head is moving. The impact is not single, it's composite. As soon as it strikes, it gets thrashed about. Anyone who has fallen off a boat or water skis knows what sort of impact occurs."

This was rock-solid testimony, free from the outlandish speculation that Luongo and O'Dea had employed, and the judge, Frank J. Murray, caught the salutary mood. When the defense overstepped the mark and tried to get Helpern to opine whether Lynn had committed suicide, Murray came down on them like a ton of bricks and threw out the question.

As was his right under Massachusetts law, van Rie was permitted to make a final unsworn statement to the jury. Looking gaunt after nearly five months in prison, he said, "As God is my witness, I am not guilty." In an accent that thickened noticeably with every sentence, he acknowledged that he had "committed a sin—of adultery—with Miss Kauffman, and I know I was wrong," With a quick glance toward Nella, he said that his wife had forgiven him.

The case went to the jury on the evening of March 1 and deliberations lasted throughout the night. The first ballot had resulted in a tie, but thereafter the doubters were whittled down. It took fifteen votes to reach a consensus, but the next day at 9:12 A.M., the jury came back. Not guilty.

A gasp of relief swept the court. There had been many female spectators throughout the trial, and several women reached forward to touch van Rie as he was bustled from the court. "God bless you, isn't it wonderful," cried one admirer, proving that the man from Holland hadn't lost his appeal for the opposite sex. Following his acquittal, van Rie quit his job as a radio officer and returned to the Netherlands to work for a publisher.

As for Helpern, he journeyed back to New York with his reputation burnished even more brightly by this triumph. He had once described the work of the OCME to a reporter in these terms: "We are strictly a discovery agency . . . We are not interested in whodunit. All we want to know is *what* did it." With the acquittal of Willem van Rie, Helpern had demonstrated to the jury in Boston the relevance of this maxim. Like his transatlantic counterpart and great friend, Professor Keith Simpson, Helpern was never afraid to stand up in court and say "I don't know." No forensic pathologist alive could say for certain how Lynn Kauffman wound up in the icy waters of Boston Harbor on that September evening. It just took Helpern to remind everyone of this fact.

All in all, these were momentous times for the man known simply as "the Chief." Just a matter of months later, on September 19, 1960, the OCME finally got the new headquarters Helpern had been angling after for so long. Built in gleaming black and white brick, overlaid with glazed blue and aluminum paneling, 520 First Avenue was, at the time of its construction, the largest and most modern forensic facility in the world. Standing on the northeast corner of Thirtieth Street, close enough to Bellevue Hospital to ensure that the old associations could be maintained, it had cost $3.7 million to build, with a further $700,000 spent on scientific apparatus.

The OCME officially took control of the building on April 12, 1961. In the lobby, on a black marble wall, it reads: *Taceant colloquia. Effugiat risus. Hic locus est ubi mores gaudet succurrere vitae.* Roughly translated, this means: "Let idle talk be silenced. Let laughter be banished. Here is the place where death delights to succor life." Someone had found the quote on the wall of an old European autopsy room and thought it appropriate for the new building. For the first time, all the OCME's administrative work and ancillary scientific services were centralized in one building, although branches would still be maintained in borough mortuaries. Inside the building were no fewer than sixty-three laboratories, a library, lecture halls, and various photographic rooms.

One much needed innovation was air-conditioning. In the old Bellevue mortuary at the height of summer, the stench from decaying bodies could become overpowering. For members of the general public who might be called to identify or claim a body, this often only added to the distress. Here, in the basement where the autopsies are carried out, there is storage space for 128 bodies in refrigerated compartments that can be accessed by steel doors. Whenever a body is required for identification, an elevator whisks it up to a glass-enclosed viewing room just off the main lobby. At every step of the way, the intent is to further insulate the bereaved from any unnecessary shock.

One floor up from the lobby is where all the administrative and statistical work is collated. It houses the records of every case investigated by the OCME. The three floors above this are mainly devoted to laboratories, where the examiners can study case notes and prepare their reports. In the toxicology labs, the work has multiplied exponentially. (When Helpern joined the OCME there were approximately thirty known toxic agents. By 1961, that number had soared to more than five thousand.) At the top of the building, on the sixth floor, is the so-called Black Museum, a collection of curiosities and noteworthy exhibits harvested from half a century of crime fighting. Helpern, like Spilsbury, was an assiduous collector of this medico-legal memorabilia, not from any morbid curiosity, but for the part that such items might play in the solving of future crimes. Murderous ice picks, sections of skull, autopsy specimens preserved in formaldehyde, and the shredded clothes of a boy who had been struck by lightning all found their way into the Black Museum. On a rather more prosaic note, this floor also housed the Milton Helpern Library of Legal Medicine, the most comprehensive collection of its kind to be found anywhere in the world.

And there were plenty of physicians who wished that Helpern would spend more time in that library. All his life he'd found certain aspects of the medical profession hard to stomach. Perhaps this distaste can be dated back to when, while still a young assistant medical examiner, he was called to testify in an insurance case that hinged on a disputed time of death and found himself opposed by two older, more experienced practitioners. To Helpern's way of thinking, their evidence was incredible, wholly unsupported by the facts. The case was eventually settled out of court, but later, when Helpern ran into the two doctors at a medical conference, he confronted them. "Would you have told your students in class the same thing that you testified to in that courtroom?" he asked.

The graying, venerable pathologist smiled patronizingly. "You've got a lot to learn. Don't ever confuse the courtroom with the class-room."

"Would you have testified that same way," Helpern asked the other man, "if this had been a murder case and the defendant's alibi hinged on the exact time of death?"

"That's the trouble with you young fellows," the doctor cooed. "You're always speculating and worrying about things that do not really happen. Come on! Let me buy you a drink."

Helpern didn't take the drink and he never forgot. Forever afterward, this case figured prominently in his lectures whenever he railed against physicians who become "more partisan than the lawyers."

Helpern's unpopularity with certain sections of the medical community was legendary. At an October 1961 gathering of the Medical Society of New York, he made his audience squirm with an eviscerating attack on what he scathingly termed the "five o'clock doctor," the physician who put private pleasure above patient need. Helpern said, "It has become hazardous to develop a serious illness over a weekend or on a holiday, and now even at night." Warming to his theme, he next delivered a stinging rebuke to those who regarded the Medical Society as "a citadel or defense against criticism." He urged those listening to speak out when a physician commits a "misdeed, either through thoughtlessness or carelessness, in not responding to a medical emergency, or over-charging." Deep down, Helpern knew he was spitting in the wind, as events in the subsequent Dr. Carl Coppolino murder trials would demonstrate,* but silence wasn't an option.

Outbursts such as this, coupled with an explosion in the crime figures, meant that Helpern was rarely out of the headlines for

---

* For a full account of this case, and Helpern's pivotal role in it, see Colin Evans, *Killer Doctors*. (New York: Berkley, 2007).

long. Noted crime novelist Erle Stanley Gardner even dedicated *The Case of the Hesitant Hostess* to the pathologist who had become the most famous medico-legal expert alive. This celebrity only added to the demands on his time. In 1966, Helpern, along-side Keith Simpson, testified at the Ottawa Supreme Court tribunal held to establish whether the Canadian teenager Steven Truscott had been wrongly convicted of murder. Neither pathologist found anything in the evidence to suggest that the original medical testimony had been flawed or that the verdict should be overturned, and the court agreed.

With so many calls on his schedule, it was a miracle that Helpern found any time for his first love—teaching. But even this had its downside. While he never doubted the willingness of his assistants, he could only watch in impotent dismay as many fell by the wayside, discouraged by the high workload and low pay. In 1966 a full-time ME in New York City could expect to earn ninety-two hundred dollars a year on average. Part-timers had to make do with a per diem of just twenty-five dollars a day. Drawn by the lure of the greater financial rewards available elsewhere—and a hell of a lot less hassle—many of Helpern's apprentices took up job offers right across America. Helpern's sole consolation in this exodus was the knowledge that his students, rigorously trained in the toughest school anywhere, would help spread the OCME doctrine of ME-based crime investigation in those states that still clung on to the coroner system. Incredibly, of these, only Louisiana and Ohio restricted their candidates to physicians. In North Carolina, for instance, applicants for the post of coroner merely had to be persons who "had not denied the being of Almighty God or participated in a duel."

Suddenly, though, Helpern was having to fight the "no coroner" battle in his own backyard. In January 1967, the New York Academy of Medicine attacked the OCME in a stinging report that recommended greater decentralization, closer links with medical schools, and more use of lay investigators. Helpern was apoplectic. This sounded like yet another attempt to hark back to the bad old days. What he needed, said Helpern, wasn't more decentralization but more money.

Certainly the battle was getting harder. All through the sixties, the homicide rate climbed with grim inexorability. When Helpern joined the OCME in 1931, New York had about four hundred murders a year. In 1969, for the first time ever, the death toll exceeded one thousand. Too many guns and too many knives, said Helpern. As it turned out, not all the knives were being wielded on the streets of New York, quite a few were being aimed squarely between the broad shoulders of the chief medical examiner. Or so Helpern suspected.

A whispering campaign against Helpern had been under way for some time. It was the age-old problem: some younger employees at the OCME felt that their career ambitions were being thwarted by Helpern's refusal to quit. At age seventy-one, Helpern had already been granted five extensions by the city to stay in office beyond the customary retirement age, leading to ugly comparisons with J. Edgar Hoover's reign at the FBI, with accusations that he had stayed in the job too long. The backbiting reached critical mass in July 1973, when a story appeared in the press alleging that certain OCME staff members were taking kickbacks from funeral directors seeking business and favors. (Under the law, undertakers were allowed to advertise, but they were prohibited from soliciting business.) An immediate investigation was announced by Nicholas Scoppetta, the City Investigations Commissioner.

Helpern came out swinging, hotly denying that any such practices existed in his office. However, one anonymous OCME employee was ready to plunge the dagger, telling a reporter that employees were being paid up to fifty dollars by certain funeral homes for each body steered their way. "It's been going on for fifty years," confided the source. The case that sparked all the kerfuffle began when two brothers from Troy, North Carolina, went to the mortuary at 520 First Avenue to claim the body of their sister. The Troy undertakers who were handling the funeral had told Richard and Amos Harris to advise the OCME that the New York Funeral Service would arrange to ship their sister's body to North Carolina. But, according to the brothers, when the mortuary assistant heard this, he was "very hesitant about calling the New York Funeral Service and suggested that we call the Metropolitan Funeral Service." Later, the Harrises learned that the MFS *was* contacted and that they, in turn, called the Troy Funeral Home, stating that the family wanted them to handle the arrangements and the shipping. When contacted about this purportedly unethical action, Richard A. Santore, president of the New York Funeral Service, stoked the flames by saying that some OCME employees had been receiving kickbacks and gratuities "all the time."

Although Scoppetta's inquiry would drag on for two more years and uncover even more egregious examples of undertaker malpractice—mainly in the handling of deceased indigents—no charges were ever leveled at any OCME staff member. But the damage had already been done. On December 15, 1973, it was announced that Helpern would be retiring at the year's end. The very next day, an obviously hot-under-the-collar Helpern appeared on TV, protesting that he had been the victim of a coup organized from within the Office of the Chief Medical Examiner. In typical fashion, Helpern didn't soft-pedal the issue. The ringleader, he said, was none other than one of his deputies, the supremely talented Dr. Michael Baden. He claimed that Baden had leaked the undertaker story to the *New York Times* in an attempt to discredit him. There had been a concerted campaign, he said, "to put me on the shelf and to insert young Sir Galahad into the position," an obvious reference to Baden. Rather unnecessarily in the circumstances, Helpern felt compelled to add that he would not be recommending Baden as his successor.

Baden wasn't about to take this accusation lying down. He strenuously refuted Helpern's allegation and picked up some vigorous support from the metropolitan editor of the *New York Times*, Arthur Gelb, who said, "None of these stories were called to the attention of the *Times* by Dr. Baden." As we shall see later, there was a long history of bad blood between Helpern and Baden—not once is the latter mentioned in Helpern's autobiography—and this episode marked a sad and acrimonious end to what had been a truly momentous career.

Shortly before his retirement Helpern estimated that he had performed more than twenty thousand autopsies and supervised and been present at perhaps sixty thousand more. It was a colossal achievement, made all the more remarkable by his fantastic powers of recall. If anyone ever harked back to an obscure case from his career, he was always able to instantly remember the details and explain why they had informed a particular conclusion. Probably no one has dominated American medical jurisprudence in the way that Milton Helpern did. His reputation circled the globe. In 1970 the University of Ghent in Belgium awarded Helpern an honorary law degree. Back home, in 1971, he was named winner of the American Medical Association's Distinguished Service Award for "distinguished service to medicine over a period of years" rather than for any single accomplishment.

After his retirement, Helpern continued to serve as a kind of emeritus consultant to the OCME. This arrangement survived for a meager eighteen months, terminating with a brutal and sudden expulsion from his office, kicked out by his successor. The few years remaining to Helpern were spent writing and testifying as an expert witness. He was appointed distinguished visiting professor at the Center for Biomedical Education at City College, but it was always a battle with his health. He was in California when the final illness struck. On April 22, 1977, Milton Helpern died at University Hospital in San Diego. He was age seventy-five.

His funeral, held at Park Avenue Synagogue on April 26, was attended by more than seven hundred relatives, colleagues, and students. Former Mayor Robert F. Wagner said, "Milton Helpern was more than a man of science. He was more than a man of letters. Above all he was a lovely man, gentle, courteous and gracious." But perhaps the most fitting tribute came from John Keenan, former chief of the homicide bureau. "As a courtroom witness [Helpern] was unimpeachable because he never testified for either side. He testified for truth and justice."

Under Helpern's leadership, the OCME had graduated from being perceived as an illegitimate offshoot of the Bellevue pathology department, to an independent and world-renowned investigator of unusual death, with a staff of 138 that included sixteen pathologists. When he started at the Office of the Chief Medical Examiner, Americans were driving Model T Fords; by the time of his retirement, men were landing on the moon. The huge technological advances that made this possible, and so profoundly influenced the direction of crime solving, also helped propel Helpern into the homes of America as the very first TV pathologist. New Yorkers who might never have picked up a newspaper in their lives grew used to seeing Helpern's distinctive visage on their TV screens. In terms of a dominant personality and the impact on his profession, Helpern stood right alongside his mentor, Charles Norris. The only difference was that Helpern operated in a harsher, more censorious age.

He'd also had to cope with a mind-bending increase in crime statistics. By 1971 the murder rate in New York had soared to an incredible 1,625, almost as many as in the whole of Europe. Little wonder that Helpern would shake his head in exasperation and declare himself amazed at "how many die of homicides in this city—it's about six a day, and that's an awful lot." With no evidence of a slowdown in the crime rate, it was blindingly obvious that whoever took over at the helm of the OCME would have his hands full. Judging from Helpern's experience, a couple of eyes in the back of one's head would be no bad thing either.

FOUR

THE BRUTAL DECADE

Filling Milton Helpern's shoes was never going to be easy. Helpern made sure of that. Being forced out of office on a technicality—he had fought like Rocky Marciano to get the Civil Service rules on mandatory retirement amended but without success—left him feeling thwarted and vengeful. His volcanic antipathy toward Dr. Michael Baden was already a matter of public record, but Helpern wasn't done yet. Behind the scenes, he groused about the qualifications and suitability of other candidates whose names were being bandied about in the press.

Some of those who came under Helpern's withering fire were none too happy either, but for an entirely different reason. It had been generally assumed that Helpern's successor would be an in-house promotion, someone already on the OCME payroll. Certainly that was the joint impression of the five deputy chief medical examiners as they readied themselves for the Civil Service promotional examination scheduled for the end of April 1974. Then came a bombshell. The Civil Service Commission decided to cancel the

John Purroy Mitchel: the New York City mayor who established the Office of the Chief Medical Examiner in 1918.
(Courtesy of The Library of Congress)

Dr. Charles Norris, the first chief medical officer.

Except where noted, all photos are in the public domain.

Dr. Norris alongside Dr. Alexander O. Gettler,
the city toxicologist.

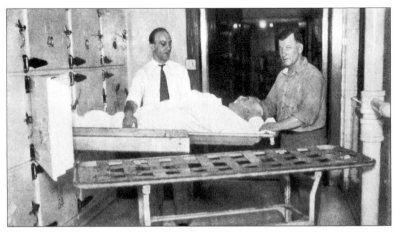

Attendents placing a body into a refrigerated compartment
at the old Bellevue morgue (c.1935).

WOMAN WRITER, 34, FOUND STRANGLED IN BATHTUB IN HOME

Mrs. Nancy E. Titterton, W of Radio Executive, Sla Beekman Place Apar

STRUGGLE IS I

Torn Clothing Dis Adjoining Room—F Was L

UPHOLSTERER'S AIDE CONFESSES MURDER F MRS. TITTERTON

FIORENZA DOOMED TO ELECTRIC CHAIR

OSSINING, N. Y., Jan. 21.—John Fiorenza, who murdered Mrs. Nancy Titterton, author, in her Beekman Place apartment in Manhattan April 10, 1936, was put to death in the electric chair at Sing Sing prison tonight with three

Press coverage of the sensational Nancy Titterton murder.
(Author's collection)

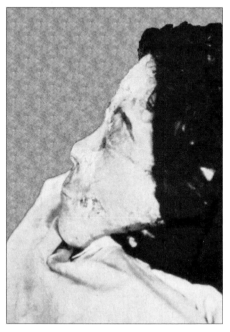

Among Dr. Thomas Gonzales's many skills was facial reconstruction. In the top photograph is what looks like garbage. From these scraps, Gonzales and other OCME pathologists were able to re-create the identifiable face of a murder victim (*right*).

Four CMEs in one photograph: In the middle, with folded arms, is Dr. Milton Helpern. Dr. Dominick DiMaio is to Helpern's right. On the extreme right of the front row is Dr. Michael Baden. Immediately behind Helpern is Dr. Elliott Gross.

(Courtesy of Dr. Vincent DiMaio)

Dr. Milton Helpern (*left*), at an international conference
with fellow pathologist and his great friend, Professor Keith Simpson.

Richard F. Biegenwald,
the Staten Isand serial killer
whose crimes were investigated
by Dr. Elliot Gross.

Dr. Dominick DiMaio, pictured with his son, Dr. Vincent DiMaio.
(Courtesy of Dr. Vincent DiMaio)

Potter's Field on Hart Island in the late nineteenth century.
This was where the body of Laura Carpi was mistakenly buried.

Dr. Charles S. Hirsch,
in charge at the darkest hour.
(Courtesy of the OCME)

The 9/11 terrorists who committed
the worst crime in American history.

examination and throw open the contest to any qualified pathologist, not just those already employed by the Office of the Chief Medical Examiner. This was a bitter pill for the deputies to swallow. An
act of intended egalitarianism backfired badly as morale inside the
OCME hit rock bottom. Ask anyone in the American forensic science community the toughest place to work and most would answer
"New York City" without hesitation. The politics, the media pressure, the unrelenting scrutiny, the mediocre pay scale, and the
nation's highest body count make the OCME a singular place of
employment, one that generates a high level of loyalty. Not unrea-
sonably, most employees expected that loyalty to be rewarded. One
of the deputies, Dr. John F. Devlin, summed up the mood of discontent thus: "If they [OCME employees] can't count on deserved promotion, why should they stay here and ride this tiger when they
could go to Oshkosh or some place and become Chief Medical
Examiner and have a nicer home and a better salary?"

This question of local experience was echoed by one of the succession favorites, Dr. Michael Baden. "Working elsewhere doesn't
prepare you for the volume and variety of work in our office and it
doesn't give you an understanding of the ethnic groups and political forces that are at play in this city," he said. "We have to be in a
position to call things as we see them, regardless of pressures from
insurance companies or hospitals or medical schools or anyone."

While the insults flew and bruised egos were nursed back into
shape, the city obviously needed someone in charge at 520 First
Avenue, and on January 7, 1974, it was announced that Dr.
Dominick J. DiMaio had been appointed acting chief medical
examiner. He had worked at the OCME for almost a quarter of a
century, first under Gonzales, then at Helpern's right hand. His
background was similar to that of his immediate predecessor. He
had been born on the Lower East Side on July 19, 1913, and after
attending DeWitt Clinton High School, he went to Long Island

University. After setting his heart on a career in medicine, he studied at Marquette University in Milwaukee. Unlike most of his class he opted for the deeply unfashionable specialty of pathology. During the war, he served in the U.S. Public Health Service, working at various Coast Guard and Maritime Service Installations in the New York area. In 1950, after a spell as a pathologist at the Polyclinic Hospital on Second Avenue, he moved just a few blocks to the Office of the Medical Examiner, joining as an assistant medical examiner to Gonzales. Under Helpern, his progress through the hierarchy had been steady, if unspectacular. Stockily built and balding with a fringe of gray hair, DiMaio's avuncular appearance concealed a restless energy that he defused when away from work by collecting stamps and playing the piano. When it came to settling the issue of permanent CME, DiMaio's name was sure to be in the mix. Provided, of course, he could survive that "temporary" period.

In many respects, DiMaio was a victim of bad timing. When he took over temporary office, there was the succession battle, of course—that was degenerating into a brutish soap opera—but other factors conspired against him. The last few years of Helpern's reign had seen a seismic shift in the way America reported its news. The seeds of journalistic change sown in Vietnam and the civil rights struggle now manifested themselves in a tougher, more confrontational press attitude toward almost every arm of government. In early 1974 Watergate was nearing its grisly crescendo, Bob Woodward and Carl Bernstein had become media folk heroes, and hungry young reporters everywhere were scrabbling under every promising rock, looking for that next Pulitzer. Nothing was off limits, and that included the Office of the Chief Medical Examiner. All at once, New York's metropolitan news pages were littered with allegations of OCME inefficiency. When Calvin Jackson, a twenty-six-year-old drifter, was arrested on September 12, 1974, for the murder of a fifty-nine-year-old widow named Pauline

Spanierman, his blithe admission that over the past fifteen months he had strangled and raped another ten elderly women in a crime-ridden neighborhood by Central Park stunned the interviewing officers. Adding to investigatorial woes was the fact that three of the alleged murder victims had not even been recognized as such: the OCME had ruled their deaths as "natural causes." To be fair, in each case the body was very badly decomposed and there was no visible evidence—no petechiae in the face and eyes, and no bruising around the neck—to suggest strangulation.* Even so, it didn't sound good, and the storm clouds that had been building around Helpern in his final months now settled on DiMaio's shoulders. The press smelled blood. They demanded to know just how many murders in New York went unreported each year. DiMaio didn't prevaricate. "I'd have to say that there are more homicides in the city than we know about," he said. It was a reply that virtually every medical examiner in the world—if they were being truthful—could have made.

Inwardly, DiMaio must have been pondering the wisdom of his promotion. Right from day one it had been one bureaucratic headache after another. Much the worst of these involved a sensational case that the crafty Helpern had kept under wraps for almost two years. The chief had sensed it was nothing but trouble. And now that trouble was about to blow up in DiMaio's face.

CASE FILE:
Colin Carpi (1971)

In the mid-nineteenth century a young woman named Louisa Van Slyke died at Charity Hospital on Blackwell's Island (later Roosevelt Island) in the East River. Her life had been brief and lonely. She was

---

* On July 6, 1976, Jackson was sentenced to life imprisonment for murdering nine women. Two of his so-called victims were later found to be alive.

just twenty-four years old when she died, an only child, orphaned at an early age, without a single living relative or friend to mourn her passing. Her death, like her life, was unremarkable in all respects save one: on April 20, 1869, she became the first person to be buried in New York's recently acquired Potter's Field, the city's brand-new public cemetery.

All major cities in the United States accumulate vast numbers of unidentified dead bodies. If they remain unclaimed, then most are buried in a local graveyard known colloquially as Potter's Field. The name is believed to derive from Matthew 27: 3–7. "Then Judas, which had betrayed him, when he saw that he was condemned, repented himself, and brought again the thirty pieces of silver to the chief priests . . . And they took counsel, and bought with them the potter's field, to bury strangers in."

It had taken New York City a long time to settle on a permanent resting place for its "indigent and unbefriended." Unclaimed bodies were first interred at Washington Square in Greenwich Village—handily adjacent to the gallows tree—until 1823, when they were removed to Bryant Park on Fifth Avenue. At the end of the following decade, as the urban sprawl pushed ever northward, this site was decommissioned and the bodies shifted to a plot on Fourth Avenue and Fiftieth Street. More upheaval came when this ground was earmarked for the Women's Hospital in 1855, leading to the removal, two years later, of more than a hundred thousand dead bodies to Ward's Island, at the northern end of the East River.

Still the search wasn't over. In 1868 the commissioners of the New York City Department of Public Charities and Correction were authorized to purchase and take title to any plot of ground, convenient and accessible to the city and large enough for a public cemetery. They set their sights on Hart Island, a scrubby outcrop of rock in Long Island Sound, owned by a family called Hunter. It was a good deal for everyone concerned. The Hunters pocketed an impressive seventy-five thousand dollars and the city finally had the space it needed for a permanent potter's field.

The cemetery itself occupies almost the entire northern half of Hart Island, and in the early part of the twentieth century it was a busy place indeed. Each year close to eight thousand unclaimed bodies were buried within its confines. By 1969 the cumulative total had reached six hundred thousand, almost two-thirds of them infants or stillborn. In recent times, better medicine, better communications and more stringent ID checks have reduced the annual intake to around twenty-five hundred, but the bureaucratic rigor is undiminished.

Any citizen who becomes aware of the death of any person is required by law to report that death to the local police precinct, which notifies the chief medical examiner. If a person dies in a city hospital or institution, and his body is not claimed within twenty-four hours, the Department of Hospitals is authorized to allow his burial at potter's field.

The body of a deceased pauper is sent to the morgue of the county in which he dies, and the medical examiner applies to the Board of Health for a burial permit. If the body remains unclaimed, the burial permit and the deceased are sent to the central morgue at Bellevue Hospital.

At the morgue, the bodies of the deceased are wrapped in shroud paper and sealed in pine coffins lined with waterproof paper. Unknowns are fingerprinted and photographed and then interred with all their clothes and belongings in case it becomes possible to identify them later. Copies of the burial certificate, chemically treated so they remain legible for decades, are placed both inside and on top of the coffins.

From the dock on City Island, in the Bronx, it's just a five-minute ferry ride out across the Sound to Potter's Field. Because of the numbers involved, a strict rota is maintained. Tuesday is reserved for bodies from Queens; Wednesday, it's the turn of Brooklyn and Staten Island; on Thursday, Manhattan dispatches its dead; Friday is set aside for the Bronx. The interments are carried out by inmates of nearby Riker's Island, who are paid between twenty-five and thirty-five cents an hour. The coffins are buried one hundred to a pit, three high and two abreast. Because of the numbers involved and multifaith issues, no rites are read out at the graveside.

All the burials are recorded in the interment registers. The entry for each body includes permit number, section number, plot number, grave number, age of the deceased (if known), date the permit was issued, date of death, cause of death, signature of the medical examiner, place of death, and date of burial. Although there are no individual tombstones, plot and section markers indicate the location of the coffin by a numerical system. Despite the daunting number of burials, the forty-five-acre site is in no danger of being exhausted. It is a grim, dignified system, and for the most part it works well. But nothing is flawless, and in 1971 Potter's Field suddenly found itself at the epicenter of the biggest PR disaster in the OCME's long history.

No one could—or would—ever say exactly how Jean Pierre Lehary came to be handling the skull on that July morning. As the curator of the OCME museum, it was his job to catalog and, if necessary, clean those items of forensic evidence deemed worthy of retention. Many of the specimens in the jars were kept for teaching purposes; some had historical significance—a major case, for instance—and some found their way onto the museum's shelves courtesy of the gallows humor that seems part and parcel of medical examiners' offices worldwide. So far as the records for this particular skull were concerned, they showed that on June 9, 1971, Patrolman Thomas Krant of the NYPD had spotted a body floating down the East River, 250 feet from Pier 70, and had summoned assistance. The female body was brought to the shore. When Detective John F. Hackett, who had been attached to the OCME for twenty years, saw the advanced level of decomposition he realized immediately that the best chance of identification would come through dental records. He contacted Bellevue, and two dentists, David E. Kenny and Carl Gardiner, duly charted the teeth in routine fashion. Although there was still some flesh attached to the skull, neither saw anything out of the ordinary. Nor did the OCME pathologist who carried out an external examination. Judging from the body's poor condition, he estimated that it had been in the water for several months.

The find was depressingly familiar. In the first half of the twentieth century, literally hundreds of drowning victims were recovered each year from the East River, with most of the bodies being found in spring.* This is because about 95 percent of victims who drown in cold weather will submerge, and their bodies linger on the riverbed until the air temperature reaches a regular 70 degrees Fahrenheit. Then, like a soggy cork, they will invariably rise to the surface. Sometimes, if the body gets trapped, it can remain submerged for so long that it is covered with barnacles when eventually dragged from the water.

In this instance, with no obvious signs of external injury, the medical examiner decided against performing a full autopsy and duly recorded the cause of death as "drowning." After twenty days in the mortuary, longer than was legally necessary for an unidentified body, the corpse was dispatched to Potter's Field—minus the head.

---

* By the mid-1990s this had fallen to thirty to forty per annum, an indication of the declining importance of the city's waterways.

Establishing exactly why the skull had been detached from the torso, and by whom, was a mystery that would exercise many an official mind over the coming months. Certainly the authorized explanation offered later has a hollow ring to it, making it easy to side with those OCME staff members who suspected the removed object had been destined for someone's desk, a paperweight, maybe, just the kind of ghoulish ornament to impress the hell out of over-awed visitors. All of which would have been fine and dandy had it not been for one slight hiccup—when Lehary was stripping the last vestiges of flesh from the skull he came across a misshapen .32-caliber copper-jacketed bullet.

This changed everything. An immediate disinterment order was issued and on July 8, workmen at Potter's Field carried out a hasty exhumation. Only at this stage did the OCME issue a teleprinter message to all law enforcement agencies in the tricounty area, advising that a young woman's body had been found and asking if the general description tallied with any of their missing persons' reports.

Eventually, the teleprinter message found its way to the New Jersey State Police headquarters in Trenton. After consulting their records, they, in turn, relayed it to the Princeton police department, as the physical details seemed to approximate those of a woman who had mysteriously vanished from that area five months earlier. Her disappearance had been the culmination to a strange and tumultuous saga.

When Laura Miller became engaged to Lieutenant Colin Carpi on February 23, 1957, the announcement was reported in the soci-ety columns of the *New York Times*. Similarly, their wedding just a few months later, on June 22 at the Church of the Messiah in Gwynedd, some twenty-five miles northeast of Philadelphia, was another highlight of the local social calendar and earned another mention in the *Times*. Friends and relatives alike agreed that theirs was a match made in heaven. Both the ravishing brunette and the handsome naval officer came from privileged backgrounds. Lynn's family was rooted in Philadelphia banking circles, while Colin's father had been executive vice president of the Penn Central Railroad. Their schooling had followed predictably similar Ivy League lines. Colin graduated from Princeton with the class of '53 with a BS in engineering, and two years later Laura emerged with equal distinction from Smith College.* Following graduation, she took a position as a clerk at the Eisenhower White House. Colin delayed his entry into the job market with a spell at Harvard's Graduate School of Business Administration. From there he enlisted in the U.S. Navy and at the time of his marriage was attached to the Bureau of Aeronautics in Washington, D.C. After leaving the White House, Laura remained in the Washington area, gaining a position on the faculty of the Potomac School, in McLean, Virginia.

When the couple decided it was time to start a family, they returned to the Princeton area. Colin, restless and eager to put his business training to good use, had left the armed forces and entered the world of management consultancy. In 1964 he took the bold step of branching out on his own. Meticulous study of the financial pages, bolstered by his own research, had convinced him that the home furniture market was an area sorely overlooked by venture capitalists. Unloved and untapped, it offered the potential for huge profits. Carpi, buttressed by an impressive array of investment bankers, singled out a Pennsylvania company called Lewisburg Chair & Furniture Corp as ripe for investment, handed over $4.5 million, and took control. Under Carpi's leadership, the company changed its name to General Interiors, and expanded at breakneck

---

* By a strange quirk of fate, Laura Miller attended Smith College at the same time as Lynn Kauffman (see chapter 3).

pace. His cash flow projections were right on the money and the benefits of life in the fast lane soon showed in the Carpi household. There were four fine children, all at private school, Laura was a regular item on the "must be seen at" social circuit, and Colin found himself featured in the February 1967 issue of *Fortune* magazine, held up as a shining beacon of how modern entrepreneurial vision was shaking up an industry notorious for its conservatism. Yes, life in the mid-1960s was very good for the Carpi family. But it didn't last.

The hairline cracks began appearing early on. Carpi's aggressive takeover campaign of rival furniture companies had tested the nerve and the patience of his fellow directors; but when General Interiors' sales figures started heading south, the boss found himself unceremoniously ousted. Carpi didn't sulk. Instead, he bounced right back by setting up his own financial consultancy business. It did well. Although Carpi had survived one major crisis, another loomed. His marriage was in freefall. In 1967, quite by chance, Laura had taken her youngest child, David, to an optometrist named Dr. William Moskowitz for treatment. Over the course of several visits, Moskowitz, by his own admission, became "intimately involved" with Laura. Nor was this any casual fling; far from it, as together, he and Laura set about writing a book on child therapy. Colin exploded. He angrily confronted Moskowitz about the relationship and reportedly kept tabs on the couple, constantly lurking nearby whenever he suspected an assignation was about to occur. Even Moskowitz's wife, Helen, marveled at the level and intensity of Carpi's obsession.

As the 1960s came to end, so too did the Carpis' marriage. By March 1970 Laura had walked out of the family home, taking the kids with her, and putting the family's future in the hands of the lawyers. For the remainder of that year and the beginning of the next, the Carpis traded figurative blows in what became a bitterly contested custody battle. By February 1971 it appeared as if Laura was getting the upper hand. But no one was prepared for what came next. On February 8, 1971, with victory in the matrimonial battle almost within her grasp, the thirty-seven-year-old mother of four just vanished.

She simply evaporated, or so it appeared. That same evening, her disappearance was reported to the police and a routine alert issued. Whether details of this alert ever reached New York remains unclear. All the evidence suggests that no one at the OCME had ever heard of Laura Carpi. Until Lehary found that bullet inside the skull.

There was still, of course, no conclusive proof to say that the skull belonged to Laura Carpi, but on July 22, 1971, a team of Princeton detectives, accompanied by Laura's dentist, Dr. Richard McClelland, arrived in New York. McClelland, who had carried out extensive and expensive work on Laura's teeth just prior to her disappearance, had already studied the OCME's dental charts, and while everything pointed to them representing the teeth of Laura Carpi, until he saw the skull itself, he wasn't prepared to commit himself. A few seconds of close inspection yielded the clinching identification.

The pathologist who had authorized the original death certificate, Dr. John F. Devlin, now conducted a full autopsy. He could find no injuries to the rest of the badly decomposed corpse; all the trauma was restricted to the skull. Closer exploration showed that the bullet had penetrated the base of the skull and the cranial cavity—execution-style—and then continued forward from the back of the head to lodge behind the face. Since family photographs showed Laura as having very thick hair, perfect camouflage for the entry wound, and because the bullet remained inside the skull and therefore made no exit wound, it had been all too easy to miss. Devlin had been sloppy, no doubt about it, in not examining the skull more thoroughly, but the pressures at the OCME were unique and, at times, overwhelming. Helpern first, and then DiMaio, had railed constantly about the appalling workload imposed on their staff. Long hours, not enough sleep, too many autopsies; was it any wonder that mistakes occasionally crept into the system? Devlin had buckled briefly under this welter burden and would suffer the humiliating consequences. But for now, he needed to issue a fresh cause of death. It was understandably terse: "Bullet wound of head, base of skull and spine. Homicidal."

Two days after the body of Laura Carpi had been identified, and one day after the autopsy confirmed that she had indeed been a homicide victim, a suspect was arrested and charged with her murder.

Interestingly enough, this wasn't the first time that someone at the OCME had missed a bullet wound to the head. Back in the Gonzales era, a machinist named George Saleeby had been charged on August 1, 1953, with felonious assault after two people in an apartment block had been wounded in two separate sniper attacks. Saleeby, age forty-three, had a long history of mental instability, and for most of his adult life had been undergoing psychiatric therapy of some kind. When arrested, he made no attempt to deny the shootings; instead, he astonished detectives by admitting he had also shot "the other guy!" This turned out to be sixty-year-old Frank Soska who on July 27 had been found unconscious on his apartment steps suffering from a head injury. He died that same day. The pathologist concerned, Dr. Emanuel Neuren, an acting assistant medical examiner, had decided, after hearing from family members that Soska suffered from severe heart disease, that the small pool of blood found at the scene was the result of Soska's hitting his head on the steps as he collapsed from cardiac arrest. With nothing to suggest otherwise, he declared this a natural death and Soska was buried. Following Saleeby's confession on August 6, Soska's body was exhumed from Ferncliff Cemetery, Hartsdale, this time for a full autopsy to be carried out by Gonzales. Sure enough, he found a .22-caliber slug that had pierced the top of the head and lodged in the right side of the brain. As noted in the previous chapter, small bullet wounds to the head are the bane of medical examiners, and Gonzales was quick to defend his assistant—a summer substitute at the OCME—by saying that even very experienced pathologists had sometimes failed to detect bullet wounds, especially within the hairline. (Saleeby was later incarcerated in a mental institution.)

Helpern, who headed up the OCME at the time of the Carpi incident, had of course been around during the Soska fiasco, and gut instinct told him that the Carpi blunder was potentially much more explosive. So he went to work. All public entities, if they are to survive and prosper, develop an instinct for damage limitation, and the OCME is no different from any other. Not a word about the Carpi debacle found its way to the media. Somehow Helpern managed to keep a lid on the story for more than two years. So far as the New York press was concerned, Laura Carpi might never have existed.

Down in southern New Jersey it had been an entirely different story. Wealthy people who disappear under mysterious circumstances invariably generate torrid headlines and plenty of speculation, and Laura Carpi was no exception. While the local press crawled all over Laura's life history, hard pressed Princeton detectives had more limited aims: they just wanted to piece together Laura's movements on what they believed was the last day of her life.

At 8:35 on the morning of February 8, 1971, after the children had gone off to school, Laura had taken a call from William

Moskowitz. Since the separation, this had been a daily ritual, him phoning every morning, as much to provide comfort and reassurance as anything else. He knew Laura was scared out of her wits. With the custody battle building to a turbulent crescendo, she had expressed concerns about her estranged husband, fearing that he would "go after her." On this particular morning she sounded on edge, but she and Moskowitz stayed talking until 8:47 A.M. Before hanging up, Laura arranged to meet Moskowitz later that morning at eleven o'clock at his Somerville office, a small town north of where she lived.

Just a few houses away, a neighbor, Mrs. Joan McAlpin, also tried to phone Laura that morning. She wanted to know if Laura would watch the McAlpin children while she (Mrs. McAlpin) went out briefly. But each time she dialed between 8:35 to 9:05 A.M. the line was busy. After that she got no answer and eventually abandoned the idea, assuming that Laura must have left the house for some reason.

When the police asked around, they found only two people who admitted visiting Laura's house on that dark, rainy morning: one was the mailman; the other was Colin Carpi.

According to his own account, he stopped by to drop off a five-hundred-dollar support check, as per his lawyer's instructions. After slipping the check through the letter box, he had gone home and talked on the phone to his mother for about three quarters of an hour. Then he'd driven to Manhattan and the Morgan Guaranty Bank at Forty-eighth Street and Park Avenue, where he kept a safe-deposit box. After extracting some documents from the safe-deposit box, he then drove back to Princeton, stopping off at his lawyer's office before going home. His first inkling that anything was amiss came when his eldest daughter, Jennifer, age eleven, had called from school to say that Laura had failed to pick her up and she wanted her father to come for her. That evening the Carpi children moved back in with their father.

Acting on a missing person's report, the police searched Laura's home. They found it neat and tidy, with no obvious signs of a break-in or theft. If Laura's disappearance was linked to a bungled robbery, as some feared, then the burglar had been very picky or hopelessly amateurish, for the dining-room table groaned beneath a display of untouched and obviously expensive silver. In the foyer, a pile of mail lay on the floor, directly beneath a mail slot in the front door. On top of the pile, and slightly to one side, lay a plain white envelope without stamps or postmark and addressed to Laura. Inside was the support check that Colin had left that morning. Thus far there was little to arouse any great concern. But a few minutes spent upstairs in the bedroom changed all that. Laura's clothes still hung in her closet. Patently, she had not packed for a trip, the strongest evidence yet that her disappearance had been sudden and unexpected. A further cursory examination failed to reveal anything else of interest, leaving detectives no alternative but to seal the house in readiness for a thorough forensic examination in daylight hours.

The next morning the police returned, accompanied by a friend of Laura's, Helen Harper, who knew the house well. One anomaly jumped out at her right away: a large dining-room rug had gone missing. This was ominous. Just two days before her disappearance Laura had thrown a dinner party, and the following day Helen had returned to help Laura clean up the house. The rug had been present then. A microscopic examination of the oak floor beneath where the rug had lain revealed four tiny stains. To the naked eye they looked like blood, but only laboratory analysis could confirm this, one way or another. Andrew J. Nardella, a forensic chemist for the New Jersey state police, continued his search for clues. On the base of the dishwasher he found another smear of what again looked like blood. These discoveries forced the investigators to reevaluate a find from the preceding night—a pink-handled mop left drying in the kitchen sink.

This mop, together with all the samples, was sent to the laboratory for analysis. The results were mixed. As Nardella had suspected, all the stains found on the mop, the floor, and the dishwasher were human blood, but, as he'd feared, all the samples were too small to type using the technology of the day. Nevertheless, these discoveries did fuel the suspicion that something awful had befallen Laura Carpi, a suspicion amplified by Laura's lawyers. They told the police of a recent stormy meeting with her husband in their presence, at which Colin had reportedly threatened Laura. Also, they alleged that one week before her disappearance, Colin had burst into Laura's house and become so violent that she had been forced to fend him off.

The marital abuse angle received a further shot in the arm with the comments of another guest at Laura's final dinner party. Mary Eager had been Colin's former secretary, and a couple of days before the party, she said, Laura had phoned and asked if she would come and stay the night before the party, because the custody battle had become so acrimonious that she feared Colin might harm her. Mrs. Eager felt torn and confused by this development, as in all the two years she had worked for Colin she had never known him to be anything other than "kind and calm." With her loyalties divided, it came as a profound relief when she heard that Helen Harper had stepped into the breach and would stay overnight with Laura.

In the days and weeks after Laura's disappearance, Colin held up well under questioning. He professed a total ignorance of her whereabouts. Investigating officers had to tread carefully. Although the circumstances of the case did, superficially at least, raise legitimate questions, there was still nothing concrete to say any crime had been committed. Without a body, the authorities were reluctant to jump the gun and start filing charges, just in case they wound up with egg on their faces.*

But five months on, with the discovery of Laura's body, it was an entirely different story. Just two days after the remains of Laura Carpi were positively identified, her husband was charged with her murder. During the interview process, Carpi agreed to submit to a polygraph test, safe in the knowledge that no matter what the outcome the results would not be admissible into evidence.

Adored by law enforcement agencies, loathed by libertarians, regarded with thinly disguised skepticism by much of the judicial system, the polygraph, or lie "detector," remains one of the most controversial weapons in the crime fighting arsenal. Some invest it with an almost mythical ability to ferret out the truth, for others it's nothing more than an overhyped bundle of plugs, pens, tubes, and graph paper, thrown together and masquerading as science. Somewhere in between these polar extremes lies the reality.

Throughout history mankind has searched for ways to trap liars. Priests in India (ca. 500 B.C.) would herd suspected thieves into a darkened room with a "magic donkey," whose tail had been daubed with lampblack. The suspects were then ordered to pull the donkey's tail, having been warned that when the genuine thief pulled the tail, the magic donkey would speak and be heard throughout the temple. When the room was emptied a few minutes later, the person who still had clean hands—having not pulled the tail—was branded the thief and punished.

The Chinese came up with an even simpler method. Suspected liars were fed a handful of dry rice. If they could spit it out, so the

---

* Their circumspection was well justified. In 2003 an Australian murder trial had to be halted after one of the alleged "victims" turned up alive and well.

reasoning went, they were telling the truth; if the rice stuck to their tongue, they were thought to have something to hide. As crude as it may seem, this Chinese "truth test" operated on exactly the same principle to that used by the modern polygraph—the belief that when people lie, their body reacts in ways that they cannot control. Whereas Chinese interrogators were on the lookout for a dry mouth as an indicator of lying, the polygraph operator searches for deception by studying changes in blood pressure, rates of breathing, pulse, and perspiration.

The first modern attempt to measure emotion as a means of determining truth and deception can be traced to the celebrated Italian criminologist, Cesare Lombroso. As early as 1895 he was recording changes in blood pressure and pulse rate in police suspects under questioning, though not with any conspicuous success. The next innovation in lie detection came in 1913 when another Italian, psychologist Vittorio Benussi, published a paper on using breath measurement as a means of determining truthfulness. During the First World War an American scientist engaged in counterintelligence, William Marston, took the process one step further, developing a systolic blood pressure gauge that he tested on German prisoners of war. Disillusioned by his results, Marston abandoned its use.

If anyone can lay claim to the title "the Father of the Polygraph," then that person has to be John Larson, a medical student at the University of California at Berkeley. In 1920, working in close conjunction with local police chief August Vollmer, Larson built the first machine specifically designed to detect lying through plotting on graph paper simultaneous measurements of blood pressure, pulse, and respiration. Several years earlier a Scottish cardiologist, Sir James Mackenzie, had designed a multifunction heart monitor that he called a polygraph, meaning "many writings," and Larson decided to appropriate the name.

Although immediately popular with police departments right across America, the polygraph suffered a major judicial setback almost right away, when the U.S. Supreme Court (*Frye v. United States*, 1923) ruled unproven scientific testimony to be legally inadmissible. As a result the polygraph was largely barred from the courtroom, even as its use in everyday life mushroomed, usually in the arena of job applications.

By the 1930s Larson had turned his back on this field of work, and it was left to his protégé, Leonard Keeler, to develop what is now regarded as the prototype of the modern polygraph. At the same time, Keeler also founded a school for the proper training of operatives.

The polygraph works by attaching rubber tubes to the subject's chest and abdomen, a blood pressure–pulse cuff to the arm, and small metal plates to the fingers. The examiner then asks the subject a series of questions, and the polygraph measures five physical responses. These are:

1. Thoracic respiration

2. Abdominal respiration

3. Perspiration (registered by minuscule changes in skin conductivity of electricity occurring at the fingertip)

4. Blood pressure

5. Blood volume

These five responses are then plotted along a horizontal graph, with the location of questions marked at the bottom of the printout. How the questions are framed is critical. Because individuals react differently, the examiner needs to know what triggers a "lie" response in that particular subject. To this end, each test contains certain "control" questions, to which the subject is directed to answer untruthfully. The concomitant anxiety usually registers as a blip on the graph. Once this untruthful benchmark has been established, the actual test can begin.

Numerous questions—some relevant to the case, some not—are fired at the subject. Each response is assigned a number from –3 (indicating a strong negative correlation) to +3 (indicating a strong positive correlation), measured by comparing the relevant response to the previously established controls. Psychology plays its part, with the skilled examiner constantly reminding the subject of just how accurate the polygraph is in catching any lies told.

Once all the responses are added together, a total score of +6 indicates a strong presumption that the subject is lying. Scores that fall between –5 and +5 are not admissible, because they are not felt to be a strong enough indication of veracity.

While no one disputes that polygraphs measure perceptible changes in human response, there can be no guarantee that these changes are prompted by the act of lying. Because stress plays a big factor in any polygraph test—even truthful subjects occasionally send the styluses haywire—much depends on how the examiner interprets the data. And herein lies much of the controversy. Give the same polygraph results to two different examiners and, as tests have shown, it is entirely possible that they will reach opposing conclusions as to the subject's truthfulness.

Supporters of the polygraph attribute such discrepancies to poor schooling and a lack of experience. A properly trained examiner, they claim, armed with a good instrument, will catch 95 percent of all liars. Critics put the figure much lower and say that with minimal practice almost anyone can be taught how to "beat the machine" by deliberately manipulating their physiological responses to give false positives.

Someone who notably failed to beat the machine was Colin

Carpi. Three times he was hooked up to the polygraph, and three times he gave responses that indicated deception.

But before the prosecutors could lay their case before a jury, they first of all had to get Carpi into court. And that was proving to be hellishly difficult. Dominating all else was the question of jurisdiction. Although the body had been found in New York, there was plenty of evidence to suggest that Laura had been killed in her Princeton house and then transported to the East River where her body was dumped. After some lukewarm interstate wrangling—New York really wanted to wash its hands of what had been a humiliating public embarrassment—New Jersey found itself saddled with the prosecution of Colin Carpi.

It was a strange case right from the beginning. Despite being indicted for first-degree murder on August 19, 1971, Carpi was released on his own recognizance in the sum of one hundred thousand dollars. This highly unusual state of affairs in a capital case persisted until the following December when a court threw out the original indictment. Carpi's triumph was short lived. A second appeal, this time by the state, led to the indictment being reinstated.

Still there seemed to be little official appetite for putting Colin Carpi on trial. The curious legal limbo dragged on all through 1972 and for most of the following year, until November 1973, when state prosecutors wearily announced a trial date set for the new year. With this announcement news of the whole bizarre saga finally broke in the New York press.

There is an old medical saw that "doctors bury their mistakes," and over the previous two years Helpern had certainly done his damnedest to bury the Carpi case. In this endeavor he'd been outstandingly successful. So much so, that when the thunderstorm finally did break above the Office of the Chief Medical Examiner, its veteran leader was on the verge of retirement. Not that Helpern got off entirely scot-free; those final few weeks in office were among the most awkward and testing of his lengthy career.

The story broke on November 28, 1973, and that day John F. Devlin was wheeled out to face a hostile press. He had first joined the OCME on a part-time basis in 1959. Three years later he became full time and in 1969 was appointed to the position of deputy chief medical examiner. He was experienced and thoroughly professional, with a strong pragmatic streak. When he told reporters that he had not conducted a full autopsy first time around because there was no reason to suspect foul play and because the office was "very busy," he was merely articulating long held office practice. He went on to explain: "We get a lot of bodies out of the river when it warms up at that time of the year and we've got to get rid of them as soon as possible. They pile up, and there's no room for them." Visions of a corpse-filled conveyor belt may have unsettled some of the more timorous, but in the day-to-day business of body disposal, practicality rules. After all, there are only so many refrigerated lockers. Pressed by reporters as to how the head came to be severed, the deputy CME said he didn't know. He flatly denied having authorized the procedure; nor did he have any idea who had done so.

Mayor John Lindsay might have just lost the recent election to Abraham Beame, but he was determined to shrug off any suggestion that he was a lame duck. One day after the story broke, he ordered an inquiry into operations at the Office of the Chief Medical Examiner. This only heightened press fervor, most of it directed at the outgoing chief. Helpern did his best to divert the attacks by saying that the impending trial constrained him from commenting about the case, but this didn't prevent him muttering darkly that details of the story had been deliberately leaked by a certain high-ranking staff member out to "besmirch" the Office of the Chief Medical Examiner. Although Helpern refrained from naming names, given his well-advertised dislike and distrust of one particular colleague, Holmesian levels of deduction were not necessary to isolate his suspect.

The inquiry into the OCME lasted for two weeks, and was headed by Gerald Frug of the Health Services Administration. So far as the OCME was concerned, his report—submitted on December 10—was like the curate's egg, good in parts. Frug's primary conclusion was that the OCME *had* acted appropriately when it severed the head, because the "expensive and highly specialized" dental work might be an aid to future identification, and that as a result of this incident the OCME was investigating the merits of having X-rays performed on all bodies brought in. So far so good; then came the zinger. When Frug went digging, he discovered that the severance had been ordered by none other than *John F. Devlin*! Having earlier denied any part in the incident, the deputy CME was now forced to come clean. He had authorized the action, he said, because the head had "decomposed to the point where [it] was merely a skull, and the removal of the skull was a convenient and appropriate way to preserve the dental work for later identification."

Bad news is often like a stone dropped into a pond. What begins as a small disturbance can, as the ripples spread outward, dislodge other problems and allow them to bubble to the surface. This case was a prime example. In short order, fallout from the report uncovered more disturbing revelations, this time concerning a perceived indifference shown toward dead people in New York City. Barely a month previously, on November 16, 1973, a fifty-six-year-old stockbroker named George Gutterman had collapsed of a heart attack on a street in Queens. He was declared DOA at the City Hospital Center in Elmhurst. Despite the fact that Gutterman was carrying substantial ID, including photographs and even fingerprint records, no city agency bothered to contact the family.

Only dogged research by family members uncovered the truth. Six days later, just as Gutterman was being prepared for a pauper's grave by Hebrew Free Burial, he was finally identified.

Even though this oversight did not reflect directly on the Office of the Chief Medical Examiner, it was yet another jab of detrimental news to greet the unfortunate Dr. Dominick DiMaio when he took over as acting CME on January 7, 1974. Ten days later, some very anxious New York eyes were focused on Trenton, New Jersey, as the trial of Colin Carpi opened.

When Mercer County assistant prosecutor Richard M. Altman made his opening address to the jury, he didn't waste any words; discard all the bizarre hoopla that attended the discovery of Laura's body and this was a straightforward case with the oldest of motives. Colin Carpi, he said, was a man consumed by hatred and bitterness toward his estranged wife, and rather than topple into the abyss of certain financial ruin, he had "carefully planned and carried out the execution [of Laura]." Altman played up Carpi's cleverness, his Ivy League schooling, portraying him as some warped genius who thought he had committed "the perfect crime." Except that, before the body was discovered, he "did something no human being in the world could have done—it was the one mistake he made." That mistake, Altman promised, would be revealed in testimony. He called it "more dramatic than anything else you will ever hear in a courtroom . . . a fatal error that bespoke his guilt loudly and clearly."

This was some boast for any prosecutor to make, and many who were familiar with the case privately questioned Altman's strategy. Promise the jury a smoking gun and you'd better deliver; come up short, and no panel would forgive you. Altman decided to get the bad news out of the way early on. Few expert witnesses have ever had to consume a larger portion of humble pie than that dished up to Dr. John F. Devlin in that Trenton courtroom. His admission that he had initially ascribed Laura's death to drowning was hugely damaging, as was the way he was made to parade—like some recalcitrant schoolboy—before the jury one by one, showing each the elusive .32-caliber slug he had missed. He explained that it was not OCME policy to remove heads unless they were so decomposed as to be skeletonized, and then only if they were needed for possible later identification. In the Carpi case, he had deemed it necessary to keep the jaws because the teeth showed elaborate dental work. The head had been severed on his orders, he said, because removing the jaws alone would have entailed more mutilation.

Altman did his best to paper over the cracks. While conceding that the OCME had fallen short of its own high investigative standards, he quite rightly praised the office as "one of the finest in the country." Only time would tell if Altman's airbrushing mission had done the trick; for now, it looked to be uphill all the way.

Originally the defense had questioned whether the body was actually that of Laura Carpi; however, the testimony of Dr. Lowell J. Levine, dental consultant to the Office of the Chief Medical Examiner and one of the world's foremost forensic odontologists, effectively demolished that thin argument early in the proceedings. As he put it, "Dental X-rays are as unique as a fingerprint for identification purposes."

Of all the components of the human body, virtually nothing outlasts the teeth after death. This durability makes them ideally suited as a means of identification. Indeed, in the aftermath of serious fires, such as the Waco inferno, teeth are often the only means of identifying scorched remains.

Identification by teeth is not new. It dates back to A.D. 49, and the time of Nero. Allegedly, Nero's mother, Agrippina, ordered her rival Lollia Paulina to commit suicide, with instructions for her soldiers to bring back Lollia's head as proof that she was dead. When presented with the head, Agrippina found identification an impossibility, until she examined the teeth and, on finding a distinctively discolored front tooth, realized that her hated enemy would trouble her no more. During the U.S. Revolutionary War, none other than Paul Revere (a young dentist) helped identify war casualties by their bridgework. Almost two centuries later and dental records again played a significant part in history, this time at the end of World War II, to identify the remains of Adolf Hitler.

It is frequently claimed that no two people have identical teeth; however, it should be remembered that unlike fingerprints, which remain unchanged from birth, dentition achieves its uniqueness through use and wear. For successful identification, both ante- and postmortem records must be available. From such data, it is often possible to make an identification from a single tooth.

There are an estimated two hundred different tooth charting methods in use throughout the world. All provide a means of identification that is elegant and almost 100 percent reliable. The American approach, called the Universal System, allocates a different number to each of the thirty-two adult teeth, beginning with the upper-right third molar (1), round the mouth to the lower-right third molar (32). Information is recorded about the five visible surfaces of each tooth, from which it is generally possible to complete a dental grid, or odontogram, unique to that individual.

As regular visits to the dentist become a way of life for more people, so the database of fillings, extractions, bridges, dentures, and deformities expands. Every addition brings an increased chance of identification, should one ever be necessary.

With all doubts about the identification of Laura Carpi cast aside, everything now boiled down to a single question: who killed her? So far as the state was concerned, Colin Carpi punched all the right buttons; he had the means, the opportunity, and certainly the motive to get rid of his wife. At stake were hundreds of thousands, if not millions of dollars, in what had degenerated into a savage divorce battle. If Laura won the case—an outcome that looked odds-on—Colin would be wiped out financially. The closer they came to the wire, the meaner Colin turned, or so it was alleged. Several people claimed to have heard him threaten his estranged wife.

One was a member of Laura's legal team, John A. Hartman III. He testified about an unpleasant incident that occurred when Carpi had been questioned for a deposition on his financial status. It had been a tense, edgy meeting for all concerned. After the deposition, both parties had entered the elevator as a group, only for Carpi to suddenly turn on his wife and say, "You've really done it this time, Laura. You've come to the end of your rope." Another attorney, Russell W. Annich Jr., who was present, said he didn't recall the exact words, but in essence they were, "Laura, you've just about reached the end of the line."

Hartman wasn't through yet. He told how Laura had also confided that on January 31—just over a week before she disappeared—Carpi had "pushed in" her front door, run upstairs "slamming" doors, then rushed back downstairs and into the dining room where she had been vacuuming. She said the defendant "had a blank stare about him" and that "his face was red, with blood vessels protruding in his head . . . he appeared to be about to do something to her." Hartman continued: "She clenched the vacuum cleaner and warned him that if he took one step toward her, she would clout him with it. He said, 'I promised my lawyers I was going to catch you this weekend and I'm going to fix you.'"

On the day following the disappearance, Hartman said, he had gone to Laura's house, and had seen Carpi sitting in his car in the driveway. He told the court that Carpi had "elongated" scratches on the left side of his face from the temple to the cheek.

Someone else who'd seen these reported scratches was Detective Sergeant Norman Servis of the Princeton Township Police Department. He had questioned Carpi that same day and saw not only the scratches but also bruises on the back of his right hand and a scratch between thumb and index finger.

These observations prompted Servis to run checks on Carpi's alibi for the day of Laura's disappearance. He paid particular attention to timings. Over numerous interviews, Carpi had maintained that he had dropped off the check at 9:30 A.M., then returned home and made several phone calls, including one to his mother that lasted forty-five minutes. At 11:05 A.M., according to Carpi, he set out to drive the fifty-five miles to the Manhattan branch of the Morgan Guaranty Bank. By his reckoning, heavy overnight rain had slowed up many of the major routes and more than two and a half hours passed before he reached his destination. Bank records logged him as having used the safe-deposit facility between 1:43 P.M. to 1:48 P.M. After this, Carpi said he returned to Princeton, stopping off briefly at his lawyer's office, before finally arriving home at around 4:00 P.M. Shortly thereafter, he had received the distressed phone call from his daughter, and had gone to pick up his children. Mindful of his precarious position in the custody battle, he had advised his lawyer that he intended taking his children to a prior dinner date he had arranged with his mother for that night.

Not so, said the prosecution. Their chronology had Carpi arriving at Laura's house on the morning of February 8, with murder in mind. At some time between 8:47 and 9:30 A.M., he had inveigled his way into the house, pulled a .32-caliber handgun, and shot Laura to death. After rolling her body in the dining-room rug, he then mopped the floor, thus obliterating most but not all traces of blood, before loading the body into his car. The visit to Morgan Guaranty was a carefully planned smokescreen thrown up to conceal the true motive for his trip to Manhattan—to dump his dead wife's body in the East River.

The state felt it had uncovered three highly significant flaws in Carpi's story. First, there was his initial insistence that he had reached Laura's house at 9:30 A.M., when phone company records showed Carpi was actually making calls from his home at this same time. (This revelation had provoked a radical revision on Carpi's part, with him later advancing the alleged arrival at Laura's by almost an hour.) Doubt, too, surrounded that supposed forty-five-minute call to his mother; according to the phone company, this was closer to two minutes. Also, all the other calls were shorter than previously claimed.

The second discrepancy came courtesy of a secretary who worked for John Cannon, one of Carpi's lawyers. Leanne Landefelt testified that at 3:35 P.M. on February 8, she took a call from Carpi, in which he left a message for Cannon, saying that the school had phoned to report Laura's nonappearance and that he was on his way to pick up his children. If accurate, this testimony could put Carpi in the electric chair, because Leanne's timings had Carpi making this call a full twenty-five minutes *before* he said his daughter had called. Only if Carpi already knew that his wife was not going to show, argued the prosecution, could he have contacted his lawyers at the time specified. Phone records at the Carpi children's private school showed no log of anyone having phoned Carpi at this earlier time. When asked by counsel if she had kept this message, Leanne said no.

Discrepancy number three was even more curious. Mailman Paul E. Stephens told the court how on February 8 he had delivered Mrs. Carpi's mail at 12:30 P.M., three hours after Colin said he dropped off the support check, and yet when detectives searched the house that evening they found the support check letter *on top* of the other mail. This incongruity obviously unsettled Carpi.

According to Detective Samuel F. Bianco, five months later at an interview held beside Carpi's swimming pool, the defendant had raised this topic and said, "I just want to get the record straight." Carpi had explained how when he took the children to the house that afternoon Jennifer had said something about the positioning of the mail. When the chief defense counsel, Gerald Stockman, tried to question Bianco about whether Jennifer handled the mail, Altman cried foul, saying Jennifer would have to take the stand if her role were to be discussed. Justice Arthur B. Salvatore agreed and threw out this line of questioning.

Carpi's prodigious bankroll meant that he could afford high-quality legal representation, and Stockman didn't let him down. Marshaling his forces skillfully and with no obvious shortage of ammunition, Stockman called John J. Scott to the stand. Quite by chance, on the night of Laura's disappearance, Scott, an old school friend of Carpi's, happened to run into Carpi at the historic General Wayne Inn in Merion, Pennsylvania. Carpi was eating there with his mother and children. Although the two men had not seen each other for twenty years, they chatted about old times, and at no time during the conversation did Scott notice any scratches or marks of any kind on Carpi's face, contrary to what the two earlier witnesses had claimed.

Stockman next disposed of that alleged confrontation in the elevator. One of Carpi's lawyers, A. C. Reeves Hicks, had also heard the remark that day and found it hard to believe that anyone would have construed it as a threat. More useful testimony came from Carpi's other lawyer, John Cannon. He told the court that on February 7 he had called Carpi and recommended that he make the support payment as soon as possible. So far as he was concerned, his client had acted impeccably throughout the painful and protracted divorce proceedings.

Everything now hinged on Colin C. Carpi. In temperament and

personality, he wasn't the type to duck the challenge of the witness stand, and when he testified he did so with an air of invincible self-confidence. His answers, forthright and punctuated with prods of his index finger, frequently irked Judge Salvatore, who ordered him not to expand his answers beyond the scope of the questions. But Carpi was determined to set the agenda. He dismissed Hartman and Annich's version of the elevator incident as a "complete fabrication . . . baloney." As for Hartman's claims that he had threatened his wife: "Nothing could be further from the truth . . . In thirteen years of married life I don't ever remember threatening Laura or ever saying anything derogatory about her to anyone." He hotly maintained that he had "absolutely nothing" to do with her murder.

On the morning of February 8, he said, he was outside Laura's house for a minute or two at most between 8:35 and 8:45, just long enough to park in the driveway, deposit the check, and drive out again. He had not seen Laura and he did not notice if her car was in the garage. By nine o'clock he was back home, phoning John Cannon's office and leaving a message with his secretary that he had followed instructions to deliver the check and would shortly be heading off to New York City on a bank errand. After working on an affidavit for the custody battle and making several more phone calls, he left for New York at 11:05 A.M., taking the Lincoln Tunnel and going across Manhattan directly to the Morgan Guaranty branch at Park Avenue and Forty-eighth Street. At approximately 2:00 P.M. he left the bank and drove back to Princeton, stopping first at the office of A. C. Reeves Hicks, at 3:30 P.M. for about ten minutes. While there he called John Cannon, only to be told that Cannon was away from the office. Carpi had hung up without leaving a message. In saying this, Carpi directly contradicted Leanne Landefelt's testimony, vehemently insisting that he had mentioned nothing about Laura not picking up the children from school.

With the trial turning into a variation on the old tangled theme of "he said, she said," suddenly one of those *Perry Mason* moments came along. A surprise witness! Four days after giving her original testimony, Leanne Landefelt was back on the stand. And what she had to say would drive a stake right through the heart of the prosecution's case.

An investigator hired by the defense had been through John Cannon's files and found a sheet of legal-size paper on which Leanne had listed calls received on February 8, 1971. Referring to this list, it reminded her that after 3 P.M., she had taken seven calls for Cannon, before taking one from Carpi. No time was specified for any of them, and the message left by Carpi was that his children had just called from school, not that the school had called.

As he listened to this astonishing reversal, Altman's world turned to rubble about his ears. No wonder the State of New York had wanted nothing to do with this case; it was a prosecutorial nightmare!

The final dagger was plunged into the state's case by two of the Carpi children. Jennifer, still only fourteen years old, confirmed that she had called her father from school at 3:50 P.M., after twice failing to get an answer from her mother. Her brother, Colin Jr., just one year younger, also testified that he'd tried unsuccessfully to contact his father.

During his closing address, Altman, in a masterpiece of understatement, professed himself "shocked" by Leanne's change of testimony. When the trial began, he had promised the jury a single "fatal error" that would prove Carpi's guilt. Having failed dismally and embarrassingly in that endeavor, he now attempted to hedge his bets by telling the jury that Carpi had committed not one, not two, but *three* "fatal errors": (1) the admission by Carpi that he visited the house on the morning she disappeared, (2) the call to his attorney's secretary on the day of the crime, and (3) his own testimony that he made the call. Altman closed by claiming that Carpi had actually made *two* calls to the secretary on that afternoon and that the first, which mentioned Laura's nonappearance, came before he heard from the children. All in all, it was a fumbling conclusion to a case that had been disastrously mishandled from the outset.

For the defense, Stockman wanted to know how on earth his client could "have gone to her house in broad daylight, killed her, taken 170 pounds or so [body and rug] to his car with nobody seeing a thing, then return, clean up with a mop, wring it out so well the state police could not even detect that the drop [of blood] remaining on the mop was human, and drive off." All of these were salient points, and all of them glided past the fact that, quite obviously, someone did exactly that.

In a final desperate roll of the dice, the state produced Eleanor Perone, a receptionist for the legal firm representing Mrs. Carpi, as a rebuttal witness to Carpi's claim that he had always treated Laura well. Mrs. Perone told how, three days before the murder, Laura had told her that the defendant had once burst in while she was vacuuming. "She said his eyes were wild and he told her time was coming near." Perone ended quietly, "She said 'he's really out to get me, Ellie.'"

Now it was up to the jury. On January 30, after two days of deliberation, they came back with a verdict of not guilty. Carpi pounded the table in triumph. Outside the court, both sides continued to trade punches. Carpi contended that the prosecution had "lied about the facts, concealed important evidence, and [engaged in running] a massive, prejudicial publicity campaign." He also declared his intention of writing a book about inequities in the legal system, a promise, thus far, unfulfilled.

For its part, the prosecution almost choked on sour grapes. No losing gracefully here. Acting prosecutor Wilbur H. Mathesius went straight for the jugular: "I want everyone to know, I want the jury to know, that he [Carpi] flunked a lie-detector test three times."

What the jury would have made of this revelation is, of course, pure conjecture, but, traditionally, juries are hostile to two things: a proven liar and flawed testimony from expert witnesses. The first speaks for itself; the second is far more insidious. As the O. J. Simpson trial demonstrated, just a whiff of forensic incompetence is often all it takes to wreck the strongest seeming case. Give a skillful defense team the tiniest of scientific blunders and you can be sure that what started life as a barely visible molehill will rapidly assume Everest-like proportions. By and large, juries put enormous faith in the testimony of expert witnesses; they expect them to be 100 percent right 100 percent of the time, and although what happened at the OCME regarding the Carpi case was incompetent and bizarre and ought not to have affected the outcome, it just didn't smell right. Few people are comfortable with the concept of medical examiners lopping off skulls to use as paperweights. Devlin's groveling explanation sounded hopelessly makeshift.

Of course, the biggest irony surrounding Devlin's bizarre conduct—largely overlooked at the time—is that had he not indulged himself in some kind of surgical conceit and removed the head, then the fate of Laura Carpi would remain a mystery to this day.

Judged on the evidence presented at the trial, Colin Carpi was rightly acquitted. No gunshots were heard at about the time that the prosecution said the murder was committed; no firearm of the type used to kill Laura Carpi was ever traced to him; no witness saw him enter the house on the morning of February 8, 1971; no one saw him leave; no one saw him dump any body in the East River; and there was not a single scrap of forensic evidence linking him to the crime. In the end the jury quite properly decided that even though the circumstantial case against Carpi raised certain legitimate questions, it fell some considerable distance short of precluding that elusive quality known as reasonable doubt.

This verdict, although embarrassing for DiMaio, did not reflect on him personally as he set himself the task of restoring faith in the OCME and consolidating his own position. Like Gonzales before him, he was hamstrung by his status as acting chief medical examiner. As the months passed, for some reason, the powers-that-be still seemed reluctant to fill the post permanently. All DiMaio could do was to keep plugging away. As always, there was plenty to occupy his mind. The surge in drug-related deaths that Helpern had first noted back in the 1930s had, four decades later, turned into a tidal wave. Much the most worrying development was the sudden appearance of methadone on the streets of New York. First synthesized in Germany during World War II, methadone was introduced into the U.S. drug treatment program in 1950 as a means of weaning addicts off heroin. For the most part it remained of peripheral interest to the drug community until 1971, when international sanctions to curb the growth of opium poppies in countries such as Turkey were put in place. While this had achieved the desired effect of shriveling the supply of heroin, it failed to take into consideration an immutable law of economics: reduced supply leads to higher prices. As the street price of heroin went soaring through the roof, junkies scrambled around feverishly for other, cheaper means of getting high. Methadone was the surrogate of choice. Cheap to produce and incredibly plentiful, it was also lethal. Addicts, used to measuring out their fixes in powder form, were completely thrown by this liquid substitute. Hundreds got it wrong, overdosed, and wound up in hospital beds if they were lucky, or on mortuary slabs if they were not. In 1974 a report compiled for DiMaio showed that in the previous year, 181 deaths had been attributed to the synthetic narcotic, as compared to 98 to heroin. Drug-related deaths were a sad and sickening trend, one that showed no sign of abating.

As DiMaio wrestled with an ever increasing workload, the city fathers, after considerable breast-beating, announced that they were finally getting round to holding an open and competitive examination for the post of chief medical examiner. The criteria for applicants were as follows: must be a graduate of an accredited medical school and licensed to practice in New York State; must have completed at least five hundred medico-legal autopsies; must have five years of full-time paid experience in a chief medical examiner's office or a comparable agency, at least two years of which had to be in a supervisory capacity. An undercurrent of resentment still bubbled within the OCME about outsiders being permitted to sit the exam, but these complaints fell on deaf ears, and eventually ten applicants took the written test on January 10, 1975.

When the scores were tallied, three candidates were deemed to have performed significantly better than the rest. Coincidentally all three happened to work at the Office of the Chief Medical Examiner. These were DiMaio; Helpern's longtime nemesis, Dr. Michael Baden; and Dr. Farouk B. Presswalla, a British subject who had served in London and Bombay before joining the OCME in 1970. He was currently an associate medical examiner.

On April 5 these three applicants passed to the next stage—the oral examination—at which they were tested for "speech, manner, and judgment." A result was confidently expected in days. But it didn't turn out that way. Instead, an ominous silence fell over the proceedings. As the weeks dragged by, the candidates became edgy, totally in the dark about the outcome. Finally, the reason for the delay became apparent: some of the original out-of-state applicants were crying foul. They felt that questions in the January test had been stacked in the "home team's" favor.

Presswalla scoffed when he heard this. "I don't see how it could be considered unfair. There was nothing in it [the test] . . . that would give the New York people an advantage. It was about principles that would apply any place in the world." Despite this protestation, Presswalla still found time to reiterate his belief that the examination should have been restricted to OCME applicants, a stance that received Baden's full support. He said, "To keep good people you have to give them the assurance that if they do well they will be promoted."

No fire, maybe, but more than enough smoke to trouble the Civil Service Commission, which ordered an inquiry into the disputed test. The results were made public on July 28, when it was announced that the January test was being set aside on grounds that some of the candidates had "a competitive advantage." Although the report could find "no evidence of willful misconduct," it was learned that some applicants knew beforehand which examiners would be preparing and grading the questions on the test and were thus able to familiarize themselves with the areas of expertise of the examiners.

DiMaio, as bewildered as everyone else by the ongoing promotion saga, was simultaneously caught up in yet another very public spat, this time between the OCME and the city's hospital system. It concerned organ transplants. Since the first successful kidney transplant, carried out in 1954, physicians had been pushing back the boundaries of transplant surgery year after year. By the mid-1970s transplants of the heart, pancreas, and liver were commonplace, along with the kidneys. Naturally, this progress was dependent on a constant supply of donors. And one of the best sources of donors was murder victims. This posed an ethical dilemma for DiMaio. He took the view that the bodies of murder victims should always remain intact until a full autopsy had been conducted. The city hospitals didn't see it that way at all; they wanted to harvest organs as soon after death as possible. The dispute peaked on March 7, 1975, when doctors at Jacobi Hospital in the Bronx defied DiMaio and removed the kidneys from a gunshot victim before an autopsy had been performed. The surgeon who carried out the procedure, Dr. Samuel Kountz, chief of surgery at the Downstate Medical Center in Brooklyn, cheekily said that Helpern had *always* permitted transplants prior to autopsy, where to do so would have no bearing on the autopsy itself. This reference to Helpern was unfortunate, as the former CME was still hovering in the background and still sniping at his successors from behind the barricades. But Kountz had a point. "There are 1,800 homicides a year in the New York area," he said, "and many of the victims are young, healthy people—the best kind of donors. If we could use a third of them, it would completely eliminate the need for dialysis treatment and for live donors."

While the ethical and succession battles raged, DiMaio struggled with the day-to-day problems of running the busiest medico-legal facility in the world. On June 24, 1975, an Eastern Airlines jet crashed in a violent thunderstorm on its approach to Kennedy International Airport, and to DiMaio and his team fell the grim task of identifying the 110 victims. Just a few months later another large-scale tragedy struck New York again when fire raged through the Puerto Rican Social Club in the Bronx in the early hours of October 24, 1975, killing twenty-five young partygoers and injuring twenty-four others who had leapt from a second-floor window. A grim convoy of four vans transported the bodies to the OCME, where DiMaio supervised a process of mass identification that had been honed into assembly-line efficiency. Each of the bodies was examined by a five-man team headed by an assistant medical examiner and including a fingerprint specialist, a photographer, a property clerk, and a stenographer.

Gasoline traces found at the club revealed the malevolent hand of an arsonist. All this carnage had resulted from a lover's quarrel, with one man enraged because his young woman friend had gone to the club with someone else. Eventually three men, none older than eighteen, were convicted of the crime and sentenced to life imprisonment.

Seven weeks later, DiMaio had to deal with the victims of yet another major fire, when the Blue Angel nightclub on East Fifty-fourth Street was engulfed by flames on December 18, 1975. This was a case where a prompt call to the emergency services might have averted catastrophe; instead, the staff took it upon themselves to attempt to extinguish a small fire backstage, only for it to spread within minutes to the public areas. Pandemonium ensued. Five of the victims were found huddled together in the ladies' room. All had died from smoke inhalation, DiMaio found, with none suffering serious burns.

Unbelievably, as the new year dawned, the vacuum at the top of the OCME had still not been filled. The bickering dragged on until spring, when the announcement of a fresh Civil Service examination held out the hope of a resolution at last. Three candidates only sat the test, DiMaio and Baden, and a newcomer, Dr. Elliot Gross, the forty-one-year-old chief medical examiner of Connecticut. When the scores were tallied, DiMaio and Baden were even with 91, six points ahead of Gross. The examining board decided that because of seniority and veteran's credit, DiMaio should be placed first, and it was assumed that he would finally be named to the $39,563-a-year post. But he still had plenty of enemies. Helpern had originally favored DiMaio's candidacy—anything to stop Baden—until the acting CME booted Helpern out of his office at 520 First Avenue. Now the former chief turned his fire on DiMaio as well. Rumors persisted that Helpern had even attempted to influence the two tests. Certainly Helpern's allies at the New York University's Department of Forensic Medicine ganged up against

DiMaio. In a bombastic statement, they expressed displeasure at the prospect of DiMaio—whom they cruelly derided as underqualified—getting the top post. According to anonymous sources deep within the Office of the Chief Medical Examiner itself, the NYU school had threatened to sever its connection with the office if DiMaio was appointed head. (Significantly, no one could ever be found to confirm this scurrilous rumor.) Muddying the waters still further was the announcement that the City Health Commissioner, Lowell E. Berlin, had, very publicly, thrown his weight behind the third-place candidate, Gross. If true, this made a mockery of the concept of an open examination.

Despite all these setbacks, DiMaio rode out the challenges and seemed just on the verge of confirmation when another bombshell struck: rumors had reached City Hall about some alleged irregularities in his business dealings. The accusations, like so many leveled against DiMaio at this time, were suspiciously nebulous. This time the suggestion was that DiMaio *might* have acted improperly by accepting nearly four thousand dollars for collating a series of statistics from the OCME's office for a California research group.

On July 30, 1976, DiMaio decided to clear the air. He went to Scoppetta and said that he "did not want the appointment with a cloud over my head," adding that while his reputation was being investigated, he would voluntarily relinquish the title of acting chief.

DiMaio was confident of exoneration and his confidence proved well placed. After a short inquiry, Scoppetta went to the mayor and announced that the practice of pathologists' accepting fees for outside work was well established and that he had found nothing to bar DiMaio from being appointed permanently. Finally, DiMaio had made it. On August 19, 1976—more than two and a half years after Helpern's retirement—New York once again had a chief medical examiner.

Even Baden professed himself delighted by the outcome. He waxed enthusiastic for the press, lauding DiMaio as a "devoted family man, which is a definite plus in this profession." Baden could afford to be magnanimous. At the back of his mind was the knowledge that unless DiMaio pulled any Helpern-like stunts with the Civil Service Commission, he had less than two years in office before the mandatory retirement age of sixty-five. His time would surely come.

For DiMaio it was work as usual. And that meant dealing with disasters. In the early hours of May 25, 1977, the third major fire to hit New York in eighteen months broke out at the Everard Baths on West 28th Street, a bathhouse that catered to homosexuals. Nine men died in the blaze. One firefighter described three of the victims as being so badly burnt that "you couldn't even tell they were bodies." The baths had a notorious reputation for promiscuity. In flagrant violation of its operating permit, many of the building's rooms had been turned into dormitories where patrons stayed overnight. Because many of the clientele had booked in under false names, it made identifying the bodies even more problematic than usual, but within a matter of just days the OCME had put names to all the victims.

The final year of DiMaio's tenure was mercifully uneventful. As 1978 unfolded, and DiMaio reached the mandatory retirement age of sixty-five, it became obvious that there would be no extension. During his brief tenure in charge he had been subjected to a relentless and at times spiteful bombardment by the press and colleagues alike. His retirement, which began on May 1, 1978, gave him the opportunity to enter private practice as a consultant and to distill the fruits of his long career into a textbook called *Forensic Pathology* (New York: Elsevier, 1989), cowritten with his son, Dr. Vincent DiMaio, the chief medical examiner for Bexar County in Texas.

But if DiMaio thought that leaving office meant putting all the OCME's cares and woes behind him, he was gravely mistaken. There were plenty of clouds to darken his retirement. In 1980 the *New York Times* revealed that DiMaio had been plagued by misdeeds at the OCME during his time in office. Those old stories about kickbacks from funeral homes were resurrected, with one OCME supervisor admitting to the Department of Investigation that he had accepted money. In return for his cooperation, the unnamed supervisor had been granted immunity from prosecution. Other names were mentioned, but no one was ever charged. A different level of dishonesty surfaced over the theft of twenty-nine pounds of marijuana from a triple-locked safe in the toxicology laboratory on the fourth floor. The marijuana, with a street value of twelve thousand dollars, had been found in the apartment of a lawyer who had committed suicide and was being kept to determine if it had played any part in the suicide's death. An OCME employee was allowed to resign after making financial restitution to the family of the deceased. DiMaio admitted having been aware of these transgressions and had passed the accusations to the Department of Investigation, but he insisted that "the end results were never given to me."

The 1970s had been a brutal decade for the OCME. Allegations of kickbacks, incompetence, other irregularities, and Machiavellian levels of interdepartmental bloodletting and intrigue meant that it was rarely out of the headlines. With DiMaio retired, most believed that rather than run the highly contentious selection process all over again, Mayor Edward Koch would save time and tax dollars and simply award the top job to the former second-place candidate, Dr. Michael Baden. With Baden in the top job, the fervent prayer was that, at last, some sense of stability would be restored to the tumultuous office. It was some hope.

FIVE

A SURGICAL REMOVAL

It all looked so preordained. After years of scrapping with bulldog tenacity to the top of the heap, Dr. Michael Baden was finally going to fulfill his apparent destiny. The official nod came on April 27, 1978. Mayor Edward Koch called a news conference to announce, as anticipated, that Baden was his choice to be the new chief medical examiner for New York City. At age forty-three, Baden was the youngest person ever appointed to the post; with good health and a fair shake from Gracie Mansion he could expect to take the OCME into the twenty-first century. Somewhat overlooked in all the excitement, however, was the fact that Baden's appointment was *provisional*. Like Gonzales and DiMaio, the man from the Bronx would have to serve a probationary period before confirmation. At the time, no one thought anything of it; just a formality, was the received wisdom.

For Baden, the promotion fattened up his paycheck to the tune of $50,000 a year, a 30 percent raise over what he had been earning as a deputy, and gave him control over a department that had grown to a full-time staff of 151 and an annual budget of $3.5 million. It also provided the front center stage that he yearned for. Of all the men who've worn the crown at the Office of the Chief Medical Examiner, none has sat so comfortably in the media spotlight as Baden. By his own admission he reveled in the attention. "I liked the public side of it," he wrote later about the job. "The excitement and the immediacy of it appealed to me."

Bronx born and Brooklyn raised, Baden was educated at City College, where he majored in biology and chemistry. In his spare time, he acted as editor-in-chief of the *Campus*, the student newspaper, a sideline so intriguing that it tempted him into seriously considering an application to the Columbia Graduate School of Journalism. But medicine won out, and after graduating Phi Beta Kappa in 1955, he went on to the New York University Medical School. Even in his first year as a student, he found himself drawn toward the morgue at Bellevue. On one of his first visits to the cavernous autopsy room he saw a group of nervous-looking doctors all huddled together, while across the room, in splendid isolation, Milton Helpern was performing an autopsy. The collective trepidation of the onlookers hinged on fears that the man on the slab had succumbed to smallpox, a disease long thought to have been eradicated in New York City. Baden shrugged off their concerns. Calmly and with great deliberation, he walked over and began observing more closely. Helpern, somewhat taken aback—not many young medical students were remotely interested in pathology, and fewer still were prepared to accept the kind of risk that Baden had just undertaken—gratefully accepted the newcomer's offer to assist as he took samples. The fact that subsequent chemical analysis showed that the man had actually died of chicken pox made not a jot of difference to Helpern. He'd been mightily impressed by Baden's chutzpah and soon took the youngster under his wing.

After graduating from NYU in 1959, Baden continued to

moonlight at the OCME—he was not allowed to process the murder cases, which were understandably regarded as far too important for a novice—before joining permanently in 1965. With Helpern as his mentor, Baden's star began its inexorable rise, and in 1968, he and Helpern combined forces to coedit a medico-legal textbook.* Articles and reports flowed from the young man's pen. Many dealt with the calamitous impact that drugs and alcohol were having on the health of America. By 1970 Baden was the undoubted wunderkind of American medical jurisprudence: a recognized international authority on the effects of substance abuse; a deputy chief medical examiner at the early age of thirty-five; and he had what looked, to outsiders at least, the inside track with Dr. Milton Helpern. Already he was being mentioned as a possible successor when "the Chief" decided to call it a day.

And then the bubble burst.

For some reason, Helpern turned against the younger man. As we have already seen, the last few years of Helpern's reign, and a hefty chunk of his retirement, were dominated by his unrelenting determination to thwart Baden's chances of succession. Since most recollections of Helpern highlight his kindness and humanity—Professor Bernard Knight, Helpern's biographer, caught the general mood when he wrote, "Above all else, [Helpern] was a gentleman, and a gentle man"—such out-of-character malevolence obviously had its roots in something bordering on the cataclysmic. Most mutual acquaintances dated the feud back to the late sixties, when Baden's then wife, Dr. Judianne Densen-Gerber, ran a controversial drug treatment program called Odyssey House. Like her husband, Densen-Gerber was not temperamentally disposed to the concealing of lights under bushels. She was brash, belligerently outspoken,

---

* Tomio Watanabe, *The Atlas of Legal Medicine,* with the editorial assistance of Milton Helpern and Michael Baden (Philadelphia: Lippincott, 1968).

a regular headline-generating machine. Her well-publicized attacks on rival state and city drug rehabilitation programs infuriated Helpern, who, as part of the city health apparatus, bridled at being criticized, however obliquely, by an underling's spouse. Helpern suspected—and later events tended to bear him out—that Densen-Gerber was more interested in financing a fancy lifestyle than in helping addicts, and he made his antipathy toward her brutally apparent.* Trapped between two warring factions, Baden inevitably caught some of the flak intended for his wife. As we have seen, Helpern's frigid hostility toward Baden did not dissipate with retirement, but Baden had youth on his side, enabling him to ride out the attacks with a certain élan. And in 1978, when the top job became vacant for the second time in two years, his longtime bête noire was dead. This time a clear run to the winning post beckoned.

Baden brought enormous credentials to his new job. He was on the faculties of three medical schools: Columbia, New York University, and Albert Einstein College at Yeshiva University in the Bronx. In addition, he taught courses on law and medicine at New York Law School. There was not a better qualified forensic pathologist in America. He first rose to national prominence in the aftermath of the Attica prison riot in September 1971, when the autopsies that he and others performed on the thirty-nine victims helped defuse the lurid myth that several hostages had had their throats slit. (All ten hostages who died were shot accidentally by troops). This led to him serving on the New York State Correction Medical Review Board, where it was his duty to investigate deaths in prisons. His appointment didn't please everyone. Many found his independence jarring. Baden was not about to button his lip for

---

* In January 1982 following a two-year investigation, Judianne Densen-Gerber agreed to repay New York City twenty thousand dollars in excessive and unjustified personal expenses she had charged to Odyssey House.

anyone; if he found any suspicious circumstances, he didn't hesitate to say so.

Candor can either help or hinder a career, and in Baden's case there was no doubt that the frankness pendulum swung decidedly in his favor. Right from his earliest days, he'd always been a lightning rod for controversy, and when he took over the reins at the OCME it was no different. Already he was embroiled in the most controversial case of his career.

CASE FILE:
Dr. Mario Jascalevich (1978)

The whispered rumors had begun doing the rounds of New York City newsrooms in the mid-1960s: Something weird was going on at a small, unnamed hospital in New Jersey. Patients were dying for no good reason—murdered, so the story went, by a doctor who had resigned from the hospital under a cloud. Inevitably, such talk revived memories of another homicidal medico, Dr. Carl Coppolino, who was currently serving a life sentence in Florida. Was it really possible that in Coppolino's adopted home state of New Jersey another murderous physician was at large? Try as they might—and to be honest, no media organization did try that hard—no one could nail down the facts. In the late sixties, several journalists heard the whispers, only to decide that the details were too vague, the case just too old, and probably not worth pursuing.

And there the story languished; interesting, no doubt, but probably nothing more than overwrought hospital gossip. Lives moved on and memories faded. Until June 1975. That was when a letter found its way to the *New York Times*. The editor thought it interesting enough to pass on to Myron Farber, a top-rate investigative journalist who regularly covered medical stories. Farber scanned the letter, which came from a New York writer and PR consultant named Eileen Milling, with an appropriately skeptical eye. In the letter, Ms. Milling claimed that a surgeon whom she refused to name, working at a hospital that she declined to identify, had gone on a two-year killing spree that left as many as thirty or forty patients dead. She described it as a "case of a warped mind playing chess with other people's lives."

At first glance the claims seemed unbelievable, the product of a febrile, possibly even deranged imagination. Yet when interviewed, Ms. Milling came across as balanced and credible, clearly not a crank, even if she was maddeningly evasive about specifics and names. Farber decided to go digging. First, he needed to identify the hospital. Trawling down through records and jogging often reluctant memories was a gargantuan task that occupied several months. Eventually a contact in the world of forensic toxicology recalled a similar story, something about strange happenings at a small private hospital out in New Jersey. The toxicologist couldn't provide any more leads, unfortunately, as it had all happened so long ago.

In the fall of 1966 Stanley Harris was a doctor at the end of his professional tether. He'd only joined the staff at Riverdell Hospital in Oradell, northern New Jersey, in February of that year, but since that time he had been plunged into a slough of utter despair. Five patients, none of whom had life-threatening illnesses, had gone under Harris's surgical knife, and all had died unexpectedly. The first had been four-year-old Nancy Savino. She had been admitted to Riverdell on March 19, 1966, suffering from suspected acute appendicitis. When Harris cut into the child's abdomen, he found nothing wrong with the appendix and identified the cause of the pain as a cluster of cysts that he removed from the mesentery, the tissue connecting the intestine to the abdominal wall. The operation was uncomplicated and went without a hitch.

Less than twenty-four hours later Nancy was dead. The end came at 8:15 A.M. on March 21. It seemed inexplicable. An autopsy could shed no light and the stated cause of death was "undetermined physiological reaction." All surgeons have either experienced or have heard of such isolated tragedies, but Harris was shaken to his core. His only hope was to put the disaster behind him and move on.

Except that one month later it happened again.

On April 22, Margaret Henderson, age twenty-six, had also been admitted with abdominal pain, but an exploratory incision, carried out by Harris, had revealed no abnormalities. After a comfortable night, Mrs. Henderson was seen by a nurse at 6:30 A.M. the following day and found to be "tense and apprehensive." At 7:30 A.M. she was given a bath. Half an hour later, according to the chart, she was unable to swallow and complained of pain in her legs and chest. Another doctor, not Harris, put Mrs. Henderson on an IV drip. At some time during the next forty-five minutes, a third doctor also examined Mrs. Henderson. Despite all this attention, at 8:45 A.M. she died. This time an autopsy was able to disclose a viable cause of death: acute hepatic necrosis, a severe and rapid form of liver failure. Harris was shattered. Twice in a month he had lost patients unexpectedly. And he wasn't alone.

When Dr. Robert J. Briski joined Riverdell as a surgeon in May 1965, he had brought with him a lengthy list of loyal patients, one expected to generate handsome revenues for the hospital. An unwritten assumption on Briski's part was that his appointment would include unrestricted surgical privileges, but within a month he was called in by the hospital's board of directors and told that his surgical performance had been downgraded to level B, which meant that, for major operations, he would require the supervision of an A-rated surgeon. Briski had bridled under this slight but continued without comment.

In May 1966, and again another three months later, Briski lost patients on whom he had operated. Neither procedure was especially difficult and both patients were expected to make full recoveries. But it hadn't worked out that way. Briski, like Harris, was stunned, and over the course of that summer, the problems for both doctors only multiplied, as their patients continued dying for no apparent reason, to the point where some began wondering if Riverdell was jinxed.

Harris had no time for any of this voodoo nonsense. These unexplained deaths, he was certain, owed nothing to ill fortune and everything to human intervention. And there wasn't a shred of doubt in his mind as to who that person might be. On October 25, 1966, unable to bottle up his suspicions any longer, Harris went to see his bosses. What he had to say would shake the hospital board to its foundations.

Six days later, Harris was in full gumshoe mode, secretly breaking into the suspect's locker. Inside he found eighteen ampoules, either empty or partially filled, of curare, and "a large syringe loaded with a needle on it." Although Harris shuddered at the discovery, part of him heaved a huge sigh of relief. Vindication had never tasted so sweet. Here was rock-solid evidence—to his way of thinking, at least—that Riverdell's top surgeon was a mass murderer.

It is a curious fact that doctors probably account for more serial killers than all the other white-collar professions combined. From Edward Pritchard and William Palmer in Victorian England, to San Francisco's J. Milton Bowers in the 1880s, and his contemporary Neil Cream who poisoned victims on both sides of the Atlantic, to the businesslike Marcel Petiot who gassed Parisian refugees during World War II after stripping them of their valuables, right through to recent times when a young intern, Michael Swango, poisoned his way across America first and then Africa, doctors feature in the serial killer statistics with startling frequency. The pinnacle of this medical mayhem, as far as we know, was reached with the quite extraordinarily lethal Dr. Harold Shipman, who over several decades murdered an estimated 254 patients (some put the death toll much higher) who attended his surgery in Manchester, England. Shipman's longevity as a killer can be attributed to one very basic human quality: trust. It would never occur to most patients that the person treating them might be more interested in extinguishing their life than in saving it. The almost mythic bond that can exist between doctor and patient offered Shipman a deadly immunity. Most of his victims were elderly women whom he had been treating for years. All were dispatched with a single overdose of morphine, with no more thought or concern than if he had been killing a fly. Eventually the sheer scale and frequency of Shipman's patient mortality rate did cause some colleagues to harbor suspicions about the avuncular doctor, but for most it was a fleeting doubt, rejected as quickly as it had occurred, pushed away to a dark corner of the mind. After all, doctors don't go around killing people for no reason . . . do they? Dr. Stanley Harris certainly thought so. Only evil intent, he felt, could explain the presence of so much curare in the suspect's locker.

Beloved by detective story writers ever since the 1920s—Agatha Christie, a trained nurse, always had a particularly soft spot for this most sinister of toxins—curare's deadly qualities were first discovered by the indigenous hunters of the Amazon basin. Monkeys might have been a prized delicacy in the village cooking pot, but their dazzling upper tree canopy gymnastics did make them damnably difficult to bring down with a blowgun. Even if the hunter's aim were true, it didn't always guarantee a tasty meal. Often the shock of being struck by a dart would induce in the monkey a cadaveric spasm—a kind of instant rigor mortis—causing its fingers to clamp viselike around a branch and enabling the beast to hang on for grim death, as it were. Scores of feet below in the undergrowth, the hungry hunter was left to gnash his teeth in frustration.

And then one day, some inventive soul realized that by dipping his dart head in a gluey liquid distilled from various local plants, when the monkey was hit, instead of becoming rigidly taut, its muscles would relax as if by magic, causing the stupefied or dead animal to tumble from the tree and into the hunter's grateful clutches.

This hunting aid was prepared from the bark scrapings of the *Chondodendron* and *Strychnos toxifera* plants. These were boiled for about two days, then strained and evaporated until one was left with a dark, heavy paste with a very bitter taste. Testing the brew's potency was rudimentary, to say the least: simply count the number of jumps a frog could manage after being pricked. The hunters called this substance variously *woorari*, *woorali*, and *urari*, all local words meaning "poison," and it is from these that we get the word *curare*.

Because curare production represented a source of considerable wealth to the various tribes, it was regarded as far too valuable for use in warfare and was kept solely for hunting. Darts, tipped with curare and fired with astonishing accuracy through blowguns made of hollow bamboo, would strike their target. Then it was a matter of waiting. A bird would ordinarily die in one or two minutes, small mammals might take ten minutes, and large mammals could survive as long as twenty minutes.

The first outsiders to note this deadly use of curare were invading Spanish conquistadors in the sixteenth century, but hundreds of years would pass before its medical properties were realized. The breakthrough came in 1811, when the pioneering British surgeon Sir Benjamin Brodie noticed a strange phenomenon: during curare poisoning the heart continues to beat, even after breathing stops. He puzzled over what could cause this effect. The answer would not be forthcoming until much later in the nineteenth century when Claud Bernard, a French physiologist, discovered that the main active constituent of curare is tubocurarine. By experiment, Bernard worked out that curare causes paralysis by blocking transmission between nerve and muscle, without affecting nerve conduction or muscle contraction directly. Bernard's findings intrigued the surgical profession. For years they'd searched for some means to keep patients absolutely still during delicate operations and curare seemed to fit the bill. The injection of curare during anesthesia produces a profound relaxation of the muscles (because the drug also relaxes the respiratory system to the point of standstill, patients administered tubocurarine have to be artificially ventilated). Typically, a dose of 20 to 30 mg induces a paralysis lasting thirty minutes. The great benefit of tubocurarine is that the patient requires less anesthesia, thus reducing risk and greatly improving the postoperative recovery rate.

In the right hands, curare is a lifesaver. Used willfully, it's one of the most efficient killers on the planet. Larger than recommended doses are almost always fatal within forty seconds, with death owing to respiratory failure. What makes curare poisoning so ghastly is that the victim is very much awake and aware of what is happening until the loss of consciousness. Doctors who have volunteered to take curare under supervised conditions have described the ordeal as horrifying, knowing they were suffocating and near death, yet being unable either to call out or gesture. A more horrible death would be hard to imagine.

Much the most insidious side effect of curare, though, is the way it disappears from the human body after it does its deadly work. And it is this quality, more than any other, that has enhanced curare's reputation as the perfect poison, virtually impossible to detect, even with an autopsy and sophisticated toxicological analysis.

Given this background, Dr. Stanley Harris's shocked reaction when he found the half-empty ampoules of curare was entirely understandable. Surely now, the hospital board would have to investigate his suspicions and look into the meteoric career of Riverdell's head of surgery, Dr. Mario Enrique Jascalevich?

The slight and bespectacled man from Argentina had been born in Buenos Aires, on August 27, 1927, the son of Italian-Yugoslav parents. After graduating from medical school, he traveled to the United States to take up an internship at Passaic General Hospital, and in 1956 began a four-year surgical residency at New York's Polyclinic Medical School. With his residency complete, he joined the surgeons' staff of Christ Hospital in Jersey City. On July 12, 1961, three months after becoming an American citizen, he received his full medical license. In January of the following year, he married Nora Caperan, also from Argentina, and a talented pianist who studied at the world-renowned Juilliard School of Music in New York City.

Jascalevich's connection with Riverdell began in November 1962, when he joined the staff as the sole general surgeon. At the time Riverdell was a small, privately run hospital overlooking the Oradell Reservoir in northern New Jersey. In its short existence—it had only been founded three years earlier—the hospital had gained an enviable reputation for providing top-quality medical care. When Jascalevich joined the staff, Riverdell had about fifty beds and plans to expand rapidly.

No one doubted Jascalevich's technical excellence. In the operating room he was fast, superbly efficient, and imaginative (in the early 1960s he had invented a stapler, used to suppress bleeding during operations, that still bears his name). The problem was that nobody liked him. He had an abrasive, hackle-raising personality.

Junior doctors who came to him for guidance and consultation on various surgical problems all too often found themselves swatted away like unwelcome flies. They soon learned that Jascalevich was brutally proprietorial with his expertise and begrudged sharing it with those whom he regarded as his inferiors. As the only surgeon at Riverdell with full operating privileges, he was much the biggest fish in a very small pond. That was how he liked it, and that was how he wanted it to remain.

But Riverdell was expanding fast, and all that explosive growth put an intolerable strain on the staff. In the summer of 1965, the hospital board decided to boost the surgical team, and to this end, appointed Dr. Robert J. Briski. Warm and outgoing, Briski was the complete antithesis of Jascalevich, popular with other staff members, prepared to share his knowledge, always available should an emergency crop up. He was also an excellent surgeon. At first all went well. The hospital board was delighted with Briski, especially with the handsome difference that his prodigious patient list made to the hospital's bottom line, but it soon became clear that his arrival hadn't pleased everyone. Jascalevich was icily furious and made no attempt to mask his anger. Personality clashes exist in all walks of life, nowhere more so than among the kind of high-octane egos that populate the operating room, so Briski just shrugged, decided it was one of those things, and got on with his job.

Continued expansion—by now Riverdell had eighty-one beds— meant that in April of the following year the hospital board hired another general surgeon, Dr. Stanley Harris. Jascalevich, who had lobbied hard against this appointment, only to be outvoted, was forced to sit and smart as his two junior surgeons began taking on more of the operations.

Shortly thereafter, the patients began dying unexpectedly. The autopsy results were vague and inconclusive, usually attributing the deaths to postoperative complications, but for young doctors trained to save lives, that summer of 1966 was a savage time. Briski's confidence plunged, bottoming out in August when he lost two patients in the space of a week. Harris, tougher minded, though no less traumatized, decided that if the pathologists couldn't find what was killing his patients, then he would.

He began by reviewing his cases. In July he had operated on Ira Holster for a diseased gallbladder. Within twenty-four hours Holster was dead. Acute coronary occlusion, said the death certificate. Then came a hiatus for the remainder of the summer. Relieved but still racking his brains to find the cause—after all, his career was on the line; many more unexplained "losses" such as these and no insurance company would touch him—Harris pored over the patients' records and charts. Suddenly, a glaring fact leapt off the page at him. Throughout August and September, during which time none of Harris's patients had died in peculiar circumstances, one person was conspicuously absent from the hospital: Dr. Mario Jascalevich. It might, of course, be nothing more than coincidence, except that Harris uncovered yet another warning flag. Just days after Jascalevich returned from vacation, one of Harris's patients had died suddenly, and the chart showed that Jascalevich had visited him shortly beforehand. Harris frowned. There was no sound medical reason for Jascalevich to be there, his presence had not been requested, and such a visit was a clear violation of protocol. Then Harris's eyes grew wider. By cross-referencing the records, he saw that *all* the patients who had died in mysterious circumstances had received a visit from Jascalevich shortly before their death. Coincidence could not explain such a bizarre chain of events; all Harris could conclude was that Riverdell's senior surgeon was deliberately killing patients. Harris took his concerns to Dr. Allan Lans, a member of the hospital's board of directors. Shortly after this came the dramatic opening of Jascalevich's locker.

Discovery of the curare prompted the board to immediately pass its suspicions to Guy Calissi, the Bergen County district attorney. This was a remarkable step. In the ordinary course of events, most members of the medical profession would rather walk barefoot over hot coals than accuse colleagues of malpractice. Their readiness to turn a blind eye is largely a matter of self-preservation. No one wants to jeopardize a hard-won career by being branded as a troublemaker or whistle-blower. After all, the reasoning goes, the next time it might be your name under the microscope. For instance, in the 1960s plenty of co-workers knew that Charles Friedgood was a lousy doctor who butchered patients, long before he got round to pumping his wife full of Demerol, but not one was prepared to pass their concerns to the relevant medical boards. As a result, despite being discreetly fired from a string of hospitals, the Long Island MD still kept finding jobs, fueling the egomania and sense of omnipotence that would eventually turn him from bungling physician to cold-blooded killer.

For the Riverdell board to act so decisively meant that it had to be very sure of Jascalevich's guilt. And after reading the report, the district attorney's office agreed. Calissi and his assistant, Fred Galda, seized the contents of Jascalevich's locker and hauled him in for questioning. The surgeon, bland and confident, offered a perfectly plausible explanation for the curare. In 1963–64, while a lecturer at Seton Hall Medical School, he had received a five-hundred-dollar grant to develop a new type of stomach feeding tube. About three hundred dollars of the funds were used to purchase twelve dogs for experimentation. Although curare was not used in this research, he claimed that he had retained his interest in dog experimentation. When the grant money ran out, the fifty-thousand-dollar-a-year doctor protested he was unable to afford to buy more dogs in the conventional way, and that this led him to obtain animals in an "unofficial" way. (He claimed that by tipping attendants after hours at the medical school, he could obtain "dying dogs" left strapped down on tables by other researchers who had completed their experiments.) For this new round of experiments, which included biopsies, Jascalevich said he required curare.

Calissi discovered that between September 21, 1965, and September 28, 1966, Jascalevich bought twenty-four 10 cc vials of purified curare from the General Surgical Supply Company of West New York. (As little as 5 cc's of the standard solution of purified curare can be lethal without artificial respiration.) When questioned about the highly unusual string of deaths at Riverdell, Jascalevich empathized with Briski and Harris, because such tragedies were an inevitable corollary of surgical life; any doctor could lose patients in such a way. He attributed it to a dreadful run of coincidences.

Clearly the hospital board was uncomfortable with Jascalevich's story and also with his presence. In November 1966 they admonished him for endangering the hospital's accreditation by failing to call meetings of the surgical department and for not providing adequate coverage at the hospital when it was considered necessary. As later events would demonstrate, Jascalevich always knew when to cut and run. In a surprise move, he tendered his resignation, on condition that no blame be attached to his conduct and that the inquiry be buried. The grateful hospital agreed, and in February 1967 Jascalevich duly resigned.

At about the same time, Calissi and Galda completed their investigation and concluded that there was insufficient evidence to pursue a case against Jascalevich. Harris succeeded him as chief surgeon and the following year performed in excess of four hundred operations. There was not one suspicious death. With Jascalevich's departure, the Riverdell "jinx" appeared to have vanished.

Almost eight years passed. Memories of the dubious doctor began to fade. Until that letter was delivered to the *New York Times*.

Although Farber had tracked down the hospital in question, the odds were still stacked against him. Loosening up tongues after so long a period of time was never going to be easy and for several months he became used to doors being slammed shut in his face and his phone calls going unanswered. Someone less diligent might have called it quits. But Farber refused to back off. And then he hit the journalistic jackpot: a source who had compiled a dossier contemporaneously with events at the hospital. What this dossier—labeled "Doctor X" by its author—had to say would change Farber's life and the course of American journalism forever. It would also lead to the OCME performing some of its finest, most innovative work, as it battled to unravel one of the most complex and sensational cases in its long history.

The dossier contained not just full details of the hospital's accusations but copies of the DA's investigation, the autopsy reports, and, critically, the name of the medical school where Jascalevich claimed to have done the illegal experiments on dogs. As Farber leafed through the paperwork he could scarcely believe his eyes. No one on the investigating team had bothered to corroborate Jascalevich's story about the dog experiments at Seton Hall Medical School; they had just taken the doctor at his word. Farber set about remedying this lapse. Three staff members at the school agreed to talk. None could recall Jascalevich's performing any alleged experiment on "dying dogs" left strapped down by other researchers who had completed their experiments. One attendant, Lee Henderson, swore that he had never received a tip from anyone in return for providing dogs "in any condition" at the school, nor did he know of anyone who had. Obviously, if true, this cast serious doubts on Jascalevich's stated reason for having the curare.

Farber continued digging and found that twenty-five patients had died at Riverdell during the time under review. Of these deaths, he wondered how many might reasonably be regarded as suspicious. Like most reporters who covered the medical beat in New York City, Farber had good contacts at the Office of the Chief Medical Examiner, and he called Dr. Michael Baden, at this time a deputy medical examiner. Baden agreed to look at the records. Eliminating those cases where the patient was obviously dying of a serious illness—such as cancer or heart disease—left him with thirteen deaths worthy of closer investigation. Of these, he isolated nine whose illnesses made it highly unlikely that they would have succumbed to sudden death. In the absence of any other indicator, to Baden's way of thinking, the likeliest cause of death with these victims was poisoning.

Baden was no fool. He knew that seeking to reopen a decade-old case would involve treading on a number of highly sensitive toes. Those doctors who had signed the original death certificates would want to defend their diagnoses; Calissi and Galda, both now elevated to the bench, would rebut any suggestion that they had taken their duties lightly; and it would also mean raising doubts about the original autopsies, performed by Dr. Edwin H. Albano, the New Jersey state medical examiner, and Dr. Lawrence Denson, Bergen County's medical examiner. A new investigation would cast a cloud over all of them.

Still, Baden decided to press ahead. Given the circumstances of the case, he felt that if the victims had been poisoned, then curare was most likely the agent of their destruction. But tempering this suspicion was the nagging realization that chances of finding curare in any body tissues after so long an interval of time were vanishingly small. Despite these reservations, Baden filed an affidavit with the Superior Court in Bergen County that, although notably light on any evidence that murder had been done, nonetheless did contain the consent for exhumations from family members of five alleged victims. A judge duly signed the order.

News of Baden's intervention lit a fire under the investigation. Suddenly every media organization in the tristate area wanted a piece of the mysterious doctor in New Jersey. (One local paper in Bergen County reportedly assigned no fewer than ten journalists to the story.) All needed to tread carefully. Because Jascalevich was still practicing medicine locally—he had operating privileges at two hospitals in Jersey City—and had not been charged with any offense, fears of transgressing the laws of criminal libel kept his name out of the public domain. This actually proved to be an editorial godsend. Lurid headlines about a potentially murderous "Doctor X" put thousands on newspaper circulations in a way that no mere name could have achieved. Media clamor reached a fever pitch as Baden readied himself to supervise the first exhumation.

The first body disinterred was that of Nancy Savino. The reasoning for this was quite calculated. Research has shown that curare tends to concentrate in the cartilage and in the soft tissues, both of which are among the earliest to decompose. Because Nancy had been embalmed, Baden felt there was a good chance the analysts would find something.

Just after dawn on January 13, 1976, gravediggers at a cemetery in Bergen County shoveled away the snow and began hacking at the frozen topsoil. Early starts are standard procedure when it comes to exhumations. The main reason is economic. If the body can be dug up, examined, and returned to the ground the same day, it costs less. Also, the emotional wear and tear on family and friends is kept to a minimum.

Two hours of backbreaking toil brought its reward; the cast-iron casket came into view. Some of Baden's anxiety thawed ever so slightly when he saw that the casket had been encased in a cement vault. This would keep out any water and hopefully retard the level of decomposition. With as much dignity as was humanly possible, the gravediggers slowly exposed Nancy's casket to the bleak January light. It was taken immediately to the OCME's Decomposed Room, where Baden performed the autopsy.

Every move he made came under the lynx-eyed scrutiny of Dr. Edwin H. Albano. When it comes to investigating crimes, the rivalry between New York and the Garden State has always been intense, and Albano was understandably miffed over a perception that he had been benched through incompetence. He was already smarting under thinly veiled press allegations that the New Jersey politico-legal machine had somehow whitewashed Jascalevich back in 1966; now he had to endure the humiliation of sitting on the sidelines while some out-of-towner reviewed his work. Albano's resentment wasn't wholly parochial. He had a serious ally in Manhattan.

The biggest beast of all in the forensic science jungle, Milton Helpern, might have been retired for two years, since which time he'd been plagued by the long-term ill health that would kill him in 1977, but his presence still cast a long shadow over the entire medico-legal community. Privately, and not so privately at times, the former CME had continued his vendetta with Baden, still convinced that he had been railroaded out of office, and he now saw the Savino exhumation as his chance to get in some shots of his own. The way that Baden told it, Helpern grumbled to anyone who would listen that exhuming bodies after such a passage of time was a monumental waste of time and tax dollars. All they would find after ten years, he confidently predicted, were a few bones and an oozy putrescence, certainly nothing to offer the toxicologists any hope. Helpern had firsthand experience of the difficulties in detecting obscure drug traces, when, back in the sixties, he had moved heaven and earth to prove that another doctor, Carl Coppolino, had used a curare-like poison to rid himself of a troublesome wife. A Florida jury had finally bought Helpern's version of events, but it had been a struggle. On that occasion, Helpern had been dealing with a recently buried body. What Baden was attempting, he thought, bordered on the ridiculous.

It was time to find out. A hush of anticipation hung in the air as the coffin lid was slowly raised. Then came a gasp. Nobody had expected this. Baden could scarcely believe the body's quite remarkable state of preservation, far beyond anything he had dared hoped for. The pink crinoline dress that Nancy Savino had been buried in was so clean and crisp it might have just been laundered, and on her chest, exactly where her parents had placed them, lay a cross and a withered rose. The cement vault had excluded the air and allowed the already embalmed corpse to become almost mummified. When Baden studied the abdomen he saw, to his delight, that the sutures that had been inserted after the operation ten years earlier were still in place. In all likelihood, this meant that the organs and tissues could be analyzed. Which was just as well, because in the four hours that Baden spent examining the body he found no evidence of gross abnormality, nothing to contradict the findings of the first autopsy. Everything now rested in the hands of the toxicologists.

Attuned to professional sensitivities and eager to stifle any possible subsequent accusations of bias, Baden opted to divide the tissue samples among four toxicology labs. The OCME's resident chemists, Dr. Donald Hoffman and Dr. Lorenzo Galante, would handle the "home" analysis, while other samples were dispatched to laboratories in New Jersey, Long Island, and California. In selecting New Jersey, Baden wasn't merely observing the proprieties, he was also firing another bullet in his ongoing feud with Helpern. The New Jersey chief toxicologist was none other than

Dr. Richard Coumbis, formerly of the New York Office of the Chief Medical Examiner, and someone who had crossed swords with Helpern over the controversial Coppolino case. At that time the director of the OCME toxicology department was Dr. Charles Umberger, a close ally of Helpern's, and Coumbis had never been happy with Umberger's methodology for establishing the amount of succinylcholine in Carmela Coppolino's body. Coumbis, who made no secret of his concerns, was asked to explain himself. Shortly thereafter, he, together with two fellow skeptics in the OCME chemistry department, paid a heavy price for their perceived revolt when Helpern fired them. (Helpern always insisted their dismissal was for an unrelated issue).

When the scientists began their analysis of the Savino tissues, nothing in the medical literature told them if curare could be detected in decomposing bodies that had been buried for so long. Ordinarily, after an injection of curare, the body rids itself of about half of the drug within twenty-four hours and the rest thereafter. On the upside, there was the knowledge that curare was a relatively stable compound, one that might remain in body tissues long after death, though ten years was struggling in the dark. Although a test had recently been developed for finding curare in blood and urine, it had not previously been used on tissues, because isolating a fraction of tissue that might contain a drug such as curare was fiendishly difficult.

One of the Long Island team, Dr. Leo Dal Cortivo, the Suffolk County toxicologist, had been wrestling with this very problem for some time. By modifying a method developed in 1963 by Dr. Ellis Cohen, a Stanford anesthesiologist, Dal Cortivo set up a series of experiments to determine if curare could be detected in tissues. Hopefully these would provide the answers to four questions:

1. What happens biologically to tissue after being buried in the ground for ten years?

2. If curare was present at death, would it still be present as curare, or might it have disintegrated into other compounds? If so, which ones?

3. Even if curare was present, would modern technology be capable of analyzing such minute traces of the drug?

4. What substances, if any, present in the earth or embalming fluid might chemically interfere with the tests and give false results, either positive or negative?

Dal Cortivo began with the liver, because as the organ that breaks down most drugs, it was most likely to reveal the presence of the poison. He added water to slivers of tissue weighing less than five grams, homogenized the mixture in a blender, and then put the macerated tissue through a series of reactions with ether, methanol, dichloroethane, and a stream of nitrogen gas. He repeated this test on tissue from the kidney and the lung. Even then, Dal Cortivo didn't know if Nancy's tissue contained tubocurarine. To answer that question, he turned to thin-layer chromatography.

Although nowadays regarded as a highly sophisticated laboratory tool, chromatography has its origins in much humbler surroundings. Early European dye makers were the first to adopt its principles, albeit in a rudimentary and unintended fashion. They found they could test their dye mixtures by dipping strings or pieces of cloth into a dye vat, then watching closely as capillary action drew the solution up the inserted material, the way that water moves up tissue paper in a glass. At various intervals, bands of differing colors appeared on the material, and by studying these the manufacturers could gauge the strength of their dyes.

This phenomenon was further explored by chemists in nineteenth-century Germany, but it wasn't put on a firm scientific footing until the Russian botanist Mikhail Tsvet began a series of experiments in 1906. Eager to find a method of separating plant pigments, he developed the basic principles that apply to this day.

Tsvet's technique was simple and elegant. He packed a vertical glass column with an adsorptive material, such as alumina, silica, cellulose, or charcoal, and then added a solution of the plant pigments to the top of the column. Next, he washed the pigments through the column with an organic solvent. During the course of this migration, the pigments separated into a series of discrete colored bands on the column, divided by regions entirely free of pigments. Because Tsvet worked with colored substances, he called the method chromatography (from the Greek, meaning "color writing"). He discovered that these different bands were the result of various elements attaching themselves to the adsorbent. Because each compound has its own distinctive adsorption rate, this adherence takes place at different times, and by plotting these variances on a chart, then comparing that chart with a set of known reference values, the compound can be identified.

This is the broad definition of chromatography. Modern improvements have refined the basics into many subdisciplines, of which thin-layer chromatography is much used. In this variation, a glass plate or plastic sheet is coated with a thin layer of a finely ground adsorbent, usually silica gel or alumina, that is mixed with a binder such as starch or plaster of Paris. The test sample is deposited at a spot near one end of the plate and a suitable solvent is allowed to rise up the plate by capillary action. The components of the sample become separated from one another because of their different degrees of attachment to the coating material on the plate or sheet. The solvent is then allowed to evaporate, and the location of the separated components is identified, usually by application of reagents that form colored compounds with the substances.

When reviewing the Savino samples, Dal Cortivo put three drops—a drop of the solvent, a drop of the known tubocurarine, and a drop of the unknown sample from the exhumed tissues—on the baseline of a silica gel plate. During the next hour, each substance left a streak as it moved up the plate by capillary action. Next, he sprayed the plate with platinic iodide, which makes the known tubocurarine turn violet at a particular point. If the spot from the unknown sample turns the same shade of violet at about the same point on the plate, presumably that sample of exhumed tissue contains tubocurarine.

This was world-class chemistry. Never before had the OCME—or any other forensic facility in the United States, for that matter—engaged in such an intensive and revolutionary bout of forensic testing. Even so, Baden wasn't out of the woods yet. Because a diagnosis of curare poisoning based simply on a positive thin-layer chromatography was certain to be challenged by other scientists, he decided to push the parameters even further. He contacted experts at Columbia College of Physicians and Surgeons and a commercial lab in California and asked them to perform two other tests on the samples from Nancy Savino's body: radioimmunoassay (RIA) and mass spectrometry.

RIA is an extremely sensitive process, capable of detecting billionths of a gram of a substance. In the two decades since the RIA test was developed by Dr. Saul Berson and Dr. Rosalyn Yalow to detect insulin at the Bronx Veterans Administration Hospital, it had been applied to an ever-growing list of substances.* So far as Baden knew, no researcher had thus far used RIA to detect curare. Dr. Richard S. Matteo at Columbia agreed to run the tests.

---

* In 1977 Yalow received the Nobel Prize in Physiology or Medicine for her work in the development of RIA. Berson had died five years earlier.

The test, in simplified terms, is based on a competitive reaction between "cold" (nonradioactive) curare—if any is present in a sample of exhumed tissue—and "hot" (radioactive) curare, and between curare antigens and the rabbit curare antibody. Tables tell the researcher how much hot curare will react with the rabbit antibody in the test tube. When cold and hot curare are added to the same test tube, a competitive reaction occurs. Both the cold and hot curare compete for the limited number of binding sites with the curare antibody. Any cold curare in the exhumed tissue would take up more binding sites, thus showing the presence of curare in the samples being tested.

The final tool in Baden's by now formidable forensic armory was the mass spectrometer. Hugely sophisticated, it can analyze an organic compound and reveal its constituent parts by bombarding the sample with electrons produced by a heated wire cathode. This breaks the sample's molecules into fragments, each of which is electrically charged, then passed through an electric field, which accelerates them. A second magnetic field deflects them from their straight path into a circular one, with the heaviest fragments following a wide radius, while lighter fragments trace a path with a smaller radius.

At the end of the mass spectrometer is a narrow slit, with a detector on the other side. When the magnetic field is weak, only the lightest fragments are deflected enough to pass through this slit. Increasing the magnetic field allows heavier particles to pass through. At the same time the detector moves across the slit, producing a spectrum of the different fragments. By studying the position of each fragment within this spectrum and its intensity, it is possible to determine the chemical makeup of each constituent in the sample.

This was the science; now Dr. Robert E. Finnigan at his laboratory in Sunnyvale, near San Jose, California, needed to compare the Savino samples against a database of more than forty thousand compounds. Finnigan had no doubt that if curare was present, this technique would find it. As he put it: "If the mass spectrometer test is positive for a compound, the identification is absolute."

All these various experiments took place over several weeks. Finally, on March 5, 1976, Baden was ready to announce the results: the scientists *had* found curare in Nancy Savino's body. Just days later confirmatory traces of curare were also found in samples taken from another alleged poisoning victim, Emma Arzt.

During the interim between these two revelations, "Doctor X" was finally unmasked. The dénouement came on March 16, when Joseph C. Woodcock, the Bergen County prosecutor, announced his intention to seek indictments against Dr. Mario Jascalevich for an unspecified number of murders. All at once the previously publicity-shy Dr. Jascalevich had to deal with the uncomfortable reality that newspapers all over North America had his name plastered across their front pages.

By the time the grand jury had heard all the evidence, the eye-watering numbers of alleged murder victims being bandied about in the press had been whittled down first to single figures, then further still. This still left enough to scare the average newspaper reader out of his or her wits, as, on May 19, 1976, Jascalevich was indicted in the deaths of five patients at Riverdell. The first four were:

NANCY SAVINO, age four; operated on for removal of intestinal cysts. Died March 21, 1966. Stated cause of death: undetermined physiological reaction.

MARGARET HENDERSON, age twenty-six; admitted with abdominal pain, exploratory incision revealed no abnormalities. Died April 23, 1966. Stated cause of death: acute hepatic necrosis.

FRANK BIGGS, age fifty-nine; operated on for a bleeding peptic ulcer. Died August 28, 1966. Stated cause of death: ventricular fibrillation.

EMMA ARZT, age seventy; operated on for removal of gall-bladder. Died September 23, 1966. Stated cause of death: acute circulatory failure.

All four patients had been recovering in their rooms from surgery, after having been operated on by colleagues of Jascalevich. The fifth indictment against Jascalevich concerned seventy-three-year-old Carl Rohrbeck who had died on December 13, 1965. This case differed from the others because this time it was Jascalevich himself who had been scheduled to operate on Rohrbeck. The procedure was relatively straightforward: the repair of a ventral hernia scar. On the morning of the operation, at about 7:30 A.M., Jascalevich visited Rohrbeck in his room for a final checkup. When he emerged a few minutes later, he stunned Rohrbeck's doctor, Jay Sklar, who was already scrubbing up, by saying that he had decided to cancel the operation. Sklar, a director of the hospital, listened in utter disbelief as Jascalevich declared that he'd had a "premonition" and did not want to proceed with the operation. Sklar couldn't swallow all this mumbo jumbo. Nor could Rohrbeck. When Sklar visited him, Rohrbeck seemed bewildered. "What's holding up the show?" he asked. Through gritted teeth, Sklar explained that he would have to double-check the patient's heart, lungs, and blood pressure. All were fine. Sklar then stormed off to find Jascalevich. After a heated shouting match between the two, Jascalevich went back to reexamine Rohrbeck, at which time he started an IV drip. Upon his return, he again told Sklar that he would not operate. Before Sklar even had time to respond, a nurse rushed in with the shocking announcement that Rohrbeck was dead! An autopsy found marked arteriosclerosis in his left main artery—a long-term condition—and his death was ascribed to "coronary occlusion." Sklar was flabbergasted. It was as if Jascalevich had known that Rohrbeck was going to die.

The Jascalevich affair was a real eye-opener for most Americans. Doctors had been accused and convicted of murder before, but in each case the victim had been someone either related to or close to the physician. Never before in the United States had a doctor been accused of randomly killing strangers. For many, such an assumption tested the limits of believability. A serial killer in the medical profession? Preposterous! Where, they spluttered, was the motive?

The district attorney's office was sure it had the answer: Jascalevich's murderous campaign had been sparked by an evil determination to discredit his professional rivals, who he feared were undermining his status and eating into his bank balance. Ironically, the defense said pretty much the same, except that their spin on events had the run-of-the-mill surgeons at Riverdell ganging up against the brilliant import from South America, using him as a scapegoat for their medical incompetence. Their client, they said, had then been the hapless victim of a vicious witch-hunt orchestrated by Farber and Baden to further their own ambitions. And those much vaunted curare tests had been flawed, the defense scoffed, and they intended producing expert witnesses to say so.

While the sniping got sharper and the insults flew like daggers, time dragged on. One year passed. Then another. It was two full years before Jascalevich stood trial. At the time of his indictment, Jascalevich had been running a popular clinic for people on welfare and had voluntarily surrendered his license to practice medicine. Now, in his hour of extremis, his grateful and idolizing former patients had no intention of abandoning their benefactor. They packed the courtroom daily, applauding wildly for every point in the defendant's favor, pointedly remaining silent when the evidence told against him. For Baden this was the biggest case of his already tempestuous career, a golden opportunity to stamp his authority on the big stage. His longtime feud with Helpern had been consigned to history, and DiMaio had just retired. By the time he took the stand—July 21, 1978—Baden was the anointed, but not permanently appointed, chief medical examiner. A strong performance here could nail down the job for life.

Unfortunately, it didn't work out that way. Long before Baden even gave evidence, the prosecution had suffered nagging doubts about two of the indictments. And so had the judge. After listening to arguments from both sides, Judge William J. Arnold ruled that for the court to accept the presence of curare in the bodies two different scientific procedures were necessary, with one corroborating the other. In neither Henderson nor Arzt had this happened. The toxicological claims advanced by the prosecution were based on a single test. As a result, Judge Arnold threw out these two charges against Jascalevich, saying, "I find that a jury could not find beyond a reasonable doubt that the defendant murdered Margaret Henderson and Emma Arzt."

This left the prosecution to concentrate all their efforts on just Rohrbeck, Biggs, and Savino. It also meant that Baden had to pick his words very carefully indeed. Unfortunately, the chief prosecutor, Sybil R. Moses, was not so circumspect. At one point she asked Baden, "Can you give an opinion as the manner of [Rohrbeck's] death?"

"The manner of death was homicidal," Baden replied. Defense counsel Raymond A. Brown was on his feet immediately. With the jury excused, he argued that there was nothing in the record to show that murder had been committed, and Judge William J. Arnold agreed. Admitting he had made a mistake in allowing the question, Arnold recalled the jury and told them to "absolutely disregard" Baden's answer and to "not consider it in any way." This ruling ripped the heart out of Baden's testimony. All he was permitted to say was that Biggs, Rohrbeck, and Savino had died from curare poisoning. It was a frustratingly limp closing to what at the outset had looked a rock-solid prosecution case.

For the defense, Dr. Henry Siegel, medical examiner for Westchester County, New York, and another OCME alumnus, took issue with the methodology used to detect the curare. "The tests do not tell me how much curare was found. Without knowing the amount, I cannot estimate whether there was a fatal effect on the patient."

Thus far the trial was following traditional lines: one expert witness says one thing; another says something diametrically opposed. But with the case dragging on through the long, hot summer, suddenly the defense was thrown a gold-plated lifeline. And it had nothing to do with science. It concerned Myron Farber.

To mount the most effective defense possible for their client, attorneys of Jascalevich decided to subpoena Farber's notes. Except that the reporter refused point-blank to hand them over. To do so, he said, would violate the journalist's code and make him reveal a confidential source. Farber's obduracy meant that, overnight, the defendant became virtually a sidebar at his own trial. Forget all the groundbreaking work that Baden and his team had so painstakingly carried out: henceforth, the Jascalevich trial was less about science and criminal culpability and more about the Constitution.

In the wake of Watergate, the power and profile of journalism in America had undergone a quantum shift. Suddenly the reporter was no longer some mere ink-stained wretch but rather a custodian of the public conscience, a gallant seeker-after-truth, with the power to topple presidents. Grabbing just a little of that post–Woodward/Bernstein kudos didn't hurt the bank balance either.

The defense now worked itself up into a self-righteous lather. They thundered that Jascalevich had been framed by a tripartite conspiracy consisting of Riverdell hospital, Baden, and Farber. The critical nature of Farber's role, defense attorneys argued, made him as much a member of the prosecution team as, say, District Attorney Joseph Woodcock, and therefore he should be stripped of any journalistic immunity. Farber, unsurprisingly, didn't see it that way at all. Like any reporter worth his salt, he was prepared to protect his source at all costs. The outcome was a legal standoff as overwrought as it was contrived. Especially when one considered the oft-overlooked irony that Farber's unidentified source was no "Deep Throat" lurking in parking garage shadows, desperate to preserve his anonymity at all costs, but someone actually *clamoring to be exposed!*

Matthew Lifflander, a lawyer friend of Dr. Allan Lans, was the person who had compiled the "Doctor X" dossier and passed it to Farber. In light of all the publicity, he felt he deserved at least some credit for his part in the investigation, credit that he now felt Farber was denying to him. Farber's holier-than-thou stance stuck in Lifflander's craw, especially when details of the hefty book deal that Farber had secured were revealed, and it turned him into a mortal enemy of the reporter. In time, Lifflander would publish his own account of the case, making plain his antipathy.*

There was plenty of moral high ground to be taken here, and Farber managed to grab it all. The courts didn't share his enthusiasm and sided unequivocally with the defense, ordering Farber to hand over his papers. He refused. Even the threat of imprisonment

---

* Matthew L. Lifflander, *Final Treatment: The File on Dr. X* (New York: Norton, 1979).

failed to budge him. What some lauded as commendable ethics, left others feeling distinctly cold. Farber's intransigence, however well intentioned, had the effect of holing the prosecution's case several fathoms below the waterline. An ecstatic defense team couldn't believe its good fortune. Their claim, that Farber's notes were needed to prove Jascalevich's innocence, was never tested in court, and we'll never know what the jury might have made of the elusive revelations.

Between July and October 1978, Farber was in and out of jail for a total of forty days, while his employer, the *New York Times*, which supported Farber up to the hilt, was initially fined one hundred thousand dollars for criminal contempt and five thousand dollars for each day that he refused to comply with the court's wishes. (Legal fees would eventually boost the bill by another million dollars). When the case reached the State Supreme Court, Judge Frederick Lacey delivered a scathing verdict on Farber's motives, saying that the book contract meant he had a financial stake in seeing the doctor convicted. "This is a sorry spectacle of a reporter who purported to stand on his reporter's privilege when in fact he was standing on an altar of greed," said Lacey. Fast losing allies, even in the press, Farber bowed to the court's wishes and handed over his manuscript to Judge Arnold.

But it had all come too late. Farber's liberty came on the same day as Jascalevich received his. On October 24, 1978, after one of the longest trials in American history, lasting eight months, the jury required less than three hours to acquit Jascalevich. His supporters in the courtroom were jubilant. Much of the credit for Jascalevich's acquittal must go to his chief defense counsel, Raymond A. Brown. He had outgunned and outmaneuvered the prosecution at every turn—some conspiracy theorists insisted Brown had deliberately engineered the Farber farrago, not because he wanted to see the notes but because he calculated that Farber would start hollering

"First Amendment!" at the top of his lungs, thereby neatly deflecting attention from his client—and he had time on his side. In some kidnapping cases victims experience what is called the Stockholm syndrome, whereby they begin to build a rapport, often even a bond, with the hostage taker.* Much the same can happen in a long trial. Over the course of several months, the jury begins to see the defendant no longer as the accused but as just another person in the courtroom. Smiles, sometimes even pleasantries may be exchanged, all of which may, even if only on a subconscious level, affect the verdict. Possibly something like that happened in this instance. Certainly, the immaculately groomed Jascalevich was affable and pleasant to everyone in court. He thanked witnesses— even when they gave evidence against him—for their testimony, and he always conducted himself in a reasonable, even-handed manner. One thing was certain: he didn't come across as any serial killer. As noted earlier, his former patients turned out in droves to support him, and it's hard to imagine that their highly vocal encouragement, combined with all the other factors, did not have some impact on the jury's decision. Some idea of Jascalevich's charisma can be gleaned from the fact that in an extraordinary display of loyalty, a few weeks after the trial the jury petitioned for Jascalevich to have his medical license restored.

But the state wasn't yet finished with Mario Jascalevich.

What the jury didn't know was that several malpractice charges remained on the docket against Jascalevich, including one of operating on a patient whom he had misdiagnosed as having cancer and others of fraud and neglect. All these cases had arisen from Jascalevich's time at another hospital in Jersey City, and none was related to the murder charges.

---

* Named after the 1973 Kreditbanken robbery in Stockholm, Sweden, in which robbers held bank employees hostage for six days. After their release, some of the hostages defended their captors.

On October 8, 1980, the New Jersey Board of Medical Examiners decided it had had enough of Jascalevich and revoked his license permanently. The following year, Jascalevich sold up and returned to Argentina where he continued to practice medicine. In 1984 he died at Mar del Plata in his home country at the age of fifty-seven.

So far as Baden was concerned, the acquittal of Jascalevich amounted to a devastating setback. His was the marquee name above the team of forensic science experts who were supposed to convict the mysterious "Doctor X," and in the end a jury had thumbed its collective nose and tossed out months of brilliant, groundbreaking work and thousands of dollars of investigative science. Baden's team had performed forensic miracles in demonstrating that curare somehow got into the bodies of at least three of the Riverdell patients. What they could not do—nor was it part of their remit—was prove by whose hand the poison had been administered. This was the prosecution's responsibility and they came up short. In truth, the case against Jascalevich was never more than circumstantial. While great swathes of suspicion adhered to Jascalevich, there was precious little hard evidence to say he was a serial killer. If Farber had handed over his notes, maybe the outcome would have been different, maybe not. Still the suspicion lingers that in the case against Mario Jascalevich journalistic stubbornness outweighed the causes of justice.

In the aftermath of this debacle, the New Jersey legislature rewrote the shield law, so that a hearing was required before a reporter could be forced to reveal his sources. Just over one year later, New Jersey governor Brendan Byrne pardoned Farber and the *New York Times*.

Baden's knack of stirring up hornets' nests stayed with him. When he took over as acting head of the Office of the Chief Medical

Examiner, it was investigating approximately twenty-eight thousand deaths a year, about one-third of all those in the city. Late in the evening of January 29, 1979, this total was increased by one. Ordinarily the death of a seventy-year-old man from cardiac arrest would be little cause for comment, except that on this occasion the victim was former vice president and four-term governor of New York State Nelson Rockefeller. When paramedics got the call at 11:15 P.M., they rushed to Rockefeller's Manhattan townhouse at 13 West Fifty-fourth Street. There they found him lying fully dressed on a couch, still warm but without a pulse. Quickly they stretchered him into the ambulance and prepared to set off for nearby St. Clare's Hospital, only to then receive instructions ordering them to Lenox Hill Hospital, some considerable distance further away. Doctors did their best, but at 12:20 A.M. on January 27 Rockefeller was pronounced dead. Thus far, it was just another tragedy. Newsworthy, of course. Controversial? Hardly. Then it became clear that something peculiar was going on. The official version had Rockefeller succumbing to a heart attack while researching a book on art history with his assistant, twenty-five-year-old Megan Marshack, who lived in a co-op apartment just a few doors down. Pretty soon the rumor mill began churning out hints that Miss Marshack's duties extended well beyond the merely archival. Whatever the truth of these stories, Baden contacted the family physician, Dr. Ernest R. Esakof, and was told that contrary to public announcements, Rockefeller's health had recently been giving grave cause for concern, and that a heart attack had come as no surprise. So far as Baden was concerned, such an assurance from the family doctor obviated any need for an autopsy. As a result, less than forty-eight hours after his death, the former vice president was cremated and his ashes laid to rest. (In his will, Rockefeller provided handsomely for Marshack; a fifty-thousand-dollar loan was forgiven, and she got to keep her co-op apartment.)

Purely by chance, a few days later, Baden happened to address a meeting of doctors at Lenox Hill Hospital on the functions of the chief medical examiner's office. The speech passed without incident or comment in the press. Baden thought no more of it and went back to running his department, wholly oblivious to the impact that this half-remembered Lenox Hill speech would later have on his career.

For now, though, he had other things to occupy his mind, and with his probationary period just about expired Baden confidently awaited confirmation. It looked to be a fait accompli when Mayor Koch started canvasing opinion about Baden's year in office. The district attorneys for Brooklyn, Staten Island, Queens, and the Bronx all provided glowing testimonials. "Thoroughly professional," was a typical compliment, followed by, "Public service in so vital an area needs a doctor of high caliber. Dr. Baden is such a man." The health commissioner, Dr. Reinaldo A. Ferrer, was especially laudatory. In a letter to Koch, written on April 11, he praised Baden for the "remarkable accomplishments" that had improved "the administrative structure and managerial procedures of the office." On the back of such radiant recommendations, Baden looked a shoo-in. Everyone seemed to be singing in harmony—except one man.

Someone once described Robert M. Morgenthau, the Manhattan district attorney, as "a good friend and a terrible enemy." Mayor Koch, who'd stood shoulder to shoulder with Morgenthau for twenty years, could attest to the former, but God help anyone who got on Morgenthau's wrong side. And in 1979 that included Dr. Michael Baden.

Morgenthau, a political super-heavyweight who carried a knockout punch in either hand, didn't want the acting CME at any price, and when Koch asked his opinion he unloaded on Baden in a long, vitriolic letter, firing accusations of sloppy record keeping and citing a lack of cooperation. Startlingly, he was joined in this con-demnation by none other than Dr. Reinaldo A. Ferrer, who just weeks beforehand had been praising Baden to the skies. The letter, jointly authored by Morgenthau and Ferrer, contained claims that the Manhattan DA's office was being stymied by OCME incompe-tence, and they identified three cases that they said had been mis-handled. In one of these, the furious Ferrer unleashed a stinging personal attack on Baden, accusing him of reneging on an agree-ment to alter specific details. Ferrer's impudence was breathtaking. For the first time in its sixty-year existence, the OCME was being ordered—against the weight of the medical evidence—to change a death certificate.

The background to this disturbing story had begun on DiMaio's watch. On May 24, 1975, Robert O. Soman, a fifty-seven-year-old electrical engineer, fell to his death from a twelfth-story apartment window. His body was found at 4:30 A.M. in front of 40 West Seventy-seventh Street. The autopsy, performed by Dr. John F. Devlin, found nothing suspicious. Death was due to mul-tiple fractures and internal injuries, stemming from a fall from height. A supplementary report filed with the OCME report showed that the "deceased was under psych. care for short time last fall." It also noted that Soman's "last few years has been very depressed. No prior suicide attempts but talked about suicide. Jumped from apt. window. Wife was sleeping at the time. No note found. No medical history." In light of this information, Devlin had no hesitation in writing "suicide" on the death certificate.

When the family heard this ruling, they became incandescent. Soman's widow, the children's author Shirley C. Soman, petitioned to have the verdict changed to accidental. Considering that Soman had to clamber across some chairs to reach the window from which he fell, this didn't sound likely. But Mrs. Soman was nothing if not stubborn and hired a prestigious firm of lawyers to fight her case. Lurking in the not too distant background of this dispute was a big chunk of money. At the time of his death, Soman was covered by a $150,000 policy with the New York Insurance Company. The company duly paid out the sum insured but refused liability under the policy's double-indemnity clause, because, as the policy terms quite clearly stated, if Soman killed himself within two years of the policy being effected, this would invalidate the double payout. (At the time of Soman's death, the policy *had* been in effect for less than two years.) However, if the death certificate could be changed to accidental, then the double-indemnity clause would apply and New York Life would have to cough up an extra $150,000.

Strong family pressure was exerted on Devlin and DiMaio to change the ruling from suicide to accidental. DiMaio, in a memo dated March 5, 1976, stated that he had reviewed the case and concluded that "there was much more reason to make it 'Suicide' than 'Accidental.'"

But the family kept pressing. And by the time the case came to a final showdown in court, DiMaio had retired and Baden was at the helm. He argued that Devlin had based his ruling on his total evaluation of the circumstances of Soman's death. Sadly, Devlin was no longer able to defend himself; on the morning of May 29, 1976, while at his weekend cottage on Block Island, Rhode Island, he suffered a massive heart attack and died. He was only fifty-eight years old and had been with the OCME since 1962. Just days before his death, he had testified at the trial of serial killer Calvin Jackson (see chapter 4). At the time of Devlin's death, Baden had described him as "a man of immense integrity and honesty, with a great concern for justice." Now, though, it was Baden's own integrity that was in question, as he fought for his own survival and the independence of his office.

Ferrer accused Baden of being "slow and unresponsive in implementing" an agreement to change the cause of death for

Robert Soman. Baden boiled when he heard this. He bitterly denied ever having given such an undertaking. Nor was he about to change his mind about the death certificate. He laid out his reason for the city's Office of Corporation Counsel: "As Chief Medical Examiner I was legally charged to maintain all records gathered in the course of such investigation—and not to alter them; and that requiring me to affix my signature to a statement which I believed to be incorrect would place me in a severe professional and ethical conflict." Baden built up a head of steam. "I know of no rule which requires the Medical Examiner to accept medical judgment from lawyers." Ethically and legally, Baden was unassailable, but he could feel the ice cracking beneath his feet. Five times the hearing to decide this case was scheduled, and five times the city's lawyers failed to show up in court to defend the suicide verdict. Understandably frustrated by such blatant stonewalling, the judge had no alternative but to award a default judgment to the plaintiffs, and the death certificate was duly altered to show that Robert Soman died accidentally.

This was yet another slap in the face for Baden, and his already considerable woes multiplied exponentially when details of the Morgenthau/Ferrer letter were made public. It contained a litany of allegations, by far the most incendiary of which was that, in one very high profile case, Baden had been guilty of "bad judgment."

It concerned that meeting at Lenox Hill Hospital. According to Morgenthau, on February 3, during the course of his address, Baden had divulged "details not previously presented in such fashion as to indicate" that Governor Rockefeller "had died during sexual intercourse" [with Megan Marshack]. This was news to the hospital. First, hospital records showed that Baden spoke on February 9, not February 3, as Morgenthau claimed; second, minutes taken at the time failed to record any mention of Rockefeller during Baden's speech.

When questioned about the incident, Baden *did* recall answering a question about the issuance of the Rockefeller death certificate, but he vehemently denied having let slip any detail regarding how the former vice president came to be dead on the couch. But Morgenthau reckoned that he had a witness, whom he refused to identify—citing the need to protect him from the possibility of litigation—who claimed to have overheard Baden making some distinctly lewd references to the manner of Rockefeller's death. In a fifteen-page response, Baden dismissed Morgenthau's accusations as "a masterpiece of distorted advocacy," before adding, "Even if these charges were true, which they are not, they would hardly justify removing me."

Koch had other ideas. Casting aside the recommendations of four district attorneys and that of Dr. Kevin Cahill, the governor's special assistant for health affairs, who described Baden as "absolutely first rate," Koch had ears only for Morgenthau. On July 31, 1979, it was announced that Baden had been demoted from the role of acting chief medical examiner and would revert to his previous rank of deputy. It was a terrible humiliation.

Baden's allies, and there were plenty, rallied to the flag. Robert Tannenbaum, former chief of the Criminal Court Bureau for the Manhattan district attorney, described the ousted CME as "too independent, that's the only slam on the guy. He cannot be leaned on and he has tremendous integrity. And so in the mentality of the New York establishment, he can't be trusted." Further afield, Dr. Cyril Wecht, the coroner for Pittsburgh and a top-rate forensic pathologist, took a straw poll of medical examiners from around the country. "All of them expressed their amazement that something like this could happen to a man of Dr. Baden's stature," he said. He blamed Baden's downfall on "political chicanery or some sort of political vindictiveness."

There can be little doubt that Morgenthau wanted Baden's

SIX

THE POISONED CHALICE

Dr. Elliot Gross was no stranger to the Office of the Chief Medical Examiner. And he knew all about Michael Baden. The two men went back a long way. They had been classmates at New York University, both had graduated in the class of '59, and over the next three decades their careers would intertwine and intersect with regularity. When one considers Gross's background, then his choice of career should come as no surprise. His father, Dr. Samuel Gross, had been a police surgeon—usually the first investigative medical officer at any crime scene—and it was from him that Gross inherited his passion for forensic medicine. After a spell as chief of the aerospace branch of the Armed Forces Institute of Pathology in Washington, where he was also a captain in the U.S. Air Force Reserve, the young New Yorker returned to his home city and joined the OCME in 1966.

At this time, the OCME was unquestionably the finest facility of its kind in the world, both in terms of technological resources and, more especially, personnel. Helpern had forged himself a global reputation, and the OCME was the main beneficiary. Pathology students from all across the United States and even further afield competed for the privilege of studying under "the Chief." He was a great teacher, in the traditional European mode of mentor and pupil, and by the mid-1960s he had attracted a following of ambitious and brilliant students. Some, of course, were hungrier than others. Gross, like Baden, was ill conditioned for the role of supernumerary, and within a few short years, he had emerged from the pack to become deputy CME in Queens. Then came a sudden and surprising dislocation. He'd always idolized Helpern, and the two had been especially close, so when the older man took Gross to one side and delivered a stark career assessment—either get some administrative experience or get used to sitting on the bench—Gross had taken him at his word. Helpern meant nothing malicious by this advice—it was just a pragmatic assessment of how the promotion game was played. Any forensic pathologist who yearned for high public office, especially in a media goldfish bowl like New York, needed far more than mere medical talent—he or she needed a master's in the bureaucratic infighting that is an intrinsic part of the modern medical examiner's job. And that meant getting some executive experience.

Gross heeded Helpern's advice, and in 1970 he spotted an opening: Connecticut was on the lookout for a chief medical examiner. Gross applied and duly got the job. A huge challenge awaited him. Before his arrival, the state did not even have a forensic pathologist and relied on the facilities of local hospitals for autopsies. Gross was charged with building Connecticut's forensic science capability from the ground up, and although his dream of a single integrated medico-legal unit would not become a reality until 1987—long after his departure—it was his groundwork that made the ultimate achievement possible. Away from the constant glare of media attention, Gross prospered. He soon found out, though, that while trading New York City for Connecticut might have halved his caseload, it did nothing to dilute the gruesome horror of the crimes he was called upon to investigate.

A particularly harrowing case began on the evening of October 19, 1974, when a harassed out-of-towner parked his car outside the Donna Lee Bakery at 1015 East Street in New Britain and hurried inside to ask directions. Thinking he would only be gone a minute at most, William J. Donahue didn't bother to switch off his car's ignition. He would never sit in his car again.

Some time later—at 8:58 P.M.—an anonymous caller contacted the police to report that the bakery lights were on, the doors wide open, and yet the store was apparently empty. Curious and more than a little apprehensive, the caller had peeked through the door to investigate, then withdrew quickly, deciding that this was a task best left to the police.

When patrol officers reached the bakery, they also found the front part of the store empty. Only after threading their way between shelves of rolls and pastries and into the rear did they uncover what one officer later described as a "slaughterhouse." Wedged between the baking ovens, dough-mixing machines, and storage racks were six bodies, among them the hapless William Donahue. Their injuries were so atrocious that the police would not allow relatives to view the bodies. When Gross performed the autopsies he was able to say that the four men and two women had all been shot in the head at point-blank range. The store owner, John Salerni, had died from a shotgun blast; the others were executed by two pistols, a .45 caliber and a 9 millimeter. All the victims had also been beaten heavily about the head before death. Judging from the ransacked cash register, this bore the hallmarks of a robbery gone horribly wrong.

Later that same evening, two members of a local motorcycle gang swung by a New Britain party, laughing and joking and generally looking pretty pleased with themselves. After a few beers, one of the men, Ronald F. Piskorski, a three-hundred-pound former club bouncer who'd made extra money by wrestling bears in a circus, persuaded a fellow reveler named Christian Noury to drive him to a pond in Berlin on Route 72. After making sure there was no one else around, Piskorski unwound a bandanna from his head, wrapped it around a pistol and some bullets, then threw the bundle into the water. Noury, unsure what was happening but convinced that his own future well-being depended on a high level of personal discretion, clammed up tight.

It took another telephone tip-off to provide the first clue as to the identity of the bakery killers. The woman's information steered detectives toward one of Piskorski's cohorts, another biker named Gary B. Schrager. Shrager was almost as big as his hulking confederate, and he and Piskorski were real tight. From the way they talked, Schrager's wife, Abigail, had no doubt that the two men were mixed up in the bakery murders. When she made the mistake of confronting her husband with her suspicions, he began lashing out with his meaty fists. The beating she received only hardened Abigail's resolve. After wiping the blood from her bruised and battered face, she called the police.

Just over a month after the killings, Piskorski and Schrager, who had been hiding out in Maine with Piskorski's sister, were arrested as they crossed the state line back into Connecticut. Schrager decided to talk. His confession, corroborated by a polygraph, revealed that the two men had gone out that night with only robbery in mind. They had targeted the bakery because at 8:15 P.M. on a Saturday they had expected it to be quiet, as indeed it was at first. When they entered, the only occupant was fifty-nine-year-old store clerk Helen Giansanti. She was quickly herded into a back room. But then other customers began showing up at the store. Thomas and Anna Dowling came for doughnuts, then William

Donahue, looking lost and bewildered. Each was rounded up and shoved into the rear of the store. In a matter of seconds, an intended routine holdup had degenerated into a preview of *Dog Day Afternoon.* The next person through the front door was John Salerni. In a bitter irony, the last customer turned out to be Schrager's own uncle, Michael P. Kron. He usually picked up his bread and pastries on a Sunday morning but decided to stop by the night before so that he could sleep late. He, too, was funneled into the back room with the other captives.

According to Schrager, he remained on guard in front of the store, while Piskorski took a hammer and began beating the hostages. Just moments later five shots were fired in quick succession. Piskorski burst back into the front, shouted for Schrager to hand over his shotgun, then retraced his steps. Almost immediately Schrager heard a sixth and final shot. The two bandits then rifled the victims' pockets, grabbed fistfuls of cash from the register, and fled. For these six lives, Piskorski and Schrager netted approximately just three hundred dollars. At separate trials, both men were convicted and sentenced to life imprisonment.

The Donna Lee Bakery killings achieved notoriety as the worst mass murder in Connecticut's history. Tragically, it was a short-lived reign. In the summer of 1977, Gross was once again called on to investigate a crime that left Constitution State residents stunned and sick to their stomachs, unable to fathom the kind of horrors that were unfolding on their own doorstep.

Frederick Beaudoin was working the nightshift at the Pratt & Whitney Aircraft plant in North Haven when he got the call. His house in nearby Prospect, a suburb of Waterbury, had burned down. When firefighters were finally able to enter the smoke-blackened shell, they stumbled across a scene of almost unbelievable heartbreak. There were bodies everywhere. Frederick's twenty-nine-year-old wife, Cheryl, all seven of their children, ages four to twelve, and a visiting six-year-old niece had died in the inferno.

It was midmorning when Gross reached the charred red-shingled house on the corner of Union City Road and Cedar Hill Drive. Arson investigators were already working on the assumption that this had been no accidental tragedy. A nose-wrinkling stink of gasoline hanging in the air and the fire's suspicious path through the house made it highly likely that the blaze had been deliberately set. After gleaning what he could from the crime scene and making his preliminary examinations, Gross supervised the removal of the bodies. Neighbors lowered their heads respectfully as the procession of nine dark green canvas body bags made its way to the waiting vehicles. Afterward, Gross spoke to reporters on the front lawn. "It was a scene of great conflagration," he said. "At the present I would classify them as highly suspicious deaths."

Autopsies performed the next day on three of the children confirmed Gross's suspicions. A boy had died of head injuries, while two of the girls were killed by "multiple head injuries and inhalation of smoke."

Another twenty-four hours later and Gross had almost completed his grim task (the autopsy of the niece, Jennifer Santoro, was performed later). The victims, he said, had all been bludgeoned about the head, in a measured and quite calculated attack. Presumably the killer had then attempted to cover his tracks by setting the blaze. Although some of the children's wrists had been tied with bootlaces, Gross quashed rumors that the victims had either been gagged or had received gunshot wounds. By the end of the second day, even before Gross could file his report, detectives had a suspect in custody.

Lorne Acquin, aged twenty-seven, had been born on an Indian reservation in Canada and had spent most of his formative years in foster care. Being shunted from one home to another was a hard life, one that left profound psychological scars. Then he met Frederick Beaudoin. For the first time in his life, Acquin found someone who wanted him as a real friend. Beaudoin treated him like a brother and for several years made him welcome at his home. It got to the point where Acquin stayed so often that the Beaudoin children called him "Uncle Lorie." (On the evening before the fire, he had even taken the kids berry picking.) The Beaudoins were the one small oasis of stability in Acquin's otherwise turbulent life. Acquaintances traced his bad behavior back to another fire, fourteen years earlier, at the house where he was then living. It had destroyed all the family possessions. Following this dislocation, Acquin had begun stealing from neighbors. This led to two short prison terms.

Now, though, he was facing nine counts of murder. The main thrust of the prosecution lay in a confession made by Acquin after fifteen hours of interrogation. In it, he described suddenly going berserk, attacking Cheryl with a lug wrench when she turned to the refrigerator to get him a beer. Then he had methodically and murderously worked his way through the one-story house, battering the children as they either lay in their beds or stood crying in their cribs. He admitted sexually molesting one of the children. When he heard groans coming from the kitchen, he went back and finished off Cheryl by stabbing her. Then he fetched a five-gallon can of gasoline from the basement and torched the house.

Such were the legal gymnastics over the admissibility or otherwise of Acquin's alleged confession that by the time his trial had been concluded, one of the chief prosecution witnesses, Connecticut's chief medical examiner Dr. Elliot Gross, had already left Connecticut and returned to his hometown.*

---

* On October 19, 1979, Acquin was convicted of nine murders and later sentenced to life imprisonment. He will be eligible for parole in 2029.

*   *   *

The news that Baden had been kicked out of office sent shock waves through the medico-legal community. So, too, did the lightning speed of Gross's appointment. On August 9, Koch announced that Gross would be taking over as CME from September 15, and yes, there would be that tantalizing one-year probationary period. For Gross, this was the fulfillment of a dream; all his life he had yearned to fill the post once held by his great friend, Milton Helpern. He was even prepared to take a sixty-four-hundred-dollar-a-year pay cut—to fifty thousand dollars—in order to follow in his mentor's footsteps. The responsibilities were enormous. In Connecticut, his office had handled eight thousand investigations a year, with a staff of just three full-time medical examiners. Now he would have to deal with almost thirty thousand deaths per annum and an often hard-to-handle staff that numbered in the hundreds. Understandably, the press baited him on the sensational departure of his predecessor. Gross, canny down to his bootstraps, neatly sidestepped the controversy by professing himself to be unfamiliar with Baden's work in the past nine years. At the same time, he had nothing but praise for Baden during the time they had worked together in the sixties.

Deep down, though, Gross sensed that Baden wouldn't surrender without a fight. Passive acceptance of a public slight just wasn't his style. Sure enough, one week after being kicked downstairs, Baden called a press conference to announce that he was suing Koch on grounds that he had been denied the due process of a hearing under Civil Service requirements. Also named in the suit were S. Michael Nadel, director of the city's Department of Personnel—and Dr. Elliot Gross.

It wasn't the most auspicious of beginnings. But it did set the tone for Gross's tenure at the Office of the Chief Medical Examiner, most of which was spent either looking over his shoulder or else fending off suspiciously well-informed reporters. The assault began immediately. Over the next few months a steady drip of rumors, innuendoes, and half-truths—none complimentary—found their way into the metro pages. According to the whispers, morale at the OCME had plunged to rock bottom; threats of resignation hung in the air; and an unbridgeable schism had divided the staff, with the pro-Gross faction complaining that the Badenites were constantly striving to undermine them and vice versa. When, on October 12, 1979, Gross married the late chief's daughter, Alice Helpern, some even chuckled that the ghost of Milton Helpern, from beyond the grave, was contributing a Jacob Marley–like piquancy to Baden's discomfort.

As the juggernaut of complaints rumbled on, Gross acted decisively to crush any possible rebellion. On February 8, 1980, he announced that Baden was being transferred to the Queens office. Another vocal critic of Gross's methods, Dr. Yong-Myun Rho, was shifted from Manhattan to the Bronx. To strengthen his hand, Gross imported Dr. Millard Hyland from Queens to head up the all-important Manhattan office.

Banishing Baden to Queens provided only temporary relief for Gross. There was still that lawsuit hovering overhead like a black cloud. The storm broke in May 1980 when federal judge Charles S. Haight Jr., ruled that Baden *had* been dismissed illegally and ordered that he be reinstated with back pay. Haight found that when Baden had been dismissed on July 31, 1979, he had already attained tenure and that under state Civil Service law he was entitled to a hearing on the charges against him. The judge wrote: "No mayor may change the rules in the middle of the game and suddenly confront an unsuspecting Chief Medical Examiner with substantially different procedures." The murkiness of this whole sorry episode was made more Stygian still by Nadel's admission in a sworn deposition that an entry summarizing Baden's work experience had been altered—after Baden was dismissed—so that it read "to serve probation." Because the Corporation Counsel announced its attention to appeal the ruling, Judge Straight stayed the order.

Gross was trapped in no-man's-land. If the appeals court upheld Straight's ruling, he would be out of the top job and most likely out of the OCME as well. Until that mess was resolved, he was still expected to run his department as if everything was hunky-dory. For the past year the OCME had been making headlines for all the wrong reasons. Gross was desperate for an opportunity to demonstrate that the office, for all its self-flagellating masochism, was still on top of the forensic game. His chance came in the summer of 1980.

CASE FILE:
Craig Crimmins (1980)

Covering an area of 16.3 acres, the Lincoln Center complex in Manhattan is the world's largest performing arts center. Its seven major halls and theaters are home to no fewer than twelve resident arts organizations, but the undoubted jewel in the architectural crown is the glistening glass and marbled magnificence of the Metropolitan Opera House. Since moving to its present home in 1966, the "Big House," as it is known to opera buffs, has strengthened its role as one of the world's most acclaimed music venues, to rival La Scala in Milan and the Bolshoi Theater in Moscow.

On the evening of Wednesday, July 23, 1980, the thirty-seven-hundred-seat auditorium was about three-fourths full for a performance by the Berlin Ballet. All eyes were on the principal dancers, Valery and Galina Panov. The couple's highly publicized struggle to immigrate to Israel from their native Soviet Union, culminating in their daring 1974 defection, had caught the attention of the Western media and made them headliners wherever they performed. On this particular night, the Panovs were presenting extracts from four ballets. First up was Stravinsky's *Firebird*, then came the pas de deux from *Don Quixote*, with music by Leon Minkus.

Down in the orchestra pit, violinist Helen Hagnes concentrated hard. Like everyone else around her, this thirty-one-year-old native of British Columbia, Canada, was a freelance musician, hired by a contractor for the Berlin Ballet's eleven-day run at the Met. With positions in the established sitting orchestras at a premium, this was how most classical musicians in New York made a living. Helen, a graduate of Juilliard and the winner of numerous awards and competitions, was top notch, a "first-call" musician in the parlance of the freelance circuit—which meant that if, say, twenty orchestra seats needed to be filled, she would be in the first ten called—and tonight she glided effortlessly through the complex scores. At the conclusion of the short *Don Quixote* piece, which ended at 9:29 P.M., she put down her violin and discreetly edged out of the orchestra pit, her blond hair vividly accentuated by the black outfit that she wore. For the next forty-five minutes she and the rest of the orchestra were on a break, as the third ballet, *Five Tangos*, by the Argentinean composer Astor Piazzolla, was being danced to prerecorded tapes. As Helen descended deep into the bowels of the Met, she did so in the knowledge that she was due back in her seat at 10:19 P.M. for the night's final ballet, *Miss Julie*, a modern piece based on the music of little-known Swedish composer Ture Rangström.

At around 10:15 P.M., the orchestra members began slipping back into their seats. Except that Helen Hagnes was nowhere to be seen. The other musicians were baffled. Normally, Helen was the embodiment of professionalism, a stickler for timekeeping; it was unthinkable that she would miss her cue. Perhaps she was unwell? Yet no one could recall her complaining of feeling ill. Her nonappearance was a real mystery. Then the conductor tapped his baton and all other thoughts were set aside as the orchestra struck up the first chord.

While the dancers pirouetted and twirled and the orchestra played, security staff scoured the backstage area for Helen. Still, there was no sign of the missing violinist. An hour passed. At 11:15 P.M., just as the final curtain was being taken and the musicians packed away their instruments, the management decided to call the police.

At about the same time, outside Lincoln Center a slim, sandy-haired thirty-six-year-old man with a beard was waiting patiently at the prearranged meeting place. It was a warm evening, with temperatures in the seventies, and Janis Mintiks wasn't overly concerned at first when his wife failed to appear on schedule. It had been almost four years since he and Helen had married, and in that time the tall sculptor and the pocket-sized musician had become utterly devoted to each other. Each night when Helen finished playing at the Met, Janis would be waiting for her after the final curtain call, and together the couple would walk the half mile to their West Side apartment.

Tonight, though, was different. Helen was nowhere to be seen. Gradually, Jan's initial insouciance gave way, first to edginess, then to open anxiety. Perhaps their wires had somehow become crossed and she'd made her own way home? He hurried off to find a phone. After calling and getting no answer, and still with no sign of Helen outside the Met, a gnawing apprehension grabbed hold and he rushed back to their apartment. It was empty. At 12:10 A.M. friends from the orchestra knocked at the door. In their hands they carried Helen's violin. Janis fretted for another twenty minutes, digesting their news and agonizing horribly, before he finally surrendered to his fears and phoned the police.

They were already ahead of him. Officers had been at the Met

since midnight, trying to unravel the mystery of the vanishing violinist. Four possibilities emerged: (1) Helen had disappeared voluntarily (tantamount to committing professional suicide in the middle
of a performance), (2) she had suffered an accident (somehow, in
some untenanted part of the building, Helen had become incapaci-
tated), (3) she had been abducted, or—and this was the possibility
that no one wanted to countenance—(4) she had been added to
Manhattan's bulging homicide count and her body had not yet
been found.

Detectives learned that security at the Met—just seven or eight
guards—was traditionally focused on the front of the house, those
areas most frequented by members of the public. Backstage, the
security oscillated between minimal and nonexistent. Here, it was
busier and more bustling than an Egyptian souk, with hundreds of
staff and performers milling up and down forty staircases and the
fifteen elevators that connected ten aboveground floors, three
underground levels of passageways, tunnels, and garages. Searching every nook and cranny of this concrete rabbit warren would be
a daunting task at the best of times; in the middle of the night it
was next to impossible. This didn't prevent the searchers from
doing their best. But by daybreak, with still no sign of Helen, it
looked odds-on that she was no longer in the building.

A few minutes past eight o'clock that morning, a maintenance
mechanic, Lawrence Lennon, made his way up to the Met's sixth-
floor roof, where many of the controls for the building's ventilation
system were housed. He needed to turn off a cooling fan. As
always, the door to the roof was unlocked and opened with a push.
The bright sunlight made him squint as he stepped out onto the
roof, but gradually his eyes had adjusted to the glare, and when
they did so they fixed upon a pair of shoes that lay next to a large
pipe. Immediately recognizing the potential significance of such a
find, he ran for help. Two detectives went to investigate. This

section of the gravel-coated tar roof was at the rear of the building, a secluded area, protected from street views by a thirty-foot-high concrete wall on the west and the granite facade of the opera house to the east. The privacy made it a popular venue for staff members to relax on a break. Bisecting this quasi-recreational area, and running almost the entire width of the building, was a huge air shaft. Inside were six hollow cylinders, each about fifteen feet in diameter and eighty feet in depth, conduits for carrying fresh air into the AC and ventilation systems.

The shoes lay next to one of these cylinders. As the officers' flashlights probed the darkness in the airshaft they picked out a terrible sight. About halfway down, between the third and fourth floors, on an orange-colored steel ledge that jutted out, lay a woman's body. The search for Helen Hagnes had ended.

Dr. Elliott Gross was immediately summoned to the scene. For him to examine the body in situ, two wooden planks were placed across the gaping air shaft. Using this makeshift platform, Gross went to work. The sight that confronted him was ugly and obscene. Helen's sightless eyes stared directly up the shaft. She had been stripped naked, bound, and gagged. The gag was formed by two napkins, one stuffed into the mouth and the other tied around it. The outer napkin covered the entire lower half of her face, but not the nostrils. Her hands had been tied behind her back with a combination of black jersey cloth—presumably slashed from her clothing—and rope. A similar length of rope, this time reinforced by a pair of shorts, was used to bind the ankles. When Gross examined the knots he noticed that all were tied in a distinctive clove hitch.

Gross reasoned that the murderer had somehow forced Helen up to the roof, where, after some kind of sexual interference—it wasn't immediately obvious if rape had occurred, only further examination could determine that—for whatever reason he had decided to kill his diminutive victim. Only an autopsy would be able to reveal if she had been alive when hurled down the shaft. After concluding that the crime scene had given him everything it could, Gross gave orders for the body to be removed.

Later that day, at the foot of the air shaft, officers found the black blouse and matching skirt that Helen had worn when she gave the last performance of her life. Both items had been slashed several times.

The murder of Helen Hagnes caused a sensation. Even in the most violent city in America, it was proof that homicide still had the ability to shock. For eighteen years the Lincoln Center for the Performing Arts had been the hub of cultural life in Manhattan, a showcase for mankind's higher cerebral endeavors; now it had hosted a spectacularly sordid and brutal murder. The city could not afford to let this killer get away; the ramifications would be enormous. Already the headlines were screaming MURDER AT THE MET and THE PHANTOM OF THE OPERA, with some commentators noting that this killing resembled the script for one of those made-for-TV movies—a victim murdered in the nation's most prestigious concert hall, with literally thousands of suspects to choose from. Little wonder, then, that by the end of day one, a team of forty detectives was poring over blueprints, floor plans, and architectural drawings of the opera house. Even so, the police openly professed themselves baffled. Captain Francis Ward of the Manhattan Detective Area didn't spare himself or his officers. "We have no suspects," he told reporters. "We are interviewing every electrician, every prop man, anyone in a situation to see [Helen] . . . that night."

The task was immense. At a conservative estimate, on the night in question more than one thousand people had access to the backstage area at the Met, and that excluded the one hundred-plus members of the Berlin Ballet entourage. Although the evidence suggested that Helen had been the victim of a random killer, detectives were leaving nothing to chance. As in most homicides, the inquiries started with those closest to the victim and then radiated outward.

The daughter of Finnish immigrant parents, Helen Hagnes was the youngest of three sisters and had been raised on a poultry farm in the tiny community of Aldergrove, British Columbia. Even before her third birthday, it was obvious that Helen had exceptional musical talent. She could hear songs on the radio and play them almost note for note on the parlor piano. Her parents, eager to encourage this unusual gift, scrimped and scraped to pay for music lessons. Their dedication and self-sacrifice paid off when at age eleven Helen won a thousand-dollar prize in a Vancouver violin contest and two years later undertook her first professional engagement. Unlike many child prodigies she didn't burn out, and in her late teens she enrolled at the Juilliard School of Music in Manhattan, where she earned a bachelor's and later a master's degree in 1976. That same year she married Janis, whom she had met while working as a counselor at a summer camp outside Montreal. They agreed that for professional purposes it made sense for her to retain her single name. Away from the rigid formality of the concert hall, Helen was happiest in T-shirts and jeans, cooking meals for a small circle of friends. Her chosen career path might have been one riddled with insecurity, but underpinning everything was one unshakable foundation: her love for Janis, and his for her. Their mutual devotion was a thing of wonderment to all who knew them. In most murder investigations, hard-boiled detectives usually fix their steeliest gaze on the surviving partner; here, they barely gave Janis a second glance. There was no faking that level of grief; besides, he didn't fit the traditional template of means, motive, and opportunity. Within hours, detectives had scrubbed Helen's heartbroken husband off the list of potential suspects.

Which meant that the killer might still be prowling the Met's red-carpeted corridors. A bizarre rumor that the murder had been carried out by someone driven into a frenzy by the ballet's tempestuous music received a suitably frosty reception from the investigators. They were more concerned with trying to fathom out how the killer managed to lure Helen up to the roof. Enticement was only an option if she knew her killer, and even then friends considered this most improbable. Helen was so guarded in any social setting that the notion of her willingly accompanying a male to such a lonely spot at night smacked of fantasy. Much the likeliest scenario involved some kind of force. For this reason, it was imperative that detectives attempted, as much as possible, to retrace Helen's final movements.

After leaving her seat in the orchestra pit, she would have stepped down a flight of wooden stairs that led into a narrow forty-foot-long cinder-block hallway on A level, one floor below the stage or street level. Overhead, ventilation pipes ran the hallway's length, while the concrete floor was lined with large crates, candy and juice vending machines, and a water fountain. After turning a corner she had entered a basement locker room labeled ORCHESTRA WOMEN ONLY. Inside this small carpeted room, Helen had relaxed on a sofa for a few minutes, chatting with another orchestra member. At around 9:30 P.M. she had left the locker room, saying she was going to keep an appointment for an "artistic discussion" with one of the stars of the show, Valery Panov, in his dressing room. Her motivation for this intended visit was wholly innocuous; she was simply trying to rustle up some work for her husband. Janis, besides being a sculptor, had done set design work and was eager to widen his experience in this field. Helen hoped that if she could talk to Panov, then maybe he would be able to pull some strings. A word in the right ear from someone of Panov's stature could open all sorts of doors.

When queried about this supposed appointment, Panov professed utter bemusement. He told detectives that he had neither expected nor did he see Helen that night, and a check on his movements seemed to corroborate this claim. At the time Helen went missing, Panov was not in his dressing room at all but was sitting in the stalls watching his wife, Galina, performing onstage. With that kind of alibi, Panov was also removed from the list of potential suspects.

Investigators, working on the premise that Helen would have been unaware of Panov's absence from his dressing room, questioned Met staff as to how she would have made her way from the basement locker room to Panov's dressing room on the stage level. Three routes were possible: in one, she would have taken an elevator up one floor and then walked around the rear of the stage; the second, involving a little-known stairway used mostly by conductors, led directly to the principal artists' dressing rooms; the third would have taken her down a long corridor under the stage, up a flight of stairs, down another corridor, past a chorus dressing room and across a loading dock. Most agreed that, of the three routes, Helen would have plumped for option one. This was the most commonly used and, during performances, would have been well trafficked. The second route was generally reserved for headliners and usually off-limits to musicians or cast members; the subterranean, circuitous route was known only to a handful of people, and it was doubtful that Helen would have been among their number.

Desperate to diffuse as much heat as possible from what had been an unmitigated PR disaster, the Met made a highly visible point of beefing up its security for that night's performance. Extra staff were drafted, and unbeknownst to the tuxedo-clad audience, among their number, suitably attired, were ten detectives, on hand in case the so-called Phantom of the Opera decided to strike again.

To no one's surprise, the performance, while hugely emotional for everyone concerned, passed off uneventfully.

The next morning, Gross began his full autopsy. It would last all day. At its conclusion, he revealed his findings. First, Helen had been alive when hurled down the air shaft. Confounding earlier rumors that she had been strangled, he reported that "the cause of death was multiple fractures of the skull, ribs and bones of the lower extremities . . . There were also contusions of the lungs. The skull fractures and other fatal injuries were the result of the fall from the roof to the ledge." After noting that "her hands were bound behind her back and her ankles were bound together," he refused to identify the items used to bind her. He was also deliberately noncommittal when asked whether Helen had been raped. However, at a separate press conference, Richard Nicastro, the NYPD's chief of detectives in Manhattan, did reveal that in a private conversation Gross said there was "no evidence of any sexual molestation."

By day's end one of the largest detective forces assembled in living memory for a single Manhattan homicide—more than fifty strong—was scouring every inch of the Met for further clues. All indicators pointed to a killer familiar with the bewildering backstage maze of corridors, tunnels, cul-de-sacs, dressing rooms, offices, storerooms, stairwells, entrances, and elevators.

One by one, the clues began to reveal themselves. On the third-floor landing of a rear staircase someone found a pen. On the next flight of stairs, just before the fourth floor, there was a hair clip. Both items were identified as belonging to the victim. Beside the pen lay a Marlboro cigarette butt. This, too, was bagged and sent for analysis. The gag used on Helen provided a strong lead. Of the two white napkins used, one was traced to the only bar and restaurant at the Met that stayed open during the summer.

By midafternoon on July 26, more than 350 persons with access to the backstage area—performers, musicians, stagehands, makeup artists, security guards, and maintenance men—had been interviewed. It was an impressive achievement until one realized that another *one thousand* employees remained to be seen! Most interviews were conducted at an ad hoc precinct station set up in the atrium at the center. It was a slow, grinding process, checking, cross-checking, and in some cases reinterviewing possible witnesses. Then came a major breakthrough: someone backstage had seen Helen just after 9:30 P.M., after she had left the locker room. Furthermore, the witness had also seen a man near Helen at the same time.

The police were unusually coy about divulging details of this witness or the information provided, saying only that she had provided a description of the man sufficiently detailed for a police artist to make a worthwhile sketch. Pointedly, the officers in charge of the investigation refused to release this sketch to the press in case it led to their being buried beneath an avalanche of false leads.

Gross, meanwhile, was finding out firsthand just how intense being the CME in New York could be. Reporters, spurred on by frantic editors desperate to outdo each other in a circulation war that had broken out over Manhattan's most notorious homicide in decades, were jumping all over Gross for more autopsy details. Most of their questions centered on the gag and what part—if any—it had played in Helen's death. Had she been suffocated? Perhaps taking his lead from the police investigators, Gross was notably evasive. "That was a factor," he said. "But I just don't want to go into further details on it. This is a complicated case." This was a strange response, one that troubled some medico-legal experts. Later, and protected by the cloak of anonymity, they shared their concerns with reporters. Suffocation was, by definition, a cause of death, and Gross had already concluded that Helen had died from injuries suffered in the fall. Now he seemed to be hedging his bets. They agreed it was not always possible to determine if a victim had been suffocated, particularly if injuries sufficient to prove fatal were sustained afterward, as only about half of all suffocation cases show the trademark pinpoint hemorrhages in the whites of the eyes and on the face. But Gross definitely seemed to be muddying the waters. The next day brought no respite for Gross. Now the reporters wanted him to nail down the time of death. Gross put it at between 9:30 P.M. and midnight. He based this on the last time she had been seen alive and the condition of food in her digestive system. This indicated that she had eaten no more than six hours before her death, and since she was known to have eaten at 6:00 P.M. this gave him the later figure. Gross also confirmed what hitherto had been widely rumored: laboratory tests had revealed no evidence of rape. Pressed as to whether there was evidence of any other kind of sexual assault, he stressed that the body had been found naked and added, "I'll leave it at that." His investigation, he said, was ongoing, and would include blood tests, a search for material under the victim's fingernails and hair fibers at the scene, and other possibly significant technical matter. Beyond that he wasn't prepared to commit himself.

While Gross took the media heat, behind the scenes, away from the cameras, notebooks, and clamoring questions, the forensic investigation moved quietly forward uncovering more clues. On the rear staircase where the pen and clip had been discovered, dark splotches, possibly blood, were found. Samples were taken and sent for analysis.

It was tough, arduous work and the pressure was remorseless. Some on the detective task force worked the case for three days straight, showering and catnapping at the station house, then back to the Met and the relentless rounds of interviewing. Others had to deal with the inevitable slew of crank letters. One, more imaginative than most and written in two lines similar to a music stave, was duplicated and sent to the *Times* and the *Post*. It declared that "to solve the opera murder case go no further than the evil bass" and was signed, "Vibrato the Great."

Exhausted detectives preferred to pin their hopes on more traditional methods. And right now all eyes were on the backstage witness. This approach, though, was generating a whole new set of problems. Laura Cutler, an American-born dancer with the Berlin Ballet, had seen someone; she just wasn't sure who. At about 9:40 P.M., after dancing the first ballet, she had decided to take elevator 12 down to a basement practice room. As she awaited the elevator's arrival, two people approached from her left. When shown photographs of the victim, she had no doubts that the woman was Helen Hagnes; her only recollection of the man was that he was nondescript. Once inside the elevator, Helen had turned to her and asked, "Where is Mr. Panov's dressing room?" Before she could answer, the man interjected, "On three." Understandably Laura thought no more of it and when the elevator reached her practice room on C level—the lowest of the ten floors—she exited, leaving Helen and the mystery man in the elevator together. The vagueness of the description given by Laura prompted investigators to ask if she would undergo hypnosis to help her recall. She readily agreed.

With a history rooted in medieval sorcery and magic, hypnosis continues to baffle to this day. Various researchers have put forth differing theories of what hypnosis is and how it could be understood, but there is currently still no generally accepted explanatory theory for the trancelike state. Its scientific use began with Franz Mesmer, a late-eighteenth-century Viennese physician who used it in the treatment of patients. Mesmer's mistaken belief that it was an occult force, which he termed "animal magnetism," that flowed through the hypnotist into the subject, led to his being quickly discredited; but "mesmerism," as it was first called, continued to fascinate medical practitioners. In the middle of the nineteenth century, it was an English physician named James Braid who, after studying the phenomenon, coined the terms *hypnotism* and *hypnosis*.

A couple of decades later, hypnosis began to be accepted by the medical mainstream, especially in France. One visitor to Paris impressed by hypnotism's possibilities was the Austrian psychiatrist Sigmund Freud. On his return to Vienna, he used hypnosis to help neurotics recall disturbing events buried deep in their subconscious that they had apparently forgotten. But he was dissatisfied with the results and soon abandoned hypnosis as a psychiatric tool in favor of free association.

Despite Freud's influential rejection of hypnosis, some use was made of the technique in the treatment of soldiers with combat neuroses during the two world wars, and it has subsequently acquired various other limited uses in medicine.

The use of hypnosis as a crime-fighting tool didn't gain any kind of serious foothold until the 1970s. Even then it was a struggle. Investigators and courts alike questioned whether it was possible, or even desirable, for witnesses to have their memories "refreshed" by hypnosis. An early proponent of the technique was an NYPD officer, Detective Charles Diggett, and in the late 1970s he won over many skeptics with his intervention in the "Son of Sam" murders. Diggett seemed the obvious choice to hypnotize Laura Cutler. But the best description she could manage was disappointingly vague. She recalled the man in the elevator as being between twenty and thirty years old, slightly taller than herself (five feet seven and a half inches), and that his hair was "not very thick, not very wavy." As she later put it, "I know only that he was not black. I was certain about that. I really noticed almost nothing about him." She constantly emphasized these doubts to Diggett, along with her nagging fear that the man she described while under hypnosis may not have been the man she saw on the night in question.

Despite Laura's misgivings, a sketch was compiled from her rec-ollections and shown to members of the Met staff. Many felt it looked familiar but few could put a name to the face, and those that did invariably came up with different candidates. In their determination to leave no stone unturned, detectives even flew the sketch down to Washington, D.C., where the Berlin Ballet was con-tinuing its U.S. tour. All they got in return were blank stares. No one recognized the face.

Treating a working building the size of the Met as a crime scene proved to be a logistical nightmare. But on August 3, eleven days after the murder, the investigators achieved a significant break-through. Close to the bottom of a cooling tower, two levels below the backstage area, they discovered two items: a tampon and a paper napkin stained with semen. The napkin was found stuffed in a pipe and the tampon lay nearby on a staircase on B level, a com-plex of work and rehearsal rooms one floor beneath the orchestra pit. Both items were sent for analysis to Dr. Robert C. Shaler, a biologist who'd recently joined the OCME after having previously worked at the Aerospace Corporation.

The finding of the tampon was especially significant as Gross's autopsy showed that at the time of her death Helen had been in a menstrual cycle. Even more excitement surrounded the discovery of the semen-stained napkin. Although Gross had seen no visible evidence of rape—a finding confirmed by Shaler's declaration that he could find no trace of semen either in or on the body—neither result swayed the police from their conviction that the crime had been sexually motivated. And finding the napkin only seemed to reinforce that suspicion. Nowadays, such a piece of evidence would be hugely, maybe even decisively important, but in 1980 genetic profiling was in its infancy, with the miracle of DNA finger-printing almost a decade away. The technology of the time restricted scientists to a rudimentary, though still telling, form of analysis that could yield the killer's blood type, his race, and a whole host of genetic characteristics that would distinguish him from more than 95 percent of the population. All this, of course, was predicated on the presumption that the semen-stained napkin actually came from the killer. There was always the possibility that the napkin might be the legacy of some other sexual encounter or experience.

As the questioning proceeded, the parameters widened: now, anyone who had been on the Met payroll since January 1, 1980—a total of twenty-six hundred people—was drawn into the interview net.

Shaler had good news. Further tests showed that the tampon *had* been used by Helen, and he had been able to extract enough material from the semen-stained napkin to give him a blood type. Now all he needed was a suspect.

A slow drip of information gradually seeped into the public domain. Sources close to the investigation revealed that the killer had most likely been armed with a knife, as some of the victim's clothes had been slashed (although Helen herself had not been cut). Then came news that Shaler had found a non-Caucasian hair on the gag. The police immediately downplayed this discovery, stressing that there was no evidence to show that it definitely belonged to the killer.

But much the most significant development came in August, almost two weeks after the murder. James Devlin, an AC engineer at the Met, suddenly recalled hearing "a sigh, a moan or a groan [between] 9:30 and 9:45 [P.M.] . . . definitely a woman," coming from the bottom floor of the building in the northwest corner. "It meant nothing to me at the time," he said. He had looked around the floor and checked elevator 11, but saw no one. Much later, under cross-examination, Devlin admitted that in the first round of interviews he had originally told detectives, "I didn't see or hear anything of a suspicious nature," but only remembered the sound "a number of days after I was interviewed."

On August 12, after a ten-day hiatus, the Met reopened amid heightened security, although the management stressed how impossible it was to police every inch of its labyrinthine corridors.

In the midst of all these developments, what neither the press nor the public knew was that from the very day that Helen's body had been discovered the police had been in possession of a critical piece of evidence—a partial palm print found on a pipe that ran across the roof, close to where the shoes had been discovered.

For most of the twentieth century, fingerprints have been regarded as the gold standard of forensic evidence. Find a print, match it to a suspect, and, bingo, case closed! In recent years, however, all that has changed. For the first time in almost a century, serious doubts have begun to be cast on the sanctity of the fingerprint as an ironclad guarantee of identification. Courts in more than one U.S. state, and also in Britain, have thrown out cases because of faulty fingerprint evidence. Perhaps the most egregious example of misidentification came in the aftermath of the Madrid terrorist bombings on March 11, 2004, in which 191 died and 2,000 were injured. An Oregon lawyer, Brandon Mayfield, found himself hauled into custody as a "material witness" after no fewer than three FBI experts matched his prints to a partial print found on a bag that contained explosives at a Madrid train station. According to the experts, they had found fifteen points of similarity. Despite the Spanish police having grave doubts about the identification, the FBI dug in its heels and kept Mayfield locked up for two weeks, before finally admitting that they had goofed: the print was actually shown to belong to an Algerian national thought to be living in Spain, named Ouhnane Daoud.* Such a blunder, once unthinkable, is becoming more common, and the possibility for mistakes is only likely to increase as fingerprint databases grow ever larger. With this expansion comes a heightened chance of two people having similar prints. The key word here is *similar,* because all the problems thus far have arisen over misidentification. No two people, not even identical twins, have ever been shown to have the same fingerprint.

For those detectives investigating the murder of Helen Hagnes, the partial palm print found on the roof was never more than a guideline, even if it did point squarely in the direction of one particular Met employee, twenty-one-year-old stagehand Craig Crimmins.

Although Crimmins denied any involvement in the murder, he freely admitted being on the roof both before and after the murder. The print, he said, could have been left on any of these occasions. This was a valid observation—after all, dozens of Met employees used the roof for work and relaxation on a daily basis—but what the print did do was to concentrate attention on Crimmins. First, there was his physical appearance, at five feet eight inches and weighing 160 pounds, he resembled the man in the elevator whom Laura Cutler had seen; second, his movements on the night of the killing were unsubstantiated and to some extent contradicted by some of the other stagehands; third, he had a history of drink problems, combined with arrests for disorderly conduct and assault.

Crimmins had been born in New York City and had quit Manhattan Vocational High School after two years to start work at the Met. He lived at Scott Towers, a well-kept cooperative at 3419

---

* A warrant was subsequently issued for Daoud's arrest. At this writing he remains at large.

Paul Avenue, in the Bradford Park section of the Bronx, where he shared a nineteenth-floor apartment with his father and sister.

And it was outside Scott Towers at 6:30 P.M. on August 29 that detectives approached Crimmins and asked him to accompany them to the 13th Precinct station house at 230 East Twenty-first Street, arriving at shortly before 7:00 P.M. It had been a low-key kind of apprehension, with no force used and no handcuffs. Whether Crimmins was actually under arrest at this point was a fine legal point that would later become crucial, but what is certain is that at some time during that night he was charged with murder and remanded to Rikers Island without bail.

With a suspect under lock and key, the police finally began to open up to the media. They revealed that during his first interview on August 6, Crimmins had aroused no suspicion, but when reinterviewed eight days later his story had changed. This time around he claimed to have been in the basement on the night in question, sleeping off a daylong bender, instead of being on duty. The night's events were a blank to him. Another lengthy bout with the detectives followed on August 17, parts of which were videotaped. Crimmins expanded on life backstage at the Met. He explained how a kind of buddy system existed among stagehands; if one of them showed up for work either feeling rough or else hungover, coworkers would cover for him. Catnapping during performances was commonplace, as stagehands with nothing to do until the next scenery change snoozed in secluded corners.

Crimmins had worked at the Met for four years. He'd obtained the job through the intervention of his father, a Met electrician with twenty years' service. (Crimmins's stepfather had also been employed at the Met for a similar period of time.) Since his hiring, Crimmins had held a variety of positions, most recently as a "grip," a stagehand who moves sets, lights, and other equipment backstage. It was a job that demanded several tools of the trade, among which were a knife and plenty of rope, the same kind of rope used to bind Helen Hagnes. Detectives also learned that when lashing scenery together, the grips all used a clove hitch, the same knot as that used to bind Helen Hagnes.

On September 5 Crimmins was indicted on two counts of second-degree murder and one count of attempted rape.

Friends and coworkers of Crimmins's were askance, unable to believe he could be the killer. Everyone knew him as a quiet, even gentle, person, very popular. They scoffed at suggestions that he might have carried Helen up the stairs, as police theorized, because he had recently hurt his right shoulder and suffered a hernia in a motorcycle accident sometime before the slaying. And they dismissed out of hand any suggestion that Crimmins might have lured Helen up to the roof with hints of sexual intrigue. As one stagehand put it: "The musicians don't associate with us." State prosecutors were untroubled by these supportive gestures from Crimmins's fellow workers; so far as they were concerned the case was in the bag. They had the most valuable piece of evidence possible—a confession.

On the night he was taken into custody, Crimmins had given a second videotaped interview, during which he appeared to admit to killing Helen. The interview in this brief tape took the form of a police officer reading out a series of set questions and Crimmins giving his replies. Defense lawyer Lawrence Hochheiser, claiming that the police "were under tremendous pressure to make an arrest in a highly publicized case," argued that his client had been coached and coerced into making the false confession. Also, at the time Crimmins was arrested—6:30 P.M. on August 29, by the defense's calculations—the police did not have probable cause to arrest, and therefore any alleged confession made after that time should be suppressed as it violated Crimmins's Fourth Amendment rights and should not be admissible in court. The police, adamant that Crimmins had not been arrested until 1:00 A.M. on August 30, insisted that all the legal proprieties had been observed. Family members of the prisoner disagreed. They complained that during both interviews police officers had willfully obstructed their efforts to obtain legal representation for Crimmins.

While the lawyers wrangled, the state reviewed its hand. Apart from the taped confession, they weren't holding any royal flush, even if the OCME had given them one vital lead, concerning that cigarette butt found on the stairway close to where Helen's pen lay. Since 1925 it had been known that some 80 percent of the population secrete their specific blood group information in various bodily fluids, such as saliva. These people are called "secretors." Craig Crimmins fell into this category. When Shaler tested the Marlboro cigarette butt found close to the hair clip and pen, the saliva stains were matched to someone with Crimmins's blood group. Again, like the palm print on the roof, it could be argued that Crimmins might have dropped this butt at any time, but the number of damning coincidences was beginning to mount.

There was also the circumstantial case against Crimmins: he knew the building well; he carried a knife and rope of the type used in the attack; he regularly used the clove hitch knot when securing scenery; and he went missing at the time of Helen's disappearance.

Offsetting all this, however, was a potentially devastating problem. When Crimmins was placed on an ID lineup, Laura Cutler failed to pick him out as the man she had seen in the elevator with Helen. Nor, it could be argued, did the face in the sketch, which showed a dark, swarthy person with short hair, a lined forehead and a stubby growth of beard, bear much resemblance to the fairer complected Crimmins.

So everything hinged on the videotaped confession. Was it admissible or not?

In such a high-profile case, the defense was always going to struggle to win this argument. And so it proved. To no one's surprise, on April 8, 1981, the courts ruled that the tapes were admissible, and the case proceeded to trial.

Dr. Elliott Gross was the first of the expert witnesses. He told how he had found Helen lying on her back, with blood covering her nostrils and ears. Death, he said, had been caused by "multiple fractures of the skull and ribs that occurred as the result of a fall." He confirmed that she had been alive when she fell. There were signs of a struggle, most evident in strands of Helen's blond hair found snagged on a hinged door nearby. The CME finished by saying that an ultraviolet light examination showed no damage to Helen's genitals, and there was no visible evidence of rape.

The testimony of Crimmins's supervisor, Frederick G. Collay, was crucial to the prosecution's case. He had last seen the defendant when the stagehands were changing scenery after *The Firebird*. This would have been around 9:15 P.M. Thereafter Crimmins was absent for every scenery change and he never saw him again that night. The next day when Collay bawled him out for going missing, Crimmins sheepishly explained that he had fallen asleep on one of the movable stages at the rear of the theater. The supervisor agreed that it was common practice for stagehands to take naps in this area, though they usually told someone, in order to be woken up.

At about 9:20 P.M., Robert Rowlands, an electrician, saw Crimmins entering the men's lounge beneath the stage. "He looked like he had been drinking." Although Rowlands couldn't swear to the exact time because he didn't wear a watch, he recalled receiving a telephone call from Collay between 9:45 and 10:00 P.M., asking if he had seen Crimmins recently. He had answered in the negative.

As the prosecution had feared, Laura Cutler was predictably vague on the stand and added little to the case against the defendant.

An illuminating and not terribly complimentary insight into life backstage at the Met was provided by one of the carpenters. Thomas Gravina told how on the afternoon of the tragedy he and Crimmins, together with a couple of other stagehands, had adjourned to a bar in Teaneck, New Jersey, where they proceeded to get blasted. By the carpenter's admittedly hazy reckoning, Crimmins sank about ten beers, sniffed diet capsules, and smoked some dope. They returned to the Met in time for the 8:00 P.M. performance. In Gravina's view, Crimmins, although obviously feeling the effects of his afternoon exertions, did not seem impaired in going about his tasks. Later that night, in between performances, Gravina also noticed that Crimmins had gone missing and the next day asked him what had happened. Crimmins said he had passed out behind the main stage.

But easily the most telling part of Gravina's testimony centered on a conversation he'd had with Crimmins on August 16. According to Gravina, Crimmins said, "If anybody asks that you had seen me sleeping in the back, say that you did." Two days earlier Gravina had told the police that no one was missing from the stage crew on the night of the slaying. "So you lied?" defense counsel Hoch asked, desperate to undermine the witness's credibility. "I lied," Gravina admitted. Urged to expand on Crimmins's reeling condition on the night in question, Gravina said that he appeared "a lot closer to being ready to pass out than just high."

Another witness told how cocaine and marijuana use was commonplace backstage at the Met, both before and during performances, and that after returning to the opera house that evening Crimmins had continued drinking, with one estimate of his intake reaching approximately twenty-six beers.

When Shaler took the stand, he described the test procedures he had conducted to determine if semen was present either in or about the body. All had proved negative. He pointed out that this didn't necessarily preclude the possibility of a seminal discharge. Semen could have been present at the time of death, but exposure to heat and moisture for more than four to six hours could destroy it. (As had already been made clear to the jury, the air shaft where Helen's body was found was dripping with condensation and wickedly hot.)

What Shaler had to say next drove yet another stake into the Met's already badly tarnished image. A drapery and three paper towels found backstage all tested positive for seminal fluid, and since two blood groups were identified, he said, the semen came from at least two men. He estimated the samples were between "one and two months" old but "could also be much older." Reporters scribbled gleefully. Shaler's testimony only added extra spice to already overblown tabloid depictions of the Met as a false-fronted meeting place, where high art in the auditorium concealed a debauched backstage world riddled with casual sex and drug use.

The final link in the prosecution's medico-legal case was made by Detective Joseph Ferraro, who said that when he dusted for prints on the sixth floor roof of the opera house July 24, a day after Helen died, he found a partial palm print on a pipe. He thought the print had been there "about a day or so at the most. It was very lucid and very clear. The clarity was very good."

That opinion was supported by another police fingerprint expert, William Plifka. He, too, had no doubt that the palm print had been made by Crimmins, and when asked how long the print had been there, hazarded a guess at "three days or less." He based this opinion on the fact that sunlight, wind, dust, and rain "adversely affect the clarity of a print."

The prosecution was now wading in dangerous waters. Trying to determine the age of a latent fingerprint is an area fraught with difficulties, as Vincent J. Scalice, a former NYPD homicide detective and now an independent forensic consultant hired by the defense, made clear. There was, he said, "absolutely no way" to determine scientifically the age of a latent print. There were just too many variables. Any estimate was a guess at best and might be off by days, weeks, even months or years.

The expert witnesses had given their testimony. Now everything hinged on the two videotapes.

In the first, made on August 17, Crimmins was questioned about his movements that night. "Well, I did miss some cues," he said, owing to the fact that he had passed out behind the main stage. When Detective Gennaro Giorgio said that other stagehands had checked the area where Crimmins claimed to have slept and found it empty, Crimmins became pensive. After a few moments he asked to speak to Giorgio alone. When the two men were on their own, Crimmins began to talk. "I'm afraid that I'm the man the cops are looking for on the elevator. I was on the elevator with that lady." He claimed that he only spoke to Helen briefly and that she exited at the second floor, after which he went to his locker, drank another six-pack and fell into a stupor. When he awoke at 11:00 P.M., he sneaked out of the building unseen, stopped off to grab a bite at a nearby fast-food restaurant, then went home.

But it was the second tape that doomed Crimmins. In it, he could be seen waiving his rights to have a lawyer present and being read the Miranda warning. The interview itself took the form of a series of confirmatory questions based on statements purportedly made by Crimmins earlier to investigators. This time he admitted sexually propositioning Helen in the elevator. Her response had been to hit him. On the second floor he stopped the elevator and pushed her into a stairwell. By this stage she was plainly terrified. When he demanded sex, she panicked and "started freaking out on me." The two fought on the stairs. "She tried to hit me. I grabbed her hand. That's when I took out the hammer. I just held it and told her to walk up the stairs." Terrified into submission by the raised hammer, Helen did as Crimmins ordered and began to undress. Crimmins, though, was incapable of intercourse, and after a few minutes of slack fumbling he told her to put her clothes back on and frog-marched her up to the roof. Once outside, he tied her with rope, intending to leave her and later notify someone where she was. However, she broke free. After a brief chase, he ran her down and retied her, this time reinforcing his rope with rags snatched from a nearby crate. When she was securely tied, he laid her on her stomach and hacked off her black skirt, black blouse, and under-clothes. "I figured if she got loose, she wouldn't run because she would be embarrassed." Then, so he said, he lurched drunkenly toward the door. Behind him, Helen let out an involuntary whimper. Something inside Craig Crimmins snapped. "And that's when it happened . . . [I] went back and kicked her off."

It was a chilling account, so graphic in its detail that it left the jury with one question only to decide: the degree of Crimmins's culpability. On June 4, 1981, after nine hours of deliberation, jurors returned a verdict of guilty in the second degree. They took the collective view that Crimmins had not set out with the inten-tion of murdering Helen Hagnes but that events had spiraled out of his drunken control. Trial judge Richard G. Denzer threw out the attempted rape charge because of a lack of evidence. At a later hearing Crimmins was sentenced to twenty years to life. At the time of writing, he is incarcerated at Shawangunk Correctional Facility in upstate New York.

This trial proved doubly satisfactory for Gross. Not only did it go a long way toward restoring the OCME's jaded reputation, but it also overlapped a court ruling that finally settled the depart-ment's messy succession wars. In December 1980 an appeals court ruled that Mayor Koch had *not* exceeded his authority when he dismissed Baden without giving him a hearing. In a 2–1 decision, the court declared that the length of the probationary period was immaterial and that the mayor could remove the CME without a hearing, even if the probationary period had expired. After a high-wire balancing act that had lasted seventeen months, Gross was civilly and judicially confirmed as the chief medical examiner for New York.

After the relative quiet of Connecticut, the new CME was pitched headlong into a caseload that rarely strayed from the headlines. In the month of his confirmation, he performed the highest-profile autopsy of his career, when the gunshot-riddled body of John Lennon was brought to 520 First Avenue. The four open-nosed bullets that took the life of the ex-Beatle caused massive internal injuries. Gross estimated that Lennon lost 80 percent of his blood volume, adding that no one could have survived such horrendous injuries for more than a few minutes.

In a foretaste of what was to come, in the spring of 1981 Gross obtained firsthand experience of the psychological damage that terrorist activity can inflict on an unsuspecting population, when at 9:30 A.M. on May 16 a bomb exploded in the men's room at the Pan Am Terminal in Kennedy International Airport. A terminal worker, Alex McMillan, took the full force of the blast. Gross's autopsy showed that McMillan had died of second-degree burns, a hemorrhage and injuries to the right forearm and thigh. A caller, speaking with a heavy Spanish accent, phoned the airport and said the bomb had been planted in the name of the Puerto Rican Armed Resistance, a group ostensibly campaigning for that island's independence. Later that day another bomb was found near a Pan Am terminal gate. Fortunately this was defused before it could do any damage. The following afternoon, yet another bomb was found in the Pan Am terminal, this time in the women's restroom. It, too, was dealt with safely. Over the next couple of days, the NYPD was inundated with more than 170 bomb threats or scares, including seven against the World Trade Center. All needed to be checked out and all proved to be groundless. Even so, this episode provided grim evidence of terrorism's multilayered assault. Overwhelming the emergency services was only half the story; the real victory lay in the trepidation felt by innocent travelers. Despite a lengthy investigation, no one was ever charged with the murder of Alex McMillan.

Murder of a more traditional kind occupied Gross when police descended on a home in the Charleston neighborhood of Staten Island on April 19, 1983, and began digging up the backyard. The house at 420 Sharrot Road was home to the mother of Richard F. Biegenwald, a paroled killer already in custody in New Jersey on suspicion of triple murder. A tip-off told the police exactly where to dig and they soon unearthed two female bodies, wrapped in green plastic bags and buried one on top of the other, thirty inches deep, in a grave next to the garage. Gross began with the body that had been buried the deepest. The two bullets he extracted from the victim's skull were sent off for analysis. Judging from the advanced decomposition, he estimated that the body had been in the ground for at least a year, probably longer. To aid in the identification process, Gross turned to odontological analysis. Dental charts showed her to be seventeen-year-old Maria Ciallella who had disappeared on Halloween night 1981 while walking to her home in Brick Township, New Jersey.

The second body had been horribly mutilated, with multiple stab wounds, and dental records were again the key to unlocking her identity. Deborah Osborne was also just seventeen years old when she left the Idle Hour Tavern in Point Pleasant, New Jersey, on April 8, 1982, to hitch a ride back to the motel where she worked as a chambermaid. Somewhere along Route 88 she was picked up by Biegenwald. In addition to her extensive dental work, Deborah was also identified by a cross found on the body.

Biegenwald was a habitual killer. At age nineteen, he was sentenced to life imprisonment for murdering Bayonne City prosecutor Stephen F. Sladowski during a botched robbery on December 18, 1958, at a delicatessen owned by Sladowski's family. Despite being repeatedly disciplined for misconduct while in prison and three times being denied parole, he was released in 1975. A string of parole violations led to more prison time, until he was once again freed in February 1981. Nine months later he murdered Maria Ciallella, the first of five more victims. Four were young women; the only male was William J. Ward, a video games operator, who had reportedly attempted to hire Biegenwald as a contract killer, only to end up dead himself.*

The positive identification of Maria Ciallella was only made possible because of the huge advances made in forensic science in recent years. But these developments were proving to be a double-edged sword. Because the detection levels of departments like the OCME seemed on a never-ending upward curve, police forces were putting an ever-greater reliance—and strain—on them to deliver the goods. Gross addressed this problem when he spoke to forty-nine medical examiners and pathologists from around the state at a two-day seminar held at New York University Medical School in May 1983. He complained that an intolerable pressure of work led to inexperienced staff dealing with cases beyond their expertise. He talked frankly about the recent death of Frank Sandola, a forty-two-year-old health club manager who was found slumped over a table in his Manhattan apartment. The assistant ME dispatched to

---

* In 1991, the original death sentences imposed on Biegenwald were overturned and substituted with life imprisonment.

the scene signed off the death as natural causes after she found a lump of meat in the man's throat, concluding that he had choked to death. Later, doubts crept into her mind. Returning to the dimly lit apartment, she found traces of blood around where the body had lain. This didn't seem right. When her doubts were passed further up the chain of command, a full autopsy was ordered. This found that a .22-caliber bullet had been fired at close range into the canal of the right ear. Because of the misdiagnosis, the crime scene was improperly processed and the killer never caught. (Even this blunder paled when set against one New Jersey case in 1982 where the medical examiner concluded that a young man in his twenties, Thomas Acevedo, had died from pneumonia. What the seventy-three-year-old medical examiner missed, the mortician did not: four bullets in the skull. No autopsy had been performed, despite a request from detectives that one be conducted.) Such sloppiness, said Gross, was unforgivable, making him speculate just how many other possible homicides were slipping through the net. For a crime to be investigated, he said, it is first necessary for a crime to be recognized. And that requires vigilant doctors. Harking back to Helpern's scathing attack on those "five o'clock doctors" in the medical profession who refused to leave the comfort and safety of their consulting rooms, Gross spoke for forensic pathologists everywhere when he said, "It's very difficult to find doctors in Manhattan willing to go to the scene."

Gross's own interdepartmental headaches, although temporarily abated, were by no means at an end. In September 1981 Baden had taken a year's leave of absence from the OCME to become chief deputy medical examiner for Suffolk County on Long Island. But the old grievances were still gnawing away at him, and in 1982 he filed a civil suit, claiming that Koch had fired him knowing that some charges against him were untrue. Baden was seeking several million dollars in damages because, he said, the groundless allegations had him "a pariah" in his profession, one whose ability to testify as an expert witness had been severely jeopardized. The battle of words, both in court and in the media, raged back and forth for two years until, in July 1984, a judge awarded Baden one hundred thousand dollars in damages for emotional stress.

Ironically, even before this judgment, Baden was once again on the OCME payroll. The controversy that had followed him to Suffolk County had blighted his chances of promotion, and as a result he decided to return to the office where he had built his reputation. In August 1983 the peripatetic pathologist announced that he was quitting Long Island and returning to New York to head the Brooklyn office.

The city and Gross certainly needed him. Record numbers of New Yorkers were being murdered each year and the OCME was close to meltdown. In 1979 the official police department tally showed that there were 1,733 murders. By 1981 that number had risen to 1,832, with one-fourth of those deaths drug related. Gross and his understaffed office were expected to investigate all these deaths. An added irritant was the mandatory requirement that in homicide cases, two qualified pathologists should be in attendance at every autopsy. The wholesale exodus of staff from the Office of the Chief Medical Examiner—largely, it must be said, inspired by disgust over Baden's original ouster—meant that corners were being cut. In the last year of Baden's tenure, ten of the fourteen full-time medical examiners had been board certified in forensic pathology; under Gross that number had shrunk to six out of sixteen. Some MEs were being called upon to perform six autopsies a day, three times the maximum number recommended by the National Association of Medical Examiners. This left little or no time for teaching and research, two disciplines that had always been central to the OCME ethos. Disgruntled former staff members lined up to take potshots at Gross, with accusations of disinterest, incompetence, and allegations that he was far too cozy with the police. Significantly, all these charges found their way into print, culminating in a series of highly critical articles about the OCME that ran in the *New York Times* in January 1985. Of these, the most damning concerned the notorious death of Michael Stewart, a twenty-five-year-old black man, arrested by transit police officers for allegedly scrawling graffiti on a subway wall. He was seized at 2:30 A.M. on September 15, 1983, in the subway station at First Avenue and Fourteenth Street while on his way home to Brooklyn after spending time at a disco. According to the officers, Stewart had resisted arrest and had to be subdued. Almost an hour later a police van pulled into Bellevue Hospital. When hospital orderlies loaded Stewart on to a gurney, they noted that he had been hog-tied—his ankles bound together, yanked up behind his back, and tied to his hands with cord. Equally obvious was the mosaic of livid bruises that covered his body. Much the greatest concern, however, centered on Stewart's heart—it had stopped beating. Although resuscitation attempts were successful, Stewart never did regain consciousness and he died thirteen days later.

His death came at a time of bitter racial strife. Congress had just concluded a hearing into charges of racially motivated police activity, and black activists seized upon Stewart's death as just the latest example of NYPD brutality. Because of the case's notoriety, Gross performed the autopsy himself, accompanied by Dr. John Grauerholz, a forensic pathologist who had been hired by the family. After an unusually long autopsy—more than six hours—during which Gross took scores of photographs, he announced that he found no evidence that any injury sustained by Stewart had contributed to his death, which he attributed to cardiac arrest. This surprised Grauerholz who thought he had seen petechial hemorrhages in the eyes—usually an indicator of asphyxia. If Grauerholz were correct, this would add muscle to the Stewart family's belief that Michael had died from a police choke hold. Unfortunately there wouldn't be a chance to test Grauerholz's findings, because one day after the autopsy, Gross returned to the autopsy room, removed Stewart's eyes, and placed them in formalin, a solution that preserves tissue but does tend to eliminate any traces of blood. When, a few days later, the toxicology report showed traces of alcohol in Stewart's blood, Gross decided that this, too, may have contributed to the death.

Then came a quite extraordinary U-turn. After conferring with other experts, Gross decided that death was due to a traumatic injury to the cervical vertebrae, with the implication that Stewart had injured himself having fallen down drunk. Gross's volte-face caused an outrage, so much so that he decided for the integrity of the department to stop personally carrying out autopsies. This, of course, only increased the burden on his colleagues. Morgenthau decided that the case stank enough to warrant charging six officers with complicity in the death of Michael Stewart.

Gross couldn't dodge the hailstorm of flak being aimed in his direction. Especially since most of it emanated from within the Office of the Chief Medical Examiner. Certain staff members there strongly believed that Stewart had died from a choke hold administered by the police, and they weren't shy about sharing these beliefs with grateful reporters.

By the time the case came to trial in June 1985, attorneys for both prosecution and defense were gunning for the beleaguered chief medical examiner. On the stand, Gross performed horribly. He now offered a third version of how Michael Stewart died—no opinion! Thereafter the trial teetered from fiasco to farce to ignominy, and on November 24, 1985, all six officers were acquitted of all charges.

Even before this debacle, Gross sensed that he was in a fight for his professional existence. In the wake of those scathing *Times* articles, he had taken a paid leave of absence to prepare his defense. This entailed him handing over day-to-day duties to his deputy, Dr. Beverly Leffers, who became the acting chief medical examiner. Gross's spell in the wilderness was brief. A mayoral report concluded that while Gross might have "mishandled" some cases, there was no underlying or systemic problem with his stewardship. Buoyed up by this verdict, Gross returned to work. Then came a more lethal arrow. This time it was fired by the state health department. In a report compiled for Governor Mario Cuomo, the department criticized Gross's management skills and lodged twelve charges of gross incompetence or neglect against him. Under fire from all sides, in August 1985 Gross was again forced to hand the reins of power to Leffers while he took a second leave of absence. His position was clearly untenable: the largest city in the United States had a chief medical examiner who was forbidden to perform autopsies. Gross fretted and fumed, absolutely convinced he knew where to pin the blame for his current predicament. Gross's lawyer, Howard Squadron, told the press that Baden and allies of Baden had been trying "to undermine Dr. Gross for years." Gross also had plenty of venom left over for the *New York Times*, and in January 1986 he filed a libel suit over that string of articles, firing the first shot in a legal battle that would drag on with Jarndyce-like longevity into the next century.*

Baden suffered his own legal setback during this period. In August 1986 a federal appeals court reversed a lower court's decision and ruled that Mayor Koch had *not* violated Baden's constitutional rights when he'd fired him. The court also overturned the hundred-thousand-dollar award. Baden, already on leave from the OCME for several months, decided that now was the time to sever all connection with the department that he had joined more than

---

* Eventually, in March 2001, an appeals court threw out Gross's suit.

SEVEN

THE DARKEST HOUR

Koch didn't pull any punches when quizzed by reporters over his reasons for firing Gross. The ousted chief, he said, lacked the "level of leadership and level of management" needed to head the Office of the Chief Medical Examiner. And just in case anyone questioned his authority to take such peremptory action, Koch cited the ruling handed down in the Baden exit. (The mayor's robust self-justification didn't prevent Gross from filing the inevitable lawsuit for wrongful dismissal.) Although the search for a successor began the day after Gross's departure, it was conducted at an unhurried, almost leisurely pace. Only one selection marker seemed set in stone; this time around there would be no in-house promotion. Years of interdepartmental score settling had taken a heavy toll on the OCME's reputation and standing within the medico-legal community, a fall from grace that a city the size and caliber of New York could ill afford. Koch decided to cut out the cancer for good by casting his selection net further afield. A few ruffled Manhattan egos, he reasoned, was a small price to pay for the restoration of public confidence. The same mayoral advisory board that just months earlier had delivered such a damning indictment against Gross was now charged with compiling a list of suitable replacements.

In the meantime, for the third time in as many years, Dr. Beverly Leffers was appointed the acting chief medical examiner. The mess she inherited was horrifying: a backlog of more than three thousand cases in the toxicology lab, autopsy reports that took as much as six months to complete—the national average was about two weeks—sagging morale, and a dire shortage of staff. It was time to get out the begging bowl. Special pleading brought a favorable response from City Hall: an additional one million dollars was tacked on to the OCME's 1988 budget request, specifically targeted to hiring more toxicologists and pathologists.

This marked a turbulent period for Leffers. On April 25, 1988, she was herself added to the list of crime statistics, when a mugger in Brooklyn struck her twice over the head with a pistol and stole her purse. Fortunately, the injuries were not severe and Leffers was able to go home after hospital treatment, nursing a sore head and ruing the theft of five hundred dollars.

She was also having to adjust to the fact that just a few days beforehand the special mayoral advisory board had announced that its headhunting quest for a permanent CME was at an end. After much sifting and competition they had reduced the short list of preferred candidates to just three names: Dr. Ross Zumwalt, the chief medical investigator of New Mexico; Dr. Brian D. Blackbourne, the CME for Massachusetts; and Dr. Charles S. Hirsch, the CME for Suffolk County, Long Island. Of these, the Chicago-born Hirsch was the panel's unanimous choice. They reckoned that he best possessed the "professional qualities" and the "administrative and personal leadership" necessary to restore the OCME's reputation.

At the time of his appointment, Hirsch was fifty-one years old and the first nonnative New Yorker since Norris to be appointed to the top position. He'd received his medical degree from the University of Illinois and his original ambition had been to open a general practice in Alaska, but during an internship in Cleveland he became hooked on forensic pathology and all dreams of the northern wilderness were pushed firmly to one side. For the next sixteen years he taught pathology in Cleveland and Cincinnati, until 1985 when he moved to the New York area, becoming the CME for Suffolk County, on Long Island.

Once in place there, he speedily carved out a reputation as a no-nonsense administrator and a first-rate pathologist. His mental toughness was never in doubt, nor was his willingness to thwart what he perceived to be meddlesome interference. When Suffolk County judge Kenneth K. Rohl was mulling over how best to sentence a teenager convicted of drug offenses, "Hizzoner" decided it would send the right message if the defendant were obliged to witness the autopsies of two drug-overdose victims. When news of this decision reached Hirsch, he took a step back and drew a deep, dark line in the sand. Turning an autopsy into a public spectacle, as he saw it, offended every ethical and professional fiber in his body. Plus, there was an added risk: some might consider that such a sentence amounted to "cruel and unusual punishment," possibly leading to all kinds of legal ramifications. He refused point-blank to accede to Rohl's wishes. Eventually the judge did find another pathologist prepared to accede to his rather curious sentencing procedures, but Hirsch had made a very public declaration of his independence.

He could be just as single minded when problems cropped up in his own backyard. On January 31, 1985, an employee at the Suffolk County morgue managed to upset just about everyone it was possible to upset with a departmental snafu as farcical as it was profoundly upsetting. The fiasco was triggered when a representative from a local funeral home called to collect the body of Patrick Hosang for cremation. The morgue attendant, James White, had gone into the refrigerated storage room and, without bothering to check the identification tag on the toe, had wheeled out Hosang's body. Except it wasn't Hosang. The body on the gurney was that of sixty-two-year-old William Podstupka. Only later, after Mr. Podstupka had been cremated, did the blunder come to light. As far as Hirsch was concerned, such insensitive negligence was unpardonable, and he wasted no time in firing White and demoting his superior.

In 1987 Hirsch carried this independent streak into the courtroom with him when he figured prominently in one of the most sensational American trials in years. The defendant, thirty-six-year-old electrical engineer Bernhard Goetz, stood accused of shooting four young black males on the New York subway system. It was a sensational story that had circled the globe. From Alaska to Australia, people got to hear about Goetz's December 1984 shooting spree that had left one man paralyzed and three others injured. His claim—that he had opened fire because the men had surrounded him and he feared being robbed—drew plenty of sympathy from some quarters. Others weren't so sure. And this included the State of New York, which portrayed Goetz as an unbalanced racist out to get revenge for having been mugged twice before. Two headline-making years passed before Goetz stood trial, during which time the defense put together an impressive lineup of expert witnesses. Among these was none other than former CME, Dr. Dominick DiMaio. He told the court that by tracking the course of the bullet wounds, it was possible to determine that the victims *were* standing in a menacing semicircle around Goetz at the time they were shot, as the defendant had claimed. Furthermore, DiMaio also stated that Darrell Cabey, the most seriously injured of the four nineteen-year-olds shot by Goetz, could not have been seated, as the prosecution alleged, when he was hit.

Hirsch, called by the prosecution as a rebuttal witness, was appalled by DiMaio's conclusions. When asked what he thought of his testimony, he replied, "In my opinion, it's completely false . . . Not only is it unsupported by fact, but it is unsupportable." This was powerful stuff. Expert witnesses, especially those in the medical profession, are rarely so critical of each other in public—behind closed doors it's an entirely different matter—but Hirsch's mold-breaking belligerence availed him and the prosecution little. When the jury came back, the so-called Subway Vigilante was acquitted of attempted murder charges and served only a few months for illegal weapon possession.

What this trial did do was to highlight Hirsch's supereffective courtroom manner. Not all experts make expert witnesses. It is a rare talent. Unlike some medico-legal specialists, whose circumlocutory style of testimony littered with non sequiturs could glaze the eyes of judge and jury alike, Hirsch was a model of lucidity on the witness stand. In this respect he was cut from the same cloth as Milton Helpern: no fancy words; just clear, concise descriptions of the matter in hand. This enviable courtroom fluency was just one of the many talents that New York City was hoping to acquire when it appointed Hirsch as its chief medical examiner.

There was just one stumbling block: nobody could agree about how Hirsch was going to be paid. A controversial proposal that Hirsch's salary should be derived from both public and private sources raised plenty of hackles and was referred to the city's Board of Ethics. After considerable head scratching, board members okayed the idea and cobbled together a package whereby Hirsch's $125,000 annual city salary could be topped up by $50,000 from the NYU Medical Center, where he would serve as chief of forensic pathology, plus another $25,000 from a consortium of local medical schools. It was an original and contentious settlement. Widespread, muttered complaints that such an arrangement opened the door to accusations of possible conflicts of interest were speedily quashed by the new incumbent. An independent autopsy, Hirsch said, "is the only kind of autopsy I know how to give, whoever I may be working for. That is my hallmark."

So it was that on January 1, 1989, Hirsch, the pipe-smoking physician who had originally dreamed of a nice quiet practice in the backwoods, officially took charge of the busiest medical examiner's office in the world. Item number one on the agenda: slashing that enormous backlog of cases. The budget increase granted one year beforehand now came into play as Hirsch went on a big hiring drive, taking on new pathologists and lab technicians. Paying staff more money is always good for office morale. Hirsch's next move, however, sent shock waves through the department. He decided to farm out some of the more complex forensic tests to private laboratories. There was no intended reflection on the abilities of those around him, just a pragmatic realization that given the pace of modern technological development, certain specialized labs already had the necessary equipment in place for the latest, most sophisticated analysis; for the OCME to duplicate these services would amount to an unconscionable waste of tax dollars. Hirsch's revolutionary approach might not have pleased everyone, but it paid off. By the summer of 1989, those six-month autopsy reports were now routinely taking a week.

Which was just as well, because this was a period when New Yorkers were slaughtering each other with Balkan-like frequency and ferocity. In 1989 the OMCE investigated no fewer than 1,905 homicides. The following year saw that number soar to 2,245. This meant that every four hours or so, somewhere in the five boroughs another life was being snuffed out. The lonely procession of bereaved relatives calling at 520 First Avenue to identify loved ones was growing at a heartbreaking rate. Like other CMEs before him, Hirsch was acutely aware of the distress this caused. Wherever possible, he arranged for identification to be done through photographs, thus sparing the bereaved the often daunting ordeal of the refrigerated steel compartments and the all-pervasive odor of formaldehyde.

Although no one realized it at the time, 1990 marked a watershed for New York's homicide rate. For reasons about which the sociologists and criminologists argue to this day—though most agree that a significantly increased uniformed police presence on the streets and markedly improved levels of forensic detection played a major role—the murder toll began, year on year, to decline dramatically.* This was great news for New York. However, it was overshadowed by another potentially far more sinister development. At 12:18 P.M. on February 26, 1993, a bomb exploded at the World Trade Center.

A van containing 1,310 pounds of explosives had been parked in the underground garage of the North Tower (Tower One). The intent of the terrorists who planted the device was for Tower One to collapse onto Tower Two after the blast, destroying them both. But the bombers had grossly underestimated the amount of explosive required to initiate such a chain reaction. Although the tower shuddered on its foundations, and six people died and more than one thousand were injured, the structure withstood the blast and remained intact.

In freezing weather, search-and-rescue teams combed the wreckage for days. The final body to be recovered came on March 15, when construction workers spotted a black boot among the rubble. Clearing away chunks of concrete and twisted steel, they

---

* The bottom of the murder graph was reached in 2005 when the number of homicides fell to 539, the fewest since 1963.

found Wilfred Mercado buried twelve feet deep. Mercado, the purchasing agent for Windows on the World, the tower's elegant penthouse restaurant, had been checking food deliveries at the time of the explosion and had plunged through three floors into the midst of the collapsed wreckage. Hirsch explained why the body had eluded searchers for so long: the icy temperatures had delayed decomposition, making it that much more difficult for the tracker dogs to detect Mercado's presence.

Although New York was no stranger to the use of bombs as an instrument of terror—the 1981 FALN (Fuerzas Armadas de Liberación Nacional) campaign and before that the eccentric sixteen-year crusade by the "Mad Bomber," George Metesky, that ended in 1957 were just two such incidents—this was the first time that Middle Eastern terrorists had carried their struggle into the heart of America's greatest city. For most New Yorkers the hellishness of what had happened was dwarfed by the prospect of what might have been. As wake-up calls go, it was brutal. Just a few hundred dollars' worth of commercially available chemicals, carefully mixed together, had almost silenced the iconic heartbeat of American capitalism.*

Besides dealing with the aftermath of terrorist atrocities, Hirsch had another problem, this time homegrown, to contend with: an awful lot of New Yorkers were dying in police custody or else following encounters with the police. The fact that many of the victims came from ethnic minority backgrounds only hardened the suspicion held in some quarters that a hard core of NYPD cops were redneck racists, patrolling the streets with a license to kill. Even those few police officers that did face charges of abusing their powers seemed to bear charmed lives once they reached the court-

---

* Six people were ultimately imprisoned for their part in this outrage. The sentences ranged up to 240 years.

room. A case in point began on December 21, 1994, when Anthony Baez, aged twenty-nine, was playing a game of touch football with his brothers outside the family's home in the Bronx. At some point the football struck a passing patrol car. When Officer Francis X. Livoti exited the vehicle and loudly ordered the brothers to quit, Anthony Baez ignored him. Livoti grabbed hold of Baez and said he was under arrest. As Baez struggled, face down beneath Livoti, family members shouted for the officer to take it easy as Baez suffered from asthma. But Livoti kept on squeezing. At some point during the struggle, Baez lost consciousness. He later died. Livoti was no stranger to violent incidents—his record listed eleven abuse and brutality complaints—and the district attorney's office decided that this time the loose cannon had let off one shot too many. Livoti was charged with criminally negligent homicide.

Whenever a cop stands trial on charges of official malfeasance, he or she can be guaranteed two things: top-quality legal representation and, if required, some very fancy-priced expert witnesses. On this occasion the defense produced a whole string of experts prepared to testify that Baez had died from a severe asthma attack after being arrested. In rebuttal, the prosecution called just one person—Dr. Charles S. Hirsch.

Now, there had been accusations in the not too distant past that certain CMEs were overly chummy with the NYPD, far too eager to testify on behalf of beleaguered officers. But Hirsch had taken office promising to "call 'em like I see 'em," and in this case he had seen petechiae in the dead man's eyes. In his book, that pointed overwhelmingly to asphyxiation as the cause of death. He said that bruises on the dead man's neck—clearly visible in the postmortem photographs—were indicative of "probably a minute or more of constant pressure. They were caused by choke marks." Again and again, Hirsch told the court that Baez had been choked to death.

Then the trial took a curious turn. The judge, Acting Justice Gerald Sheindlin, who was hearing the case without a jury, asked Hirsch to play the devil's advocate. Assume for a moment, said Sheindlin, that Baez was released from the neck grip, regained consciousness and struggled, whereupon he was pinned facedown and one or more officers put pressure on his back. "And I also want you to assume that as a result of that activity, Mr. Baez suffered an acute asthma attack." Hirsch listened closely as Sheindlin warmed to his theory, certain he knew where this was heading. Would it be possible, the judge asked, for this set of circumstances to produce results consistent with what was found at autopsy? It was a skillfully framed question and, of course, left Hirsch with no alternative but to reply, "Yes, sir, it could."

On October 10, 1996, Judge Sheindlin announced his verdict. After condemning Livoti's quick temper and unprofessional conduct, and also denouncing Livoti's fellow officers for having engaged in a "nest of perjury," the judge then proceeded to acquit the defendant. It was all too bewildering.*

Verdicts such as this did nothing to undermine a commonly held belief in the mid-1990s that New York cops were untouchable. And weary veterans of the civil liberties wars weren't holding out too many hopes the following year when yet another NYPD officer found himself in court on charges of unlawful killing.

No one disputed that Patrick "Hessy" Phelan died from a gunshot wound in the early hours of January 22, 1996. Far more contentious was the answer to this question: whose hand held the gun that fired the bullet? The jockey-sized Phelan—he stood less than five feet tall and barely nudged the scales over one hundred

---

* Two years later, the city settled a civil suit with the Baez family for $2.94 million. In 1998 Livoti was convicted of violating Baez's civil rights and sentenced to seven and a half years imprisonment.

pounds—had spent most of the preceding day drinking at the Oak
Bar on 206th Street, a popular hangout for Irish immigrants in the
Bronx. According to his barroom buddies, the thirty-nine-year-old
housepainter was a bad drunk, and this particular midnight found
him reeling on his feet and belligerent. The bartender, Margaret
McGrath, worried that Phelan was too inebriated to find his way
home, asked her boyfriend to help the little fellow across the road
to her apartment, where he could sleep it off on her couch. Richard
J. Molloy, an off-duty cop, stood on little ceremony as he bundled
Phelan roughly from the bar. Too roughly, in the view of most who
witnessed the incident. According to Molloy, after they reached
McGrath's apartment, just as he was laying Phelan down on the
couch, the Irishman suddenly yanked Molloy's service revolver
from its holster and shot himself to death. Acquaintances of both
men pondered the likelihood of a skinny little guy like Phelan getting the better of the hulking Molloy in a fight for possession of a
pistol. Some scoffed, some shrugged; everyone agreed it didn't
smell right.

So what would Hirsch make of Molloy's story? Phelan had
been shot once, through the left eye at close range, and when
Hirsch opened up the skull, he was able to track the path of the
.38-caliber slug, which had traversed the brain and exited the back
of Phelan's head. Judging from the angle of fire, and allying this to
an estimate of the shooting distance—the scorch marks and powder burns around the entrance wound had been minimal—Hirsch
was able to pour cold water on any notion that this gunshot had
been self-inflicted.

Hirsch's doubts received strong corroboration when a hitherto
unknown witness named Cormac Lee suddenly materialized.
Investigators from the Internal Affairs Bureau had stumbled across
Lee during the course of their inquiries. Lee, it transpired, had been
in the kitchen when the two men entered the apartment. They were

unaware of his presence, and he'd overheard them arguing heatedly in the lounge. At one point he had peeked in, only to recoil quickly when he saw Molloy brandishing a gun. Retreating to the bedroom, Lee had then heard Phelan yell challengingly, "Go on! Go on!" Almost immediately a shot rang out. When Lee rushed into the room, Molloy was standing no more than two feet from the stricken Phelan, who lay on the couch, blood pumping from a head wound. There was no gun in sight. (Investigators later found the revolver, with one spent shell and five live rounds, in Molloy's possession.) The next day, Molloy, bristling with menace, had cornered Lee at the Oak Bar and warned him to keep quiet about what he had seen.

Around the neighborhood Molloy was feared as a bully with a hair-trigger temper. In 1993 he had shot and killed an ex-con named Granson Santamaria, using the excuse that he thought Santamaria was reaching for a gun. No weapon was ever found. Six months later, Molloy was again spraying bullets around, when he opened fire from his patrol car at a man named Paul Lipsy. One of the bullets passed through Lipsy's jacket but did not hit him. Since Lipsy was found to be carrying a gun—he had been mugged twice and claimed to be carrying the weapon for self-protection—he was sentenced to one year's imprisonment for illegal possession of a weapon, despite the trial judge's condemning Molloy's actions as "offensive and shocking" and also branding Molloy's testimony as "incredible." Molloy's record was littered with other disciplinary infractions, most for excessive violence. In his career, Molloy had fired his gun on no fewer than nine separate occasions and had been on the receiving end of fifteen complaints.

Notwithstanding Hirsch's findings and Molloy's dubious track record, on April 18, 1997, a judge threw out an indictment for second-degree murder, saying there was insufficient evidence to prove reckless behavior by the officer. Once again, or so it seemed, the cowboy cop had slipped through the net. But the district attorney's office wasn't about to roll over without a fight. On appeal the indictment was reinstated, after it was discovered that the gun in Molloy's holster was secured by a leather strap that ran from the outside, over the handle, behind the hammer, and snapped on the body side. Tests showed it was physically impossible to pull the gun from the holster with one hand while the strap was snapped shut. There was one other anomaly: how many suicides, after shooting themselves in the head, are thoughtful enough to return the weapon to its owner before they expire?

On April 20, 1999, Molloy, who had also waived his right to a jury trial, was found guilty and later sentenced to a maximum of twelve years. Most trial watchers agreed that Hirsch's testimony had been crucial. And controversial. Plenty of NYPD officers grumbled that they had been stabbed in the back by a rogue public official with a vendetta against New York's finest. Those able to see the big picture recognized that Hirsch's independence was utterly essential if public confidence were to be restored in what had become a very shaky institution indeed.

Not long after the conclusion of this trial, the OCME proudly presented the latest addition to its ever-expanding array of technical resources—six enormous refrigerated trucks that could be used to store bodies if the city mortuaries lost power or in the event of a mass fatality. There were two for Manhattan and one each for the other boroughs. Ellen Borakove, a spokesperson for the OCME, explained that the mortuary at 520 First Avenue could house only about 200 corpses. For just a few hundred dollars a month, the city gained six rolling morgues, each five feet high and forty-five feet long, that together could store about 250 bodies. New York was taking the possibility of catastrophe seriously. Ever since the beginning of the decade, the city had maintained a contingency plan that called for up to eight thousand body bags to be on hand should they ever be needed. "We have the ability to get a significant number more," said Ms. Borakove. "Of course, we all hope it won't be necessary."

Twenty-one months later that hope collapsed in rubble.

CASE FILE:
September 11, 2001

Sixty-six years to the day after New York's first chief medical officer, Charles Norris, died, his successor, Dr. Hirsch, was in his office at 520 First Avenue. Outside, it was a glorious fall morning with bright sunshine and promised highs in the eighties. Inside, Hirsch had his hands full. A training session on dealing with biohazards and airborne pathogens had been scheduled, and the OCME was once again up to its elbows in yet another headline-making case. This time it concerned an off-duty cop, Joseph Gray, who, after an all-day drinking binge, had plowed his car into a family group, killing three people. One of the victims, Maria Hererra, had been pregnant at the time. Despite urgent medical attention at the hospital, her unborn baby also died. Because the baby, which had been delivered by Caesarian section, never took a breath on his own and lived only for half a day with the aid of drugs, Hirsch felt justified in declaring it to be stillborn. But the Brooklyn DA's office—with one eye on an upcoming election and urged on by the victims' furious relatives—decided to take a stand. Suddenly everyone wanted little Ricardo Hererra's name added to the murder victim list. When Hirsch refused to change his finding, the DA's iron fist came down, and in a showy announcement Hirsch was overruled.* It was a rare public reversal for Hirsch, but he was ready to put all

---

* In May 2002 Gray was sentenced to five to fifteen years for second degree manslaughter.

that behind him now. Win some, lose some; as far as Hirsch was concerned, this Tuesday morning was shaping up to be just another day at the Office of the Chief Medical Examiner. Until just before 9:00 A.M.

That was when the phone rang. The message was terse—a plane, thought to be a commercial airliner, had struck the North Tower at the World Trade Center, barely three miles away.

During its brief and hectic history, New York City had suffered some quite appalling accidents, none greater than the *General Slocum* disaster of June 15, 1904, when a steamship burst into flames on the East River with the loss of more than one thousand lives. But a modern airliner slamming into one of the world's tallest buildings threatened to dwarf even that catastrophe. Those with long memories recalled that once before a plane had hit a Manhattan skyscraper. On July 28, 1945 a twin-engined B-25 army bomber, hopelessly lost in blinding fog, had careered into the Empire State Building, 915 feet above street level, killing thirteen persons and injuring twenty-six more. Shocking as that incident had been, today's sounded much, much worse.

Over the previous decade, the OCME, in concert with New York City's various emergency response agencies, had repeatedly practiced drills based on simulated plane crashes and attacks with biological weapons, so while other staff members set in motion this well-rehearsed disaster plan, Hirsch and five aides readied themselves for the short drive to the scene. Their first task would be to establish a temporary morgue for the inevitable victims. But just moments before they left, another message came through—a second jetliner had smashed into the World Trade Center's South Tower.

In an instant it became clear that the first crash had been no random accident but part of a well-coordinated attack. An aerial assault of this nature on a major city was entirely unprecedented;

the body count could be astronomical. On any given day, upward of fifty thousand people worked at the Twin Towers, with visitors more than doubling that total. Faced with numbers like that, Hirsch and his department were potentially dealing with the greatest act of mass murder in American history.

The OCME team threaded its way through streets filled with screaming sirens, firefighting trucks, and just about every kind of emergency vehicle imaginable. When the congestion turned to gridlock, they parked a few blocks up from the disaster zone and completed the rest of the journey on foot. As they reached the World Trade Center Plaza, a vision of Dantean horror reared up before them. The peaks of both towers were ablaze, and columns of smoke billowed from raw holes in the structure, blackening the lower Manhattan skyline. But it was unable to block out the most horrific sight of all—a ghastly human confetti, as scores of trapped workers chose to jump a thousand feet to their doom in order to escape the raging infernos. Very few medical examiners are eyewitnesses to the deaths they investigate. Here, Hirsch could only look on, as helpless as everyone else around him, as the bodies rained down.

Amid the pandemonium, news came through that the carnage wasn't confined to New York alone. Just before 9:45 A.M., the networks began reporting that 240 miles southwest of Manhattan, another hijacked airliner had careered into the west wall of the Pentagon in Arlington, Virginia. The devastation there was also colossal.

As dazed onlookers in Lower Manhattan stared up at the stricken towers, struggling to digest the magnitude of what was happening about them and elsewhere in America, suddenly, at 9:59 A.M., the air bulged with a fearful cry from the disbelieving onlookers—the South Tower was falling!

In a matter of just ten seconds, the 1,368-foot-tall building simply ceased to exist. Its concertina-like collapse squeezed all the life from sixty million cubic feet of space, generating a lethal windstorm that roared with hurricane force through the concourse, killing scores more and filling the air with shards of steel, flying concrete, and choking smoke.

Among those flattened by the blast was the OCME team. One investigator broke her leg so severely that the bone gaped through; another, felled by a blow to the back of the head, would take months to recover. Amy Mundorff, the city's first forensic anthropologist, was thrown forty feet headlong into a wall and fractured two ribs. Hirsch got lucky. He happened to be standing on West Street beneath a pedestrian footbridge when the tower fell and was shielded from the worst of the blast. Even so, he too was hurled like a rag doll, sustaining bruises all over his body and spraining an ankle. When he picked himself up he resembled a ghostly wraith, blanketed from head to toe in white dust.

Suddenly news came over the wires of yet more insanity. Another hijacked airliner—the fourth—had crashed, this time in a rural part of Pennsylvania, eighty miles southeast of Pittsburgh, and twenty minutes' flying time from Washington, D.C. Apparently en route to a target in the nation's capital, for some reason it had crashed short of its destination. Only in the fullness of time would cell phone transcripts reveal how heroic passenger intervention had most likely averted yet another national disaster.

Meanwhile, in the World Trade Center Plaza at 10:28 A.M., one hour and forty-two minutes after being struck, the North Tower went the way of its twin, collapsing with hellish, almost unbelievable rapidity.

In the midst of all this madness, with hundreds of emergency personnel milling everywhere, Hirsch fought to coordinate the OCME's response. His arm had been badly gashed in the hail of debris belched out by the South Tower's collapse, but he calmly sutured the wound himself and remained at his post. No other medical examiner in history had had to deal with death on such a monumental scale. Although the number of casualties was as yet unknown, whispers from some shell-shocked authorities were putting the death toll as high as ten thousand. Such a loss of life on American soil had not been seen since the bloodiest days of the Civil War.

When Hirsch reached the end of that dreadful day, he made a chilling discovery: his pockets were full of dust. He shuddered inwardly. If the blast had been able to pulverize concrete and steel to this fine powder, what on earth would it have done to human bodies? In the normal course of events, the medical examiner's function is either to determine or confirm the cause of death. Here, Hirsch sensed that his overriding concern would hinge on simply finding enough human matter to identify.

All through the night the disaster management plan swung into action. By first light, less than twenty-four hours after the atrocity, a barge tied up at a pier in Lower Manhattan. On board were pallets of ice, designed to preserve any human remains as they were recovered from the rubble. Later that morning a convoy of refrigerated trucks lined up along Second Avenue, adjacent to the medical examiner's office. They would provide space to store about a thousand bodies. More than eleven thousand body bags were delivered in two loads, with no one yet knowing how many would ultimately be needed.

As work began on clearing the devastation, logistical nightmares were uncovered at every turn. It wasn't just the Twin Towers that had suffered. Sixteen other major buildings in and around the plaza were either partially destroyed or else had sustained significant damage, and although hygiene requirements mandated that the rubble be cleared as soon as possible to minimize the risk of disease, medical urgency was tempered by the realization that among this debris lay the remains of thousands of murder victims. Some compromise had to be found, a kind of clearinghouse for the World Trade Center debris. It was decided to recommission the Fresh Kills Landfill, a three-thousand-acre site on the northwest of Staten Island that had been the city's main garbage dump until it was closed down earlier in the year. Once there, every scrap of the 1.6 million tons of rubble would be sifted by hand by FBI agents, and any body parts discovered put on ice and transferred to 520 First Avenue.

Investigators began the task having no idea how much—or how little—they would find. The manuals told them that jet fuel burns at about a maximum of 1,500 degrees Fahrenheit, depending on circumstances. Temperatures of this magnitude would ordinarily consume human remains beyond recognition. But there was another element at work here. Experts calculated that after the initial impacts numerous fires broke out at the core of the buildings, raising the temperature ever higher. And it was these fires that did most of the damage. Sucking in energy from floors full of office supplies, they reached temperatures of over 2,000 degrees Fahrenheit, hot enough to buckle the buildings' steel frames and weaken them to the point where collapse was inevitable.

The quite extraordinary violence of the disaster and the fires at Ground Zero that would ultimately burn for months among the rubble made the problems of identification almost unimaginably difficult. There would be fingerprint records for the scores of government officials who died in the inferno, provided there was a print to match. Dental records, too, were expected to play a big part. Of all the tissues in the human body, nothing is tougher than teeth. But everything has its destruction threshold and even teeth can be incinerated at the kinds of temperature levels reached in the Twin Towers. The hope was that most victims would have experienced only minimal exposure to these extreme temperatures.

To aid in the identification process, staff at the OCME issued a seven-page form to relatives and friends of those thought to have died in the tragedy. The questions were necessarily intimate: What was the blood type? Were there any distinguishing scars? What about facial hair? Had he been circumcised? Did she or he wear any distinctive jewelry? A wig, perhaps? Had they undergone expensive dental work? Or cosmetic surgery? Were they tattooed? What was the color of her favorite nail polish? The list was comprehensive and heartbreaking. Once a form had been completed, its answers were fed into a giant database supplied by the Disaster Mortuary Operational Response Team (DMORT), a special unit designed to assist local agencies in the event of natural and man-made disasters. In time, they would provide more than two hundred investigators ranging from pathologists to investigators, X-ray technicians to dentists. Many were veterans of the 1995 Oklahoma City bombing that had left 168 dead, but nothing could have prepared them for the kinds of numbers they were dealing with here. This was domestic tragedy on an entirely unprecedented scale.

To understand just how so many people could have died so quickly, it was necessary to piece together the series of events between impact and collapse. At 8:46 A.M. American Airlines flight 11, which had been hijacked shortly after taking off from Logan Airport, Boston, flew into the upper portion of the North Tower, slicing through floors 93–99, rendering all three of the building's stairwells impassable from the ninety-second floor up, and killing all eighty-one passengers and nine crew. One astonishing fact emerged: within the space of the tower's 209-foot width, the plane was brought from *586 mph to a dead stop!* Yet even this stupendous amount of energy—sufficient to sway the tower a foot on its foundations—failed to make it collapse. That would come later. Countless workers were pulverized instantly as they sat at their desks. Hundreds, perhaps a thousand or more, survived the impact, only to be trapped on the floors up to the top of the 110-story building.

Many of these would have been helpless spectators when, at 9:03 A.M., a second Boeing 767 hijacked out of Logan International that morning, United Airlines flight 175, tore into the South Tower between the seventy-seventh and eighty-fifth floors, killing all seventy-four passengers and crew. For some reason the plane had banked just before impact, a maneuver that left portions of the building undamaged on the impact floors. The most significant outcome of this abrupt shift was that it allowed one of the stairwells to remain passable from at least the ninety-first floor down and likely from top to bottom.

Within minutes of the dual impacts, emergency rescue personnel were inside both buildings. Their actions that day have entered the pantheon of human courage. Fighting their way up smoke-filled stairways, often in pitch darkness, they found terrified workers and shepherded them to safety. Then it was back into the choking smoke to hunt for more survivors. But their bravery came at a terrible cost. When the roll call was taken, history would remember this as the blackest day ever for the world's fire and rescue services. The numbers were staggering. Three hundred and forty-three members of the Fire Department of New York (FDNY) were killed, the largest loss of life of any emergency response agency in history. The Port Authority Police Department (PAPD) suffered thirty-seven fatalities—the largest single day loss of life of any police force in history. Their colleagues in the NYPD lost twenty-three—the second-largest loss of life of any police force in history, exceeded only by the number of PAPD officers lost the same day. And yet, amid all this tragedy for the emergency services, a single beacon of brilliance gleamed through. Miraculously, twelve firefighters, one PAPD officer, and three civilians—all of whom were descending stairwell B—survived the collapse of the North Tower and somehow managed to emerge alive from the wreckage.

But thousands had not, and it was the OCME's grim duty to put names to as many victims as possible. Two days after 9/11, Mundorff, both eyes blackened and her face puffy and bruised, reported back for work. Hirsch welcomed her with a hug. In many ways Mundorff's resilience became a metaphor for the OCME and its staff in the face of such a crisis. Her role would be crucial in analyzing remains from the catastrophe. The whole bodies and larger body parts came in body bags, the smaller pieces were in red plastic biohazard bags. There was one unexpected problem. To an untrained eye, one bone looks pretty much the same as another, and as the World Trade Center had housed a dozen restaurants, serving twenty thousand meals a day, this meant that many of the bones sent to Mundorff actually came from chickens and other animals. First she needed to eliminate these; then it was a matter of sorting through the human parts, looking for anything unique, like a healed fracture or an operation scar, that might help identify the victim. Parts obviously not from the same person were placed in separate containers for subsequent DNA analysis.

Hirsch had a fine balancing act to perform—weighing the sensibilities of an intense human tragedy against his department's role as a medico-legal facility. Because a crime had been committed, and because the FBI and other law enforcement agencies were working round the clock to track the source of the conspiracy, it was essential, as much as possible, to identify the remains of the hijackers. An examination of passenger manifests for the hijacked planes, combined with close study of CCTV footage taken at Logan International and other airports, did provide clues to the whereabouts of the hijackers in the days before their final act. If they had left any personal items in hotel rooms—hairbrushes, soiled clothing, washcloths, that kind of thing—then the chances of extracting useful and identifying DNA were high. This in turn might lead to other conspirators, ones who had taken no physical part in the atrocity but who might be actively pursuing further outrages. There was another factor at work here. In the event of a possible mass burial, rigorous DNA profiling would allow the investigators to segregate the remains of the attackers from those of their victims, thereby diminishing the distress felt by the victims' bereaved relatives.

With thousands of body parts buried under a debris field that stretched for sixteen acres, progress was mind-numbingly slow. By mid-morning on September 13, crews had recovered just ninety-four bodies; of which, forty-six were identified. Once the legal proprieties had been observed, vehicles from funeral homes began arriving to pick up the first named victims.

For most relatives the wait was much longer and much more painful. A family assistance center was established at the Lexington Avenue Armory on Twenty-sixth Street to deal with anyone desperate for news of missing relatives. Some brought photos, little realizing that chances of a visible recognition were vanishingly slight; others held out hairbrushes and razors, having heard that such personal items might hold DNA traces of their missing loved ones. Blood relatives were asked to provide a swab sample from the inside of their cheeks in hopes that it would yield a DNA match for any fragments found. At the same time, every relative was asked to complete the seven-page questionnaire.

As the rescue effort began to gather pace, a string of mobile mortuary containers was flown in by DMORT, and a temporary morgue was set up in a hangar at LaGuardia Airport, complete with its own generators, X-ray equipment, cooling units, desks, chairs, lights, and medical equipment. Most of the bodies and body parts were brought here first.

At the OCME, details of the victims were stored in more than fifty file drawers labeled RM DM, for Reported Missing/Disaster Manhattan. Among these was Father Mychal Judge. Known to everyone in the fire service as Father Mike, the sixty-eight-old Franciscan priest had been the FDNY chaplain since 1992, and in that time he had attended scores of fires and seen almost as many tragedies, providing comfort to victims and firefighters alike. His was a regular face on news broadcasts. When the second plane struck the World Trade Center, Father Mike was already in the North Tower. Documentary film cameras show him as being everywhere, counseling, tending the injured, praying. At one point he went to the side of a firefighter who, bizarrely, had been struck by a falling body. When it became clear that the man was not going to survive, Father Mike removed his fire helmet and began administering the last rites. At that moment a fresh avalanche of debris engulfed both men. Neither survived. As a mark of respect to Father Mike's supreme self-sacrifice, it was decided that the first death certificate for 9/11—officially listed as 00001—should be in his name.

At first the rescuers were pulling whole bodies from the twisted steel and concrete, but gradually the remains became smaller, harder to seek out. And all the while the fires burned, and the hoses gushed, and the evidence slowly turned to mush. Bodies had been incinerated, mangled, crushed, mingled with others, often to the point of oblivion. As early as September 15, Hirsch declared his belief that in the future most identifications would be made through DNA analysis. Although the OCME had long practiced for a major catastrophe, the sheer scale of the 9/11 DNA effort was beyond the capability of any single agency. For this reason, it was decided to contract several private companies to help. The Laboratory Corporation of America, with nine hundred offices across the country, was brought in to analyze the personal items of the missing and the cheek swabs of their kin.

The DNA samples from the recovered bodies would be handled by two companies, Myriad, based in Utah, and Celera, a Maryland company. To minimize the ever-present risk of error, all the analyses would be double-checked by New York State Police laboratories. Then came the announcement that the database of genetic material would be moved from the armory to a new unit situated at Pier 94, near West Fifty-fourth Street. The city promised it would be open from 8:00 A.M. to midnight, seven days a week. At the same time, adjacent to the OCME a large tent had been erected. Filled with wreaths and votive candles, it served as a kind of ecumenical chapel and soon became known as Memorial Park. Here grieving relatives could come and, perhaps, find some comfort. Meanwhile, just next door, in the blue and black tiled building, the relentless identification process continued without pause.

There was still no exact figure on how many people had died. Initial estimates in the tens of thousands looked to be wide of the mark, and steadily the numbers were pared down. By October 23, the number had fallen to just over four thousand. Of the 478 victims confirmed dead, 425 were identified. At first the identifications were running at ten a day, but as the difficulties multiplied the identification numbers dwindled markedly, and it soon became clear that this would be a mammoth undertaking. The medical examiner's office remained tight lipped as to how long the operation might take.

With the OCME and almost every other government investigative agency working flat out, the unimaginable happened. On November 12 at approximately 9:00 A.M., another American

Airlines jet, flight 587, bound for the Dominican Republic, crashed just minutes after takeoff from Kennedy Airport. The first reaction everywhere was that terrorists had once again targeted New York City.

The plane came down in the Rockaway Beach section of Queens, an area that had been home to dozens of firefighters who had lost their lives at the World Trade Center. Within twenty-four hours, crash investigators were able to issue assurances that there had been no terrorist involvement. Mechanical malfunction, not malevolent intervention, had brought down the Airbus 300-600. For Hirsch and the OCME the lack of terrorist involvement provided cold comfort; there were still another 265 bodies to autopsy and numerous grieving families and friends to counsel and comfort.

At times, fate can deal hands of almost indescribable cruelty, and for one woman, Naomi Gullickson, this crash was especially gut wrenching. Just two days beforehand, she had attended a memorial service for her firefighter husband who had died saving lives at the Twin Towers. Now she had to absorb the crushing reality that her father was on board flight 587 when it crashed.

Others, too, were similarly devastated. On September 11 Rafael Hernandez had been seriously injured while escaping the Twin Towers. Even so, he and his family counted him lucky to be alive. In the days and weeks following 9/11, Rafael had been tortured by nightmares of planes crashing, but he was finally making some headway and had raised no objection when his wife said she was taking their three-year-old daughter on vacation to the Dominican Republic. They, too, were aboard flight 587. Rafael learned of their fate from watching TV footage, standing dumbstruck as the cameras showed how his wife and daughter had been snatched from him. For those working at the OCME such random and terrible tragedies don't just occur at times of national disaster—they are regular events. This is the part of the job that rarely makes headlines: having to look into the eyes of people struck down by unfathomable levels of human suffering. For Hirsch, it strikes to the very heart of his responsibilities. "The real test of a place like ours," he once said, "is the service we deliver to anonymous citizens at the worst times in their lives: Someone you loved walked out the door and now you'll never see them again. At times like that, people need not only technical excellence but they need to be treated with compassion and creativity. And doing that day in and day out is [our greatest] challenge."

In the meantime, the recovery mission at Ground Zero continued with quiet determination. But the problems of identification were getting tougher with each passing day. There were no more intact bodies being pulled from the wreckage. The human remains were getting smaller and smaller. By the end of November, Hirsch hadn't seen an entire corpse in weeks. At first, victims' remains had been identified using conventional methods that relied on the human eye. Dental records alone were responsible for 187 identifications. Fingerprints added another seventy-one to the identification total, while photo identification and miscellaneous X-rays boosted the numbers by sixteen and forty-five, respectively.

But year's end brought the grim realization that many of the missing would never be identified or even found. No one wants to be the bearer of such ill tidings, and at a public meeting Hirsch's sad but honest observation that many victims had been simply vaporized caused uproar among some bereaved relatives, many of whom either refused or else struggled to comprehend a reality in which their loved ones had simply vanished from the face of the earth with no trace.

Just about the only glimmer of hope in all this darkness was a marked improvement in data management. Originally, the OCME had been inundated with human fragments—they were, after all,

dealing with more homicide victims than most forensic pathologists see in a lifetime—and all too often scientists and technicians
found themselves testing samples from victims who had already
been identified. (When one considers that as many as two hundred
human fragments had been linked to a single person, it was a
miracle that so few duplications actually occurred.) As discrepancies and repetitions in the victim details were rectified, it led to a
dramatic decrease in the estimated number of victims.

One year from Black Tuesday and the verified identification toll
had reached 1,401. Given the circumstances—bear in mind that only
293 bodies were recovered intact, an incredibly low percentage for
such a large-scale disaster—this was a quite astonishing achievement. The OCME and its satellite laboratories spread right across
the United States were performing miraculous feats of identification,
but one fact was now glaringly obvious—henceforth DNA typing
would offer the only hope of identifying the victims of September 11.

Overseeing the DNA effort was Dr. Robert C. Shaler, the OCME's
forensic biologist. Initially, his hope was that conventional DNA
analysis would be able to provide the answers he was looking for.
From each collected fragment of remains, three rectangular plates
of DNA samples were preserved at the medical examiner's office
and frozen at −80 degrees Fahrenheit. A computer software program then collated all the data from the different tests, recalculat-
ing the percentage of identification certainty each time a new result
came in.

But conventional DNA analysis requires high-grade genetic
material and here so many of the samples were too crushed, burned,
or decomposed to yield useful DNA. (At one stage more than a
dozen tractor-trailers were packed with human remains too small
or too degraded even for DNA analysis.) As already minuscule

human body parts decompose, the roughly three billion base pairs that make up a strand of DNA in the nucleus of a cell begin to disintegrate. Any fragments left are likely to be worthless when tested using standard DNA profiling methods. This posed a problem for Shaler. To achieve the level of certainty demanded by both the scientists and the families, he turned to new technologies that had been under development for some time but never used in forensic investigations.

One, known as mini–short tandem repeats, or mini-STRs, was developed at the National Institute of Standards and Technology in Gaithersburg, Maryland. The other, called single nucleotide polymorphism analysis, or SNP, was created by Orchid BioSciences, of Princeton, New Jersey. The beauty of both methods is that they require far smaller intact pieces of DNA than the standard process used globally for everything from crime investigations to paternity tests.

To give an example of the mini-STR's sensitivity, whereas scientists customarily analyze DNA samples of about four hundred base pairs, which form the signature double helix of human DNA, the mini-STR can evaluate pieces of DNA as short as one hundred base pairs.

A SNP—pronounced "snip"—is a small genetic change, or variation, that can occur within a person's DNA sequence. There are four chemicals that make up DNA: adenine (A), guanine (G), cytosine (C), and thymine (T). Strung together in an extremely long sequence, the chemicals on one chromosomal strand align with the chemicals on the other strand; that is, A always joins with T, C always joins with G. Thus, a section of DNA code might be arranged thus:

C A G T T C A
G T C A A G T

But occasionally irregularities occur, and an example of an SNP is shown in the following:

CAGTTCA

GGCAAGT

Note that the second adenine in the first snippet is replaced with a guanine in the second snippet. For a variation to be considered a SNP, it must occur in at least 1 percent of the human population.

The effectiveness of these new DNA techniques can be demonstrated by the case of forty-six-year-old Manhattan firefighter Thomas J. McCann, who had disappeared during the rescue effort. Distraught family members had brought a toothbrush to the OCME, hoping that it would contain DNA from the missing McCann. It did. Now it was a question of matching McCann's DNA to any of the thousands of human fragments recovered. Eventually investigators at the OCME compared it to a three-by-two-inch piece of muscle that had been recovered from the site. By July 2003 they were confident that they had a DNA match between the muscle fragment and the toothbrush, but the numbers weren't statistically strong enough. According to the calculations, the probability was one in 4,600, considerably below the threshold that had been agreed in order for an identification to be cited as positive. (At the beginning of the investigation at least five samples were misidentified and had to be reclaimed from disappointed relatives.) For Mr. McCann, it was an SNP test, more than two years after the small bit of muscle had been recovered, that finally produced the requisite degree of certainty—one in a trillion. For his widow, Anne Marie, it was a miracle worth waiting for. "I wanted *something*," she said.

In the understandable desire to identify victims, it was, at times, easy to lose sight of the fact that the OCME was still involved in a homicide investigation. There were guilty parties that needed to be named. When Shaler found, against all the odds, that he was getting DNA identifications from passengers on the planes, he pondered the possibility of obtaining DNA from the terrorists. However, when inquiries were made to the FBI, asking if they had managed to obtain any DNA from the suspected hijackers, all that came back was a thudding silence. If the FBI—notoriously parochial in matters of jurisdictional authority—did hold this evidence, then they were clearly not about to surrender it without a struggle. Only after a year of hectoring and exasperation did the FBI reluctantly hand over ten DNA profiles, presumably from the hijackers. Shaler was able to make two matches almost immediately. A third came soon afterward. This surprised him. The commonly held wisdom was that all the hijackers had been grouped together in the cockpit, and would have therefore been vaporized when the planes made impact. Shaler's findings forced a rethink. Now the likeliest scenario had one cadre of hijackers storming the cockpit and overpowering the flight crew, while their co-conspirators herded passengers into the rear of the plane. Shaler hypothesized that when the planes struck the towers, those hijackers at the controls would have been consumed by the main fireball, and that therefore the traces of DNA he found had originated from the guards. Like everyone else at the OCME, Shaler was kept in the dark about the identities of those hijackers whose DNA he had matched. The FBI decided to sit on this information. Another closely guarded secret surrounds the current whereabouts of the hijackers' remains. Besides the ethical considerations—most sensibilities would rebel at the thought of any cross-contamination between remains from victims and hijackers—these samples are still classed as evidence from a crime scene and have been preserved by the FBI at an undisclosed location. Not even the OCME is privy to the secret.

Identifying the victims, though, would always be the OCME's main mission. And that meant cross-checking every possible detail before a death certificate was issued. The first question to be answered: Was this person actually dead? This information— seemingly so prosaic or unnecessary, even—was vital for insurance companies to begin settling claims that were expected to run into the millions of dollars. Most insurance adjusters have a predictably jaundiced view of human nature, even in the aftermath of a national tragedy. Someone, somewhere, they suspect, will try to turn a quick buck. And so it proved. Across the United States no fewer than two dozen fraud cases linked to the 9/11 disaster eventually went to court. Of these, the most egregious involved a Georgia couple, Alan and Cynthia Gavett. Like millions of Americans that fateful day the Gavetts watched events unfold on their TV screens, but where others saw only horror, they spotted a business opportunity. Just days later Alan Gavett filed insurance claims that could have netted him upward of a half-million dollars, saying that forty-year-old Cynthia had been a victim of the tragedy. She had, he said, traveled to New York for a 9:00 A.M. job interview on the morning of September 11 with Cantor Fitzgerald, an investment bank at the World Trade Center. Choosing Cantor Fitzgerald was a crafty ploy. It had been well publicized that in terms of human loss Cantor Fitzgerald was the worst affected company at the World Trade Center, losing 658 employees. Of even greater significance to an aspiring fraudster, was the accompanying revelation that the company's records and paperwork had been almost entirely destroyed. This made the Gavetts' version of events virtually impossible to verify. (In truth, his wife had never left the family's comfortable seventy-four-acre spread in Concord, Georgia.) When an insurance company ran some background checks, it was puzzled to learn that no obituary for Cynthia Gavett had appeared in the Georgia press. Thinking they needed to straighten out their records, they contacted the local sheriff's office to verify the Gavetts' address. Now, it just so happened that the person to whom they spoke knew the Gavetts. Not only that, but he had seen the allegedly deceased Cynthia, very much alive and well and making no attempt to pretend otherwise, in the days following the tragedy. Following this disclosure, the Gavetts' scam unfolded in double-quick time. On November 26, Alan and Cynthia Gavett were arrested and charged with fraud. In May 2002, each was sentenced to ten years imprisonment.*

Inevitably, as time passed, the OCME's investigation reached a point of diminishing returns. In the immediate aftermath of 9/11, about seventy staff members were assigned to the World Trade Center identification unit. By 2005 that number had fallen to just two. In April of that year, families of the victims of the 9/11 attacks gathered at an interfaith service where they thanked Hirsch and his staff for the quite extraordinary job they had done. He promised that the identification work would never end, but after three and a half years of work costing a total of eighty million dollars, there was the frank admission that the OCME had reached the limits of current scientific technology when it came to identifying victims.

But that didn't mark the end of the story. In September 2005 workers clearing Ground Zero for future redevelopment set about preparing the adjacent Deutsche Bank Building at 130 Liberty Street for demolition. A section of the South Tower had gouged an ugly gash in the facade of the forty-one-story building as it collapsed. Workers on the roof made a startling discovery: fragments of what looked like human bones. These ranged in size from a half-inch to two inches. They were immediately taken to the OCME to

---

* Both have since been released.

determine if they were human. (Back in August 2003, similar fragments had been found at the Deutsche Bank, but testing showed these to be nonhuman.) Further searching of the building revealed a total of 760 body fragments. Sophisticated analysis confirmed that the bones *were* human, and subsequent DNA testing was able to identify yet another victim of the atrocity.

In October 2006 yet more human remains—some as large as arm or leg bones—were found in rubble excavated from a manhole. These will obviously be analyzed, and hopefully more identifications will follow.

At the time of writing, 58 percent of the victims of the trade center attack—1,603 persons—have been identified. Of the 20,730 body parts recovered, so far only 10,933 have been matched to a known victim, while 9,797 remain unidentified. Those that remain have been dehydrated and placed in storage to await advances in DNA techniques. It's also why the remains will stay in separate bags with separate numbers even after they are placed in the Ground Zero memorial tomb. It is sobering to think that if this tragedy had occurred just fifteen years earlier—before the advent of DNA typing—then the number of identifications would have numbered in the hundreds. Cutting-edge science has brought a grain of comfort to thousands of bereaved relatives, and the work will go on. As Ellen Borakove, a spokesperson for the Office of the Chief Medical Examiner put it, "This office has given a promise to the families that we are never going to stop trying. We are never going to give up."

Wartime has a knack of accelerating technological progress, and the war against terror has been no exception. Identification techniques pioneered in the aftermath of 9/11 have since been employed in Thailand to identify victims of the 2004 tsunami in

Southeast Asia. And the next generation of DNA analysis is already under way.

In February 2007 the OCME opened a new high-sensitivity forensic biology DNA laboratory at 421 East 26th Street. Costing in excess of $250 million, it is the finest facility of its kind in North America, and as good as any in the world. Everything is top of the line. And to make sure it all functions as intended, a sophisticated laboratory battery backup power protection system has been installed to ensure that the lab suffers no potentially calamitous power fluctuations of the kind that might damage both crime-related samples and expensive hardware.

Within this cutting-edge laboratory, scientists are able to carry out a still controversial technique known as low copy number DNA analysis. In the past, conventional DNA testing required approximately 150 cells of genetic material for testing. But all too often, crime scene investigators were harvesting samples of less than that amount, samples that were, in evidentiary terms, worthless. And then, in 1999, British scientists pioneered a method of microanalysis whereby they could obtain a DNA profile from as few as thirty cells. At this new laboratory, OCME scientists have lowered the threshold to an astonishing *six cells'* worth of genetic material! Sensitivity of this order allows them to test, say, even skin cells left on a smudged fingerprint.

The technique works by amplifying, or copying, the DNA in cycles, as in conventional testing. Where the difference lies is in the numbers. Conventional testing generally calls for twenty-eight cycles; low copy testing will require at least thirty two-cycles. Unfortunately, with each cycle, the DNA lose clarity. Think of it as a photocopy of a photocopy; the first copy might be acceptable but with each repetition thereafter the image degrades.

Not everyone is convinced by low copy number DNA analysis. They argue that the smaller the sample the greater the risk of contamination. Concerns have also been raised about the process's heightened sensitivity. Say, for example, you shake hands with someone and that person then goes on to commit a crime, it is not beyond the realms of possibility that your DNA might be transferred to the crime scene. If it has, the chances are that low copy number analysis will find it. Taken in isolation this would be cause for considerable concern, but there is another, much bigger drawback to low copy number DNA analysis: the process actually destroys the sample. It may be all well and good for a prosecutor to claim that low copy number DNA analysis has placed a person at a crime scene, but if the defense is unable to physically examine the sample themselves, then they are in no position to test the truth of that allegation. The legal ramifications of such an imbalance are all too obvious.

For now, though, the OCME's new high-sensitivity laboratory is an example of life imitating art: *CSI: New York* in the real world. A series of rooms is connected by sanitized glass cabinets, through which evidence is passed by technicians wearing gowns, gloves, masks, even bootees. Everything is done to ensure that purification levels are the highest possible. Test tubes, instead of being sterilized, which guards against just bacteria, are irradiated to destroy potentially harmful stray chromosomes.

In the past the high cost and time-consuming nature of DNA testing meant it was reserved for only the most serious offenses, typically homicides and sex crimes. This new laboratory's capabilities will allow the OCME to assist in burglaries, home invasions, and other crimes of this type. Another useful corollary is that it will significantly increase the number of forensic samples that New York City contributes to the state's DNA database. (Pending legislation, the state hopes to require that all convicted criminals provide DNA samples for inclusion in the state DNA and the FBI's Combined DNA Index System databases.)

*   *   *

When Charles Norris took charge of the OCME in 1918, the popular notion of forensic science was embodied in an image of Sherlock Holmes, magnifying glass in hand, crouching over some half-glimpsed clue. The reality wasn't so very different. Investigative procedures, where they existed at all, bordered on the risible. Crime scenes were poorly processed, clues were misinterpreted, evidence was often lost or else contaminated. All in all it was pretty shambolic. Just about the only identification tools available to the crime scene investigator—beyond an often unreliable eyewitness—were fingerprint analysis and blood grouping, both of which were in their infancy. Yet within a decade or so all that changed. Suddenly Norris and his staff had a whole new range of forensic tools at their command. There was the comparison microscope for ballistics analysis; then came the first electron microscope, which offered hitherto unimaginable powers of magnification. Year after year the array of toxicological identification techniques grew exponentially. Whenever these innovations led to the capture of some callous killer, the press coverage was suitably wide eyed. As a result, chemists like the reclusive and brilliant Dr. Alexander Gettler became almost household names. Suddenly it was a time when science promised everything and all things seemed possible. If the hyperbole occasionally got out of hand, well, that was the press just doing its job, and generally there was someone like the sage and sanguine Milton Helpern on hand to rein in the excess.

As forensic science has moved on, so have the crimes it investigates. In Norris's earliest days, it wasn't uncommon for newspaper editors to splash 40-point headlines on the kind of domestic murder case that nowadays would struggle to make the metro section. Homicide has become so commonplace and we have become so case hardened to its incidence, that, without a noteworthy participant or some compelling backstory, a single murder rarely makes the front pages. The days when thousands would stand bareheaded in the streets to witness the funeral of a hitherto unknown murder victim such as Jennie Becker are long gone. In the modern world we have had to adjust to a reality in which fanatics ram canisters of steel, bulging with jet fuel, into skyscrapers, obliterating thousands at a time. However, while the numbers might have escalated hugely, one factor hasn't changed: the utter wastefulness of murder, any murder. A life taken and countless others ruined—these remain the immutable constants of homicide investigation.

As the OCME enters its tenth decade, it does so bearing a burden of pressure and expectation that would have made Charles Norris blink with disbelief (and possibly reach for another martini). Progress in any field or institution is rarely linear; to get the highs, one must endure the inevitable lows, and the OCME is no exception. Its unique standing on the national stage guarantees that it is rarely out of the spotlight, and any problems it encounters are magnified a hundredfold. As we have seen, most of the major difficulties have arisen not from any technological or professional deficiencies but because of personality clashes and thwarted ambition. When Dr. Charles Hirsch assumed leadership of the OCME in 1989, he inherited a department demoralized by years of internal feuding and outside meddling. Its international reputation for probity, impartiality, and top-quality science had taken a big hit since the glory days when Helpern had been at the helm. Perhaps one of Hirsch's greatest achievements has been the restoration of that status. Under his auspices, the OCME investigated the worst crime in American history, and it did so with a skill, dedication, and sensitivity that few, if any, medico-legal facilities in the world could have matched.

But, of course, you can't please everybody all the time. And the snipers are always well within range. You can almost bet that whenever the OCME investigates a headline-making death or homicide, some opportunist will emerge from the woodwork bellowing demands for an "*independent* autopsy!" Hirsch makes no secret of his contempt for this oblique slur. In November 2003 he crystallized his disgust thus: "I believe it impossible for a well-informed, fair-minded person to have any doubt whatsoever about the independence of New York City medical examiners." Then, in a barb directed at those experts who might be financially motivated to reach a particular conclusion, he added caustically, "My paycheck is going to be the same whatever we conclude."

It was this desire for independence that led to the establishment of the Office of the Chief Medical Examiner, and for the most part it has performed magnificently. Thousands of murderers have been brought to justice by the OCME's expertise. But catching killers has been only part of the story. In its ninety years of existence, the OCME has investigated well over one million deaths, a herculean achievement by any reckoning and one made more remarkable still by the fact that the only beneficiaries of all this endeavor are the millions of New Yorkers who daily go about their lives with scarcely a thought for the blue and black tiled building that stands on First Avenue. For, as Dr. Hirsch once remarked, "We're not doing our job for the sake of the cadavers."

INDEX